Children's Literature in Second Language Education

Also available from Bloomsbury

Children's Literature in Context, Fiona McCulloch
Corpus-Based Approaches to English Language Teaching, Mari Carmen Campoy,
Begona Belles-Fortuno and Maria Lluisa Gea-Valor

Children's Literature in Second Language Education

Edited by
Janice Bland
and
Christiane Lütge

B L O O M S B U R Y
LONDON • NEW DELHI • NEW YORK • SYDNEY

Bloomsbury Academic
An imprint of Bloomsbury Publishing Plc

50 Bedford Square	1385 Broadway
London	New York
WC1B 3DP	NY 10018
UK	USA

www.bloomsbury.com

Bloomsbury is a registered trade mark of Bloomsbury Publishing Plc

First published 2013
Paperback edition first published 2014

British Library Cataloguing-in-Publication Data
A catalogue record for this book is available from the British Library.

ISBN: HB: 978-1-4411-8352-1
PB: 978-1-4725-7627-9
ePDF: 978-1-4411-2978-9
ePUB: 978-1-4411-8276-0

Library of Congress Cataloging-in-Publication Data
A catalog record for this title is available from the Library of Congress.

Typeset by Newgen Imaging Systems Pvt Ltd, Chennai, India
Printed and bound in Great Britain

Contents

List of Contributors

Grit Alter received a teaching degree for English and Philosophy at secondary school in 2007 and completed her teacher training in 2009. Subsequently she worked as research assistant at the Universities of Hildesheim and Mainz, Germany. At Hildesheim University she was actively involved in organizing the international conference *Children's Literature in Language Education – from Picture Books to Young Adult Fiction*. Since 2011 Grit has been a research assistant for the TEFL Chair at the English Department of Münster University, Germany. Her research interests include inter- and transcultural learning, teaching literature and Teaching English as a Foreign Language (TEFL) methodology as well as North American studies.

Janice Bland is an experienced English teacher, and joined the English Department at Hildesheim University in 2007, and the Department of English and American Studies at the University of Paderborn in 2012. Her interests are Children's Literature in education, the subject of her PhD at the University of Jena, Germany, and Drama and Creative Writing in EFL teacher education. Janice has published widely, including *Children's Literature and Learner Empowerment: Children and Teenagers in English Language Education* with Bloomsbury Academic, EFL textbooks for German and international publishers and four collections of plays for schools, with Players Press. Janice co-edits the new international peer-reviewed CLELEjournal: *Children's Literature in English Language Education*.

Eva Burwitz-Melzer is Professor of English as a Foreign Language (EFL) Teaching at the Justus-Liebig-University in Giessen, Germany. After finishing her PhD in American literature she worked as a teacher and as a lecturer at the Universities of Frankfurt, Jena and Giessen, Germany. She has done empirical research in the fields of EFL Teaching in primary schools and in secondary schools, mostly in the field of reading, writing, teaching intercultural communicative competence and reading literary texts. Her current fields of research interest are the development of language and literary competences of EFL students in grades 3 to 12 as well as teacher education.

Maria Eisenmann is Professor of EFL Teaching at the University of Duisburg-Essen, Germany. After finishing her PhD and working as a teacher in school and as a lecturer at the University of Würzburg, Germany, she taught at the University of Education in Freiburg, Germany, and held a deputy professorship for EFL Teaching at the University of Erlangen-Nuremberg, Germany. Her primary research interests lie in the field of teaching literature, media literacy and intercultural learning including individual differences.

Maria Teresa Fleta Guillén has taught the *Teaching Young Learner's Module* of the Teaching English as a Foreign Language (TEFL) Master Programme at Alcalá de Henares University, Madrid, Spain, since 2005. Prior to joining the AHU, she worked at the British Council School of Madrid, Spain, in the Early Years and Primary sections. Her work and research studies focus on child second language acquisition and bilingual education. Her attempts to combine theory and practice can be seen in published reports and articles on the theoretical underpinnings of child second language acquisition and on practical issues concerning content and language teaching to young learners.

Maria Luisa García Bermejo is an Associate Professor at the School of Education, Complutense University of Madrid, Spain. She holds a PhD in English, an MA and MEd in Teaching English to Speakers of Other Languages (TESOL) and an MA in Spanish. She conducts seminars in English, didactics and the teaching of literature. Her research focuses on Second Language Acquisition (SLA) and Information and Communication Technology (ICT) and language and literature teaching.

Carola Hecke teaches English and Spanish at the School of St Ursula, Hanover, Germany. She studied Art History at Georg-August-University Göttingen, Germany and UC Berkeley, the United States and majored in English Language Teaching and Spanish Language Teaching in Germany. Between 2006 and 2011 she worked as teaching and research assistant in English teaching methodology at Georg-August-University Göttingen. Her doctoral dissertation (2012 forthcoming) is on the impact of visual culture on the use of pictures in ESL teaching. Her major interests are visual media in EFL teaching and intercultural learning with the help of literary texts.

Annika Kolb is a Junior Professor in the Department of English of Heidelberg University of Education, Germany. She holds a PhD from Hamburg University, Germany, is a trained primary and secondary school teacher and has taught in schools and at Freiburg University of Education, Germany. Her research interests include teaching English in primary school, continuity between primary and secondary EFL and teaching literature in the EFL classroom.

Stephen Krashen is Emeritus Professor at the University of Southern California, the United States. He is best known for developing the first comprehensive theory of second language acquisition, introducing the concept of sheltered subject matter teaching and as the co-inventor of the Natural Approach to foreign language teaching. He has also contributed to theory and application in the area of bilingual education, and has done important work in the area of reading. He was the 1977 Incline Bench Press champion of Venice Beach and holds a black belt in Tae Kwon Do. His recent papers can be found at www.sdkrashen.com.

Li-Feng Lee earned her bachelor's degree in English from National Changhua University of Education, Taiwan, her master's degree in English literature from National Chengchi University, Taiwan and her PhD in English education from Ohio State University, the United States. She has taught at National Formosa University, Taiwan, since 2008, specializing in Children's and Young Adult Literature. She is an

Assistant Professor in the Department of Applied Foreign Languages. Her current research is in the areas of teaching literature and culture in the secondary and tertiary EFL classroom, reading preferences of English as a Second Language adolescents and cultural studies approach to literature for children and young adults.

Christiane Lütge is Professor and Chair of EFL Teaching at the University of Münster, Germany. Previously she was Professor at Mainz and Hildesheim Universities, Germany. She also worked as a teacher at secondary schools for several years. Her research interests lie in the fields of teaching literature, cultural studies in the EFL Classroom, media literacy, global education, inter- and transcultural learning and teacher training. She co-edits the new international peer-reviewed ejournal: *Children's Literature in English Language Education.*

Alan Maley has been involved with English Language Teaching (ELT) for 50 years. From 1962–88 he worked for the British Council in Yugoslavia, Ghana, Italy, France, China and India. He then became Director-General of the Bell Educational Trust in Cambridge from 1988–93. This was followed by five years as Senior Fellow at the National University of Singapore. He went on to set up an MA course in ELT at Assumption University, Bangkok. He is currently Visiting Professor at Leeds Metropolitan University, the United Kingdom. He has published over 40 books and numerous articles. His main research interests are in innovative methodology, creative writing, extensive reading and teacher development.

Beniko Mason is a Professor at Shitennoji University, Osaka, Japan. She has been interested in comprehension-based methodology since 1985 when the Comprehension Hypothesis (a.k.a. Input Hypothesis) and the related Reading Hypothesis were first introduced. Her classroom research has been designed to determine the effects and efficiency of this methodology. After almost three decades of study she no longer has any doubts about the power of reading on language acquisition.

Sandie Mourão is a freelance teacher, teacher educator and materials writer based in Portugal specializing in early years language education, with a particular interest in picturebooks, free play and the use of the mother tongue in second language learning. She has an MA in TESOL from the University of Manchester, the United Kingdom and a PhD in language didactics from the University of Aveiro, Portugal. Sandie has edited, authored and contributed to a number of ELT-related publications, and is currently co-editor of *Children's Literature in English Language Education* CLELEjournal.

Susanne Reichl is Associate Professor at the English Department of the University of Vienna, Austria, where she teaches and researches literature, cultural studies and teaching methodology. She has previously taught at the University of Münster, Germany, and, supported by a grant from the Austrian science fund, spent two years in Frankfurt and London working on her postdoctoral qualification (*Habilitation*). Her research interests include the teaching of literature and culture in secondary and higher education, children's and young adult literature, teacher education, postcolonial studies, British cultural studies and time travel stories.

Sigrid Rieuwerts is Senior Lecturer at the Johannes Gutenberg University Mainz, Germany (British Studies) and Fellow at the University of Edinburgh, the United Kingdom (Celtic and Scottish Studies). She was educated at Justus-Liebig University Giessen, Germany and the University of Lancaster, the United Kingdom, and completed her first and second state examinations for secondary schools (subjects: English, German, Theology). She received her doctorate from the University of Mainz and her postdoctoral qualification (*Habilitation*) from the University of Siegen, Germany. Her teaching and research focuses mainly on storytelling, Anglophone cultures and literatures and their use in the EFL classroom.

Johan Strobbe is a teacher of English at a secondary school in Brugge, Belgium. He is a member of staff of the Teacher Training Department of the University of Leuven, Belgium. He specializes in extensive reading and its effects on language acquisition. He is the editor and co-author of *Enter*, published by Plantyn, a series of EFL textbooks that integrate the use of teenage fiction in language learning. He also lectures in English for business and law at the University of Leuven, Belgium.

Paola Traverso is a teacher, teacher trainer and children's author. She works in Italy at ANSAS Liguria, an Institute of Educational Research. She is a member of LEND, the Italian Association of Foreign Language Teachers. She specializes in teaching English to young learners and storytelling. She has contributed to the Italian Ministry of Education website for long distance teacher training for primary-school teachers of English, offering workshops on storytelling and creative writing.

Andrew Wright is an author, illustrator, teacher trainer and storyteller. For 15 years he was Principal Lecturer in Art and Design at what is now the Manchester Metropolitan University, the United Kingdom. As a TEFL author two of his recent titles are *Storytelling with Children* (2008), with Oxford University Press, and *Writing Stories* (2008), together with David A. Hill, with Helbling Languages. As a storyteller and a story maker with children, he has worked in over 30 countries. He has also contributed to international storytelling conferences, for example, in Turkey and in Japan. He is a member of the Society for Storytelling.

1

Introduction

Janice Bland

While this volume has been guided by research questions that are significant for English as a Foreign Language (EFL) and second language (L2), the contributions address issues that are highly relevant for language teaching from preschool to the upper secondary school classroom. The book has come about because the studies of literary texts both as literature and language-acquisition input below the upper secondary level are to date very few. 'Children's literature' as a term is generally used to cover all literature for children and adolescents, including oral literature, such as fairy tales and nursery rhymes, graphic narratives and young adult literature, reflecting the eclectic interests of children (see Hunt, 1996 and 2001; Watson, 2001; Nodelman et al., 2003; Rudd, 2010). A number of different directions have been chosen from which to approach and discuss the advantages of children's literature for L2 education, including examples of good practice and the presentation of research results. The first approach, in Part One, is extensive reading, also called free reading, with literary texts ranging from picturebooks (usually written as one word in recent scholarship to emphasize the word/image interdependency) to teenage fiction. Research studies are introduced and quoted in Part One that strongly indicate that free or extensive reading is both a pleasurable and highly effective path to familiarity with diverse meanings and language patterns. However, educationalists know that the path to becoming a reader is paved by texts for young readers, such as picturebooks: 'Books in childhood initiate children into literature' (Meek, 1982, p. 285). Therefore a closer study of what is meant by picturebooks and graphic novels, and the significance of visual literacy in L2 education is the focus of Part Two. The English language as the object and sole focus of study is gradually diminishing, and content-based EFL classrooms are becoming the norm in many types of school. As Intercultural Communicative Competence (ICC), in contrast, is likely to gain further in importance, Part Three considers the manifold opportunities children's literature affords for developing ICC. In Part Four it will be shown how primary and secondary school students are able to take an active role in their literary education from the outset with children's literature, which entices a different creative response with each rereading. Part Four illustrates the close connection between storytelling and creative writing and focuses on the affective dimension and empowerment with the playful language of children's literature and culture.

Why use children's literature in language education at primary and secondary school?

Multilayered literature and multilayered readers

Multilayered literature refers to literary texts that are readable in different ways at different levels of sophistication and maturity. This applies to all worthwhile literary texts, of course: '*Reading a story is unique yet repetitive*. As with the performance of a play or symphony, each "reading" is a unique experience' (Benton, 1992, p. 18, emphasis in the original). Particularly children's literature is multilayered, in that it has a dual audience, adult and child, and often a multiple audience, as is the case with crossover literature. However, children's literature scholars and educationalists emphasize that already a picturebook 'invites all kinds of reading and allows the invention of a set of stories rather than a single story' (Meek, 1982, p. 288). Multimodal texts such as picturebooks and graphic novels, that create narrative through 'written language, visual image and graphic design – to tell a story' (Serafini, 2009, p. 11), demand repeated readings, for 'we can never quite perceive all the possible meanings of the text, or all the possible meanings of the pictures, or all the possible meanings of the text-picture relationships' (Sipe, 1998, p. 101).

A related term, the 'multilayered reader' should be applied to L2 readers just as much as to L1 readers, as students live complex lives in a complex world and deserve best quality texts to serve as a motivating literacy and literary apprenticeship. And as Bassnett and Grundy (1993, p. 7) maintain, 'literature is a high point of language usage; arguably it marks the greatest skills a language user can demonstrate. Anyone who wants to acquire a profound knowledge of language that goes beyond the utilitarian will read literary texts in that language'. The resistance towards employing children's literature in language teaching mirrors the historical, now largely overcome resistance of many scholars towards including the study of children's literary texts in literature courses in academia. However, in Europe as in the United States the lack of respect for children's literature in teacher education can still be observed, as Allison Hoewisch (2000) maintains when she centres on the need for ongoing teachers to study children's literature as both a powerful educational tool and significant literary form.

The trajectory of EFL learning towards ever-younger students

Students now start learning English around the world at an ever-younger age. David Graddol writes: 'The trend has gathered momentum only very recently and the intention is often to create a bilingual population' (2006, p. 88). Due to the many competing disciplinary demands at secondary-school level, primary English should be seen as the all-important foundation. Referring specifically to preparing young learners for the English-medium upper secondary-school EFL classroom, Ghosn considers that communicative courses may be an insufficient preparation for the cognitive demands of the advanced academic classes, whereas 'a syllabus that is based, or that draws heavily on authentic children's stories, provides a motivating medium for language learning while fostering the development of the thinking skills that are needed for L2 academic literacy' (Ghosn, 2002, p. 172).

The motivational force of storytelling and picturebooks in language teaching to young learners has already been chronicled (Garvie, 1990; Brewster et al., 2002; Enever et al., 2006 and Wright, 2009). However, few primary English teachers and even fewer secondary-school teachers are really conversant with the literary and ICC potential of children's literature. Yet children's literature has 'a massive cultural influence' (Hunt, 2001, p. 2), and furthermore, if students whose English language exposure solely consists of functional communicative learning, are later plunged straight into canonical adult literature as advanced learners, they miss out on the affirmative and self-esteem-promoting educational potential of children's literature, which is a vital apprenticeship to life and to becoming a reader.

What hinders the use of children's literature in language education?

Access to motivating books

Time and opportunities are needed for a reading apprenticeship, including reading both inside and outside school. The choice of texts in formal education is of the utmost importance, as many school children do not have any access to suitable books in the home. A study conducted in the United States by Hart and Risley (1995) shows the impact of the socioeconomic status (SES) of students on their reading. It was demonstrated that an enormous gap in language input at the start of school (children of poverty had heard and seen circa 32 million fewer words) was linked to a discrepancy of attainment at age 9. Schools must at least attempt to compensate for the disadvantages of a lack of books in the home environment, particularly as extensive reading supports the development of learner autonomy as well as language acquisition (Krashen, 2004 and 2007; Renandya et al., 2002; Grabe, 2009). And due to the linking of life opportunities with skilled reading abilities, it is 'an important societal responsibility to offer every person the opportunity to become a skilled reader, and in many cases, this means becoming a skilled L2 reader' (Grabe, 2009, p. 6).

The availability of children's literature is a crucial issue. A four-year reading project in the EFL classroom in Hungary established that the children's enthusiasm was largely due to the high quality of the picturebooks: 'According to the teacher from the socially disadvantaged school (T2) "some of the children have never in their lives seen books of this quality, and maybe they never will"' (Lugossy, 2006, p. 28). Children and teenagers have tremendous trouble finding books they like, even in their mother tongue (Yankelovich, 2006, p. 34). Without school libraries with a good variety of children's literature, also in the L2, the chances for children to become readers, and all the empowerment that being a reader entails, are extremely unequal, and an extensive reading programme has little chance to be persuasive and successful (Krashen, 2004 and in this volume).

The CEF versus the transactional approach to reading

Booktalk in the classroom with children's literature can be student-centred, transactional meaning making. This constructivist approach contrasts with the trend of teaching with L2 texts in many countries, for example those that follow the model of the *Common European Framework of Reference for Languages* (CEF). Some deficits have been identified in this framework. The CEF lacks content specifications (Fulcher, 2004) and particularly there is little description of educational processes in language learning (Bredella, 2003). Further, according to Quetz and Vogt, the pragmatic orientation towards adult learners (2009, p. 68) and disregard of the affordances of fictional texts, drama processes and creative writing (2009, p. 83) mean the CEF is a less suitable framework for school-aged learners. Moreover, striving for communicative competences should not be seen as language acquisition only. Mike Fleming asks whether literature should be separately taught and assessed or included in the teaching of language, as it 'is literature that encapsulates the language in its most subtle and intricate forms where nuances of meaning and ambiguity have to be embraced' (Fleming, 2007, p. 55). In literature the content is inseparably woven into the language; this is a tremendous aid to children who, within their own horizons, are experts (for instance fairy tales, animals alive and extinct, sports, games and fantasy), and can use their expertise when both the content and language of stories are ingredients of the EFL classroom. On the other hand, children who are starved of stories lack the words and ideas that underlie confident, well-chosen action: 'Deprive children of stories and you leave them unscripted, anxious stutterers in their actions as in their words' (MacIntyre, 1981, p. 216). Michael Rosen expresses this in a way that highlights classroom malpractice: 'Children who come from homes where books are being read get access to the kinds of abstract and complex ideas that you can only get hold of easily through exposure to extended prose. The rest are being fed worksheets' (Rosen, 2009). The complexities of multimodal and multilayered children's literary texts are very far removed from filling in gaps in worksheets.

Children's culture in teacher education

Literacies and the canon

The Pedagogy of Multiliteracies argues that 'what students needed to learn was changing, and that the main element of this change was that there was not a singular, canonical English that could or should be taught anymore' (New London Group, 1996, p. 63). According to Richard Kern (2000, pp. 16–17) the following principles of literacy, or multiple literacies, are applicable to language teaching: interpretation, collaboration, conventions, cultural knowledge, problem solving, reflection and self-reflection and language use. Kern highlights interpretation as the central construct of literacy that connects communicative competence and literary studies, as both revolve around interpretation. Hybridization, boundary breaking, a sense of parody and irony, to mention just a few elements of postmodernism that require an interpretative response, are observable in much contemporary children's literature (Lewis, 2001; Goldstone,

2001), ensuring that one and the same text addresses a multiple audience. It is thus essential to provide university students in teacher education with criteria for selecting complex yet linguistically appropriate children's literature, so that the higher levels of maturity of the L2 learners, who will typically be a year or two older than an L1 reader of the same book, can be a distinct advantage. In fact school students as digital natives are used to combinations of text, image and dynamic layout, and find multimodal texts such as picturebooks and graphic novels stimulating. Multimodal texts do not demand linear reading but allow a *choice* of reading path, recalling the multiple windows simultaneously open on computer screens. Serafini argues that teachers must become 'more discerning readers and investigators of the picture books they choose to read in their classrooms. Being able to lead sophisticated discussions with their students requires teachers to become more sophisticated readers themselves' (Serafini, 2005, p. 63). Students need to perceive a connection between the EFL classroom and their world beyond school, therefore the school canon of literary texts should be extended beyond monomodal texts such as print media.

Carney and Levin (2002) report in their research on reading that images help not only in contextualizing the topic of the text, but also allow students some autonomy in their predicting and interpreting meaning. The ability of students to create mental images while reading in a foreign language needs to be trained in order for them to achieve fluency and pleasure (Stevick, 1986; Tomlinson, 1998). The extremely valuable asset of visualization and imagining for language learning should be taken into consideration beyond the primary school. Arnold refers to creativity and emotions in the language-learning context when she observes that in many educational programmes 'words and numbers have pushed imagery "out of the picture", and in the process much is lost. When used appropriately, images can provide a strong impetus for learning' (Arnold, 1999, p. 262). Marsh and Millard (2000, p. 104) maintain many teachers mistakenly 'consider the movement from pictures to words largely as an intellectual progression', and in the US educational context, Sipe argues that 'picturebooks are valuable resources for developing visual aesthetic understanding in all grades, including middle school and secondary school' (Sipe, 2008, p. 131).

The storyworld as a microcosm of children's culture

The relationship between images and imagining, creativity, emotions and the empowering of language learning is crucial. High-quality children's literature can help students learn to map the world story by story, while successively acquiring competences such as visual, literary and intercultural literacy, concurrently with language acquisition. Quoted in White (1998, p. 75), the influential writer of fantasy Alan Garner compares his young adult fiction to onions, in that an onion has many layers, but is in every layer whole in itself. In this multilayered way narrative is a secretive, magical affair; in many storyworlds 'there is a whole cast of witches, monsters, dragons, goblins and others who are pictured for us but which have parallels, if at all, only in our heads' (Graham, 2005, p. 212). As children's literature is enmeshed in the cultural world of the child, it should be a central study for ongoing teachers. Learning to enter a storyworld imaginatively and mindfully should be considered a pivotal competence in the intercultural communicative classroom:

> the grounding of stories in storyworlds goes a long way towards explaining narratives' immersiveness, their ability to 'transport' interpreters into places and times that they must occupy for the purposes of narrative comprehension. (. . .) storyworlds are mentally and emotionally projected environments in which interpreters are called upon to live out complex blends of cognitive and imaginative response. (Herman, 2005, p. 570)

Claire Kramsch (1996, p. 3) argues that culture 'constitutes itself along three axes: the diachronic axis of time, the synchronic axis of space, and the metaphoric axis of the imagination'. Through the 'metaphoric axis of the imagination' the reader enters the storyworld and learns to be able to see from another perspective. The presentation of cultural information in current EFL textbooks is still frequently factual cultural information 'reduced to teachable and memorisable chunks' (Teske, 2006, p. 26). While this does not facilitate an imaginative leap and change of perspective, it also ignores what Harold Rosen (1985, p. 6) calls the 'nurture of narrative'. A salient aspect of children's culture is the patterned and playful language that belongs to the 'organic language' of childhood (Ashton-Warner, 1963), in that it grows out of the child's own emotions and needs. Nursery rhymes and vigorous rhythms in stories encourage young EFL students to experiment with the language they are just beginning to acquire. Narrative or storying is central to children's culture, and then 'stays with us as a cognitive and affective habit all our lives long' (Meek, 1982, p. 287).

Approaching children's literature in second language education

It is mistaken to believe that children, teachers or university students can read literature in an interpretative way just because they have mastered how to read (Perloff, 1997). The chapters in this volume have been brought together hopefully to show that for EFL students, as for L1 students, 'Literature, not reading lessons, teaches children to read in ways that no basal reader can, because literature is read, if at all, with passion, with desire' (Meek, 1982, p. 290).

Part one: Extensive reading with children's literature

Krashen with 'Free Reading: Still a Great Idea' produces a wide-ranging overview of recent empirical research to confirm, in Chapter 2, that more free reading leads to better reading, writing and many other language skills, as well as less boredom in the classroom. Mason, in Chapter 3, reports on 'Efficient Use of Literature in Second Language Education: Free Reading and Listening to Stories'. She moves beyond the efficacy of free reading combined with listening to stories, to give an account of her studies that equally show the efficiency of this method. An early start to extensive reading is recommended by Day and Bamford (1998, p. xiv), who consider, provided the children have learned to read in their first language, that 'extensive reading is appropriate at all stages of language learning; it is never too early – or too late – to learn to read a second language'. Kolb documents in Chapter 4, 'Extensive Reading of Picturebooks in Primary EFL', a recent case study with 9 and 10-year-olds in Germany, in their fourth year of EFL, who extensively read picturebooks. The study concerns itself with the students' reading motivation, confidence and reading competence. Two of the most important ingredients in the EFL-literature classroom are surely interest and enthusiasm on the part of the reader and the literary worth of the text. In Chapter 5, 'Free Space: An Extensive Reading Project in a Flemish School', the challenge of reading with teenagers is taken up by Strobbe, whose project reveals that motivation through a wide and eclectic choice of books is key to a pleasurable reading experience as well as language acquisition.

Part two: Visual literacy with picturebooks and graphic novels in ELT

In Chapter 6, 'Approaching Literary and Language Competence: Picturebooks and Graphic Novels in the EFL Classroom', Burwitz-Melzer illustrates the challenge of literary literacy and visual literacy. She highlights the need for the 'visual turn' in language teaching to be better prepared for in teacher education. In Chapter 7, 'Picturebook: Object of Discovery', Mourão has produced evidence that already preschool Portuguese children in an EFL context are able to use the peritextual features of picturebooks, such as book covers and titles, to develop cognitively by practising inferential thinking. Bette Goldstone considers postmodern picturebooks as 'renegades from (the) traditional picture book'; among the playful characteristics of postmodern literature are 'a greater power given to the reader/viewer encouraging cocreation with the author or artist; and a juxtaposition of unrelated images creating nonlinear formats' (Goldstone, 2001, pp. 362–3). This is explored in Chapter 8, in which Bland describes achieving a meaningful crossover from the primary to the secondary classroom with multimodal texts in 'Fairy Tales with a Difference: Creating a Continuum from Primary to Secondary ELT'.

Part three: Intercultural encounters with children's literature

The connection between imagined storyworlds and intercultural communicative competence is highlighted in Chapter 9, 'Otherness in Children's Literature. Perspectives for the EFL Classroom', in which Lütge discusses the experience of 'otherness' and diversity that can be afforded through the imaginative world of fantasy and magic realism.

In Chapter 10, 'Doing Identity, Doing Culture: Transcultural Learning through Young Adult Fiction', Reichl considers intersubjective learning processes with diverse cultural contexts, which may lead to cognitive dissonances and constructive understanding. In Chapter 11 'Developing Intercultural Competence by Studying Graphic Narratives' Hecke produces evidence for the development of intercultural communicative competence with graphic novels. Rieuwerts in Chapter 12 '"We are Britain!" Culture and Ethnicity in Benjamin Zephaniah's Novels' argues for a multicultural and anti-racist dialogue in the L2 classroom with Zephaniah's writings. In Chapter 13, 'Taiwanese Adolescents Reading American Young Adult Literature: A Reader Response Study', Lee documents the nature of her EFL students' experience with authentic literary texts, and in particular their development of intercultural awareness and understanding. Teachers and students can profit from a wider range of literary texts than ever before in different modes and different media, however this does not obviate but rather necessitates the need for a critical scrutiny. In Chapter 14, 'Developing Intercultural Competence through First Nations' Children's Literature', Alter examines the ideological implications of children's literature. A scrutiny of popular texts for children shows the frequently demeaning representation of indigenous cultures, whereas children's literature titles by Native American authors can help develop a respect for 'otherness'.

Part four: Empowerment and creativity through story

Creative writing and performance are important elements of active literary interpretation, and the ludic nature of children's literature and culture encourages a vital first step to linguistic creativity. The interaction of aesthetic reading and creative writing is described by Maley in Chapter 15, 'Creative Writing for Second Language Students'. An aspect of learner empowerment is routinely neglected in language education, although it would be particularly relevant for intercultural learning: that teachers use the diverse 'cultural information students bring into the classroom as legitimate and important constituents of learning' (McLaren, 1988, p. 214). In Chapter 16, 'Young Adult Literature in Mixed-Ability Classes', Eisenmann refers to the political and cultural environment of the school, as well as the emotional and social differences of the students. Not only the classroom texts and their selection must be examined, but also the way they are implemented. Student-centred methodologies are described, including extensive reading, keeping a reading log and literature circles. While English learning is so time-consuming throughout schooling and beyond, it is surely unacceptable that the potential for humanist discourse that arises through interaction between language learners and first-rate children's literature is so manifestly under-realized. In Chapter 17, 'Enhancing Self-Esteem and Positive Attitudes through Children's Literature', Traverso outlines the humanist school of thought on language teaching, and the role school can play towards students' emotional development. She concludes that employing children's literature in the EFL classroom can be a tremendous support towards fostering positive feelings. In Chapter 18, 'The "Art" of Teaching Creative Story Writing', Fleta Guillén and García Bermejo illustrate the close relationship between music and literacy, the rhythmical patterns and the qualities of sound, and how this can be exploited for creative story making and storytelling. In Chapter 19 'Stories as Symphonies', Andrew Wright demonstrates from his perspective as storyteller and illustrator how the many modes of communication, generally too little developed in teacher education, can be exploited holistically and with all senses to enrich creative storytelling and creative writing.

English language teaching is usually considered to embody a key role in education as a whole, also as an opportunity for the development of intercultural learning and tolerance, parallel to mother tongue education. Children's literature and young adult English language literature across the world displays a stunning diversity, yet often remains entirely undiscovered by English language teachers, and consequently also by English learners. We hope with this volume to provide arguments for employing valuable works of children's literature by leading authors that should be at the top of any list, to counteract an overreliance on worksheets, and the 'tendency of fossilisation of the literary canon at schools' (Lütge, 2012, p. 191).

References

Arnold, J. (1999), 'Visualization: Language learning with the mind's eye', in J. Arnold (ed.), *Affect in Language Learning*. Cambridge: Cambridge University Press, pp. 260–78.

Ashton-Warner, S. (1963), *Teacher*. New York: Simon and Schuster.

Bassnett, S. and Grundy, P. (1993), *Language through Literature*. London: Longman.

Benton, M. (1992), *Secondary Worlds: Literature Teaching and the Visual Arts*. Buckingham and Philadelphia: Open University Press.

Bredella, L. (2003), 'Lesen und Interpretieren im "Gemeinsamen europäischen Referenzrahmen für Sprachen": Die Missachtung allgemeiner Erziehungsziele', in K.-R. Bausch, H. Christ, F. Königs and H.-J. Krumm (eds), *Der Gemeinsame europäische Referenzrahmen für Sprachen in der Diskussion. Arbeitspapiere der 22. Frühjahrskonfererenz zur Erforschung des Fremdsprachenunterrichts*. Tübingen: Narr, pp. 45–56.

Brewster, J. and Ellis, G. (2002), *Tell it Again – The New Story Telling Handbook for Primary Teachers*. Harlow: Pearson.

Carney, R. and Levin, J. (2002), 'Pictorial illustrations still improve students' learning from text', *Educational Psychology Review*, 14(1), 5–26.

Council of Europe (eds) (2001), *Common European Framework of Reference for Languages: Learning, Teaching, Assessment*. Cambridge: Cambridge University Press.

Day, R. and Bamford, J. (1998), *Extensive Reading in the Second Language Classroom*. Cambridge: Cambridge University Press.

Enever, J. and Schmid-Schönbein, G. (eds) (2006), *Picture Books and Young Learners of English. Münchener Arbeiten zur Fremdsprachen-Forschung*. München: Langenscheidt.

Fleming, M. (2007), 'The use and mis-use of competence frameworks and statements with particular attention to describing achievement in literature', in *Towards a Common European Framework of Reference for Languages of School Education? Selected Conference Papers*. Poland: Waldemar Martyniuk, pp. 47–59.

Fulcher, G. (2004), 'Are Europe's tests being built on an "unsafe" framework?' *Guardian Weekly*. Accessed 18.03.2004 at www.guardian.co.uk/education/2004/mar/18/tefl2

Garvie, E. (1990), *Story as Vehicle: Teaching English to Young Children*. Clevedon: Multilingual Matters.

Ghosn, I. (2002), 'Four good reasons to use literature in primary school ELT', *ELT Journal*, 56(2), 172–9.

Goldstone, B. (2001), 'Whaz up with our books? Changing picture book codes and teaching implications', *The Reading Teacher*, 55(4), 362–70.

Grabe, W. (2009), *Reading in a Second Language. Moving from Theory to Practice*. Cambridge: Cambridge University Press.

Graddol, D. (2006), *English Next*. British Council.

Graham, J. (2005), 'Reading contemporary picturebooks', in K. Reynolds (ed.), *Modern Children's Literature*. Basingstoke: Palgrave Macmillan, pp. 209–26.

Hart, B. and Risley, T. (1995), *Meaningful Differences in the Everyday Experience of Young American Children*. Baltimore: Paul Brookes Publishing.

Herman, D. (2005), 'Storyworld', in D. Herman, M. Jahn and M.-L. Ryan (eds), *Routledge Encyclopedia of Narrative Theory*. Oxford: Routledge, pp. 569–70.

Hoewisch, A. (2000), 'Children's literature in teacher-preparation programs: An invited contribution', *Reading Online*. Accessed 28.05.12 at www.readingonline.org/critical/hoewisch/childrenlit.html#author

Hunt, P. (ed.) (1996), *International Companion Encyclopaedia of Children's Literature*. London: Routledge.

— (2001), *Children's Literature*. Oxford: Blackwell.

Kern, R. (2000), *Literacy and Language Teaching*. Oxford: Oxford University Press.

Kramsch, C. (1996), 'The cultural component of language teaching', *Zeitschrift für Interkulturellen Fremdsprachenunterricht*, 1(2), 1–13.

Krashen, S. (2004), *The Power of Reading* (2nd edn). Portsmouth, NH: Heinemann.

— (2007), 'Extensive reading in English as a foreign language by adolescents and young adults: A meta-analysis', *International Journal of Foreign Language Teaching*, 3(2), 23–9.

Lewis, D. (2001), *Reading Contemporary Picturebooks, Picturing Text*. Oxford: Routledge.

Lütge, C. (2012), 'Developing "literary literacy"? Towards a progression of literary learning', in M. Eisenmann and T. Summer (eds), *Basic Issues in EFL Teaching and Learning*. Heidelberg: Universitätsverlag Winter, pp. 191–202.

Lugossy, R. (2006), 'Browsing and borrowing your way to motivation through picture books', in J. Enever and G. Schmid-Schönbein (eds), *Picture Books and Young Learners of English*. München: Langenscheidt, pp. 23–34.

MacIntyre, A. (1981), *After Virtue*. London: Duckworth.

McLaren, P. (1988), 'Culture or canon? Critical pedagogy and the politics of literacy', *Harvard Educational Review*, 58(5), 213–34.

Marsh, J. and Millard, E. (2000), *Literacy and Popular Culture. Using Children's Culture in the Classroom*. London: Paul Chapman.

Meek, M. (1982), 'What counts as evidence in theories of children's literature?', *Theory into Practice*, 21(4), 284–92.

New London Group (1996), 'A pedagogy of multiliteracies: Designing social futures', *Harvard Educational Review*, 66(1), 60–92.

Nodelman, P. and Reimer, M. (2003), *The Pleasures of Children's Literature* (3rd edn). Boston: Allyn and Bacon.

Perloff, M. (1997), 'Literary Literacy', *Chronicle of Higher Education, 9 May 1997*. Accessed 30.05.12 at http://epc.buffalo.edu/authors/perloff/chron.html

Quetz, J. and Vogt, K. (2009), 'Bildungsstandards für die erste Fremdsprache: Sprachenpolitik auf unsicherer Basis. Antwort auf das Positionspapier der DGFF', *Zeitschrift für Fremdsprachenforschung*, 20(1), 63–89.

Renandya, W. and Jacobs, G. (2002), 'Extensive reading: Why aren't we all doing it?', in J. Richards and W. Renandya (eds), *Methodology in Language Teaching: An Anthology of Current Practice*. New York: Cambridge University Press, pp. 295–302.

Rosen, H. (1985), *Stories and Meanings*. Sheffield: National Association for the Teaching of English.

Rosen, M. (2009), 'The ups and downs of a story', The *Guardian*. Accessed 09.06.2009 at www.guardian.co.uk/education/2009/jun/09/michael-rosen-creativity-in-the-classroom-teaching

Rudd, D. (ed.) (2010), *The Routledge Companion to Children's Literature*. Abingdon: Routledge.

Serafini, F. (2005), 'Voices in the park, voices in the classroom: Readers responding to postmodern picture books', *Reading, Research and Instruction*, 44(3), 47–65.

— (2009), 'Understanding visual images in picturebooks', in J. Evans (ed.), *Talking Beyond the Page. Reading and Responding to Picturebooks*. Oxford: Routledge, pp. 10–25.

Sipe, L. (1998), 'How picture books work: A semiotically framed theory of text-picture relationships', *Children's Literature in Education*, 29(2), 97–108.

— (2008), 'Learning from illustrations in picturebooks', in N. Frey and D. Fisher (eds), *Teaching Visual Literacy Using Comic Books, Graphic Novels, Anime, Cartoons, and More to Develop Comprehension and Thinking Skills*. Thousand Oaks, CA: Corwin Press, pp. 131–48.

Stevick, E. (1986), *Images and Options in the Language Classroom*. Cambridge: Cambridge University Press.

Teske, D. (2006), 'Cultural studies: Key issues and approaches', in W. Delanoy and L. Volkmann (eds), *Cultural Studies in the EFL Classroom*. Heidelberg: Winter, pp. 23–33.

Tomlinson, B. (1998), 'Seeing what they mean: Helping L2 readers to visualise', in B. Tomlinson (ed.), *Materials Development in Language Teaching*. Cambridge: Cambridge University Press.

Watson, V. (2001), *The Cambridge Guide to Children's Books in English*. Cambridge: Cambridge University Press.

White, D. (1998), *A Century of Welsh Myth in Children's Literature*. Westport: Greenwood Press.

Wright, A. (2009), *Storytelling with Children* (2nd edn). Oxford: Oxford University Press.

Yankelovich (2006), *Kids and Family Reading Report*. New York: Scholastic. Accessible at www.scholastic.com/aboutscholastic/news/reading_survey_press_call_2.pdf

Part One

Extensive Reading with Children's Literature

2

Free Reading: Still a Great Idea

Stephen Krashen

I have been writing papers on the benefits of free voluntary reading since the early 1980s. My interest was stimulated by reading Frank Smith's book, *Reading without Nonsense*, and my realization that Frank Smith and Kenneth Goodman's hypotheses about learning to read were very similar to what I had proposed for second language acquisition: I had claimed that we acquire language when we understand it. Smith and Goodman hypothesized that we learn to read by understanding what is on the page. Their conclusions, based on entirely different evidence from mine, provided a comforting confirmation of the 'Comprehension Hypothesis'.

Readers read better

My papers over the last three decades on this topic have reviewed the impact of self-selected or free reading on literacy development. Case studies, correlational studies and experimental studies have all confirmed that more free reading results in better reading ability, better writing, larger vocabularies, better spelling and better control of complex grammatical constructions. Much of this research has been reviewed in several publications (summarized in Krashen, 2004; Mason, 2010; Cho, 2010) so I will restrict this part of the paper to a brief update.

Early studies on sustained silent reading (self-selected reading in school) were done in the United States with children who spoke English as a first language. In these studies, the students in both the experimental and comparison classes had traditional instruction, but those in the experimental classes were given some class time to do self-selected reading with little or no accountability. Experimental students typically did better than comparisons in longer-term studies, and in short-term studies there is either no difference or the readers did better on tests of reading comprehension. Subsequent studies confirmed that free reading worked for English as a foreign language with children (Krashen, 2004; Cho, 2010).

The subjects in the studies in Table 2.1 were students of English as a foreign language at the high school and university level. These studies are of great practical

Children's Literature in Second Language Education

Table 2.1 Studies of English as a foreign language – self-selected in-class reading

Study	N	Duration	Cloze	RC
Yuan and Nash, 1992	37	One year	0.38	
Sims, 1996	30	One year		0.81
Sims, 1996	30	One year		0.65
Mason retakers	30	One sem	0.702	
Mason Jr college	31	One year	1.47	
Mason university	40	One year	1.11	
Mason: response L1	40	One year	0.24	0.61
Mason: response L2	36	One year	0.63	0.48
Lituanas et al., 1999	30	Six months		1.7
Bell, 2001	14	One year	1.31	3.14
Sheu, 2004	31			0.71
Sheu, 2004	34			1.04
Lee, 2005	65	12 weeks	0.24	
Hsu and Lee, 2005	47	One year	0.58	
K. Smith, 2006	51	One year	0.47	0.39
Lee, 2006	41	One year	1.02	
K. Smith, 2007	41	One year	0.56	
Liu, 2007	46	One year	1.59	

interest, and are also experimentally relatively clean: students in these studies generally have limited input in English outside of class.

The studies were done in Taiwan (Yuan et al., 1992; Sims, 1996; Sheu, 2004; Hsu et al., 2005; Lee, 2005 and 2006; K. Smith, 2006 and 2007; and Liu 2007), Japan (Mason et al., 1997), the Philippines (Lituanas et al., 1999) and Yemen (Bell, 2001). In all studies, time was set aside for self-selected reading and readers were compared to similar students who did not have reading time included as part of their English programme. Only studies in which students are tested on reading (reading comprehension and cloze tests) were included.

The readers did better than those in the comparison group in every study. This is shown in the Cloze and RC columns, which contain effect sizes, a measure of the impact of a treatment. All effect sizes are positive and the average effect size for cloze tests was .46, which is considered modest, which increased to .73 when sample size was taken into consideration. For reading comprehension, the average effect size was a substantial .87, which increased to .88 when weighted for sample size. This is a remarkable confirmation of the power of reading.

Readers know more

A series of studies by Stanovich and colleagues show that readers know more than non-readers do about literature and history (Stanovich et al., 1992), science and social studies (Stanovich et al., 1993), have more 'cultural literacy' (West et al., 1993) and even have more 'practical knowledge' (Stanovich et al., 1993).

Another contribution to this area of research is Filback et al. (2002), who reported that among practicing Christians, those who reported more self-initiated reading of the Bible had more knowledge of the Bible than those who did less reading. More formal Bible study, however, was not related to more knowledge of the Bible.

The cognitive benefits of reading

Older people who read more do better on tests of mental ability. The standard test used to detect dementia is the MMSE, a short test of arithmetic, memory and spatial relations. A research team (Galluccia et al., 2009) found that older people (average age 84) who said they read novels and non-fiction averaged 27.3 on the MMSE, which is in the normal range (27–30). Those who said they only read newspapers averaged 26, which is just below normal (20–26 = 'some impairment'), but those who said they did no reading averaged 21, well inside the 'impaired' range. Frequency of reading was a significant predictor of MMSE scores even when other factors, such as physical activity, chronic diseases, socializing and hearing ability were controlled.

A popular research design in dementia studies is to test older people who don't have any signs of problems, and then retest them years later, comparing those who develop problems and those who don't. In one of these 'prospective' studies, Verghese et al. (2003) reported that 68% of those who developed dementia five years after initial testing said they read books or newspapers frequently (at least several times per week), but 86% of those who did not develop dementia were frequent readers, a significant difference. Geda (2009) reported similar results.

Studies also show that bilingualism is related to delay of the onset of dementia, as is drinking coffee. In fact, recent studies with mice suggest that drinking five cups per day can reverse Alzheimer's (Arendash et al., 2009). The research, however, provides no evidence that caffeine improved the memory of normal mice, even if administered from youth through old age. The effect, so far, appears to be specific to dementia. Coffee, in other words, keeps you normal but won't make you super-normal.

We need to know the effect of combining all three, reading, bilingualism and coffee. Note that it is easy to do them at the same time: hang out at a coffee shop (drink about three regular cups of coffee a day, according to the research), and read a book in another language. I would be happy to volunteer as a subject in such a study. Maybe the experimenters will pay for my coffee.

Are readers nerds?

Some people think that readers are nerds, 'book-worms' who don't get out much, don't do much and are simply boring, dull people. The research, however, does not agree with this characterization. In fact, the results of a number of studies of adult readers show that readers are 'active and social' (Bradshaw et al., 2004).

Table 2.2 presents data originally published in 1982, from Zill et al. (1990), comparing literature readers (those who reported reading 'any creative writings, such as stories, poems, plays and the like' for the last 12 months), those who read any kind of a book or magazine and those who reported no reading. The results are remarkably consistent, with readers reporting being more active in all categories.

We cannot, however, conclude from this data that reading is directly associated with being active and social. As Zill et al. point out, the amount of leisure reading done is also closely associated with education and affluence (for confirming data, see Bradshaw et al., 2004). It may be the case that those who are more affluent have more time and money to engage in these activities. However, this is probably not the case for visiting museums. Bradshaw et al. (2004) present a multiple regression analysis showing a relationship between reading and visiting art museums and attending performing arts events, even when income and education were statistically controlled.

Table 2.2 Leisure activities of literature readers, non-literature readers and non-readers (1982); adults 18 and older

LEISURE ACTIVITIES	Literature readers (%)	Readers, not of literature (%)	Non-readers (%)
Amusements			
Play card, board games	77	62	27
Attend movies	75	59	25
Visit amusement park	57	49	19
Attend sports events	59	43	17
Exercise, Sports			
jog, exercise	65	43	18
play sports	48	36	14
camping, hiking	43	34	14
Home-based activities			
Repair home, car	66	60	28
Gardening	69	53	34
Gourmet cooking	38	22	8
Collect stamps, coins	20	10	3
Charitable work			
Volunteer, charity work	36	21	9
Cultural attendance			
Visit historic sites	50	28	8
Go to zoo	41	25	11
Visit museums	32	15	4
Art and crafts			
Weaving, needlework	42	29	18
Pottery, ceramics	17	9	3
Photography, video	14	6	2
Painting, drawing, sculpture	14	6	2

Source: From Zill and Winglee, table 2, p. 15.

Controlling for background variables

To control for education, income and other related variables, my colleagues and I approached the question in a different way: the subjects in this study came from one social class, children in schools with high levels of poverty (90% or more free or reduced price lunch). All children were in grades four and five in four different schools in Austin, Texas.

We asked the children about people they knew who read a lot, whether they were 'not interesting and fun', 'kind of interesting and fun' or 'very interesting and fun'.

As presented in Tables 2.3 and 2.4, the results are clear and consistent. Very few children felt that readers were not interesting and fun, and about two-thirds felt they were very interesting and fun. The percentages are nearly the same in all four schools and in both grades.

Attitudes may change as children get older, but this data suggests that fourth and fifth graders do not think that readers are nerds.

Encouraging reading

Despite the prevalence of rewarding children for reading, and claims made on behalf of reading management programmes, the last decade has produced no evidence that such programmes work or do not work. Krashen (2003, 2005) reviewed research on Accelerated Reader, easily the most popular reading management programme in the United States, and reported that no study looked specifically at whether the tests and

Table 2.3 Responses to people I know who read are interesting and fun: Grade four

School	N	Very (%)	Kind of (%)	Not (%)
1	44	68	25	7
2	101	62	32	6
3	43	69	29	2
4	48	74	26	0

Table 2.4 Responses to people I know who read are interesting and fun: Grade five

School	N	Very (%)	Kind of (%)	Not (%)
1	43	53	44	2
2	99	62	32	6
3	49	67	27	6
4	51	68	32	0

prizes that are an integral part of Accelerated Reader add anything to the gains one would expect just from self-selected reading. We thus have no evidence one way or the other on the effectiveness of this programme.

The last decade has, however, given us a better idea of what does work to encourage reading. Three small-scale studies confirmed Jim Trelease's idea (Trelease, 2006) that one book, one positive reading experience (called a 'home run' book), can create a reading habit (Von Sprecken et al., 2000; Kim et al., 2000; Ujiie et al., 2002).

Natural partners

Research has also confirmed another Trelease idea, that read-alouds and free reading are 'natural partners' in that read-alouds stimulate interest in independent reading, as well as provide some of the linguistic tools that make reading more comprehensible (Trelease, 2006).

One study had the self-explanatory title, 'Sixteen books went home tonight: Fifteen were introduced by the teacher' (Brassell, 2003). In another study, Wang et al. (2007) observed children in EFL classes in Taiwan who had clearly enjoyed hearing series books such as the Marvin Redford series read aloud. This led to an eagerness to read books from the same series on their own during SSR time.

Lee et al. (2009) examined the texts used in Wang and Lee and compared them to assigned pedagogical texts. The 65 storybooks the class used over 4 years provided a richer source of vocabulary, with twice as many nouns and 3 times as many verbs and adjectives as the textbooks, suggesting that comprehensible authentic material may be much better for language acquisition and literacy development than traditional texts.

Access!!

The research of the two decades on the impact of libraries has repeatedly demonstrated the fact that more access to books results in more reading and hence better reading. Library quality (books and staffing) has been shown to be related to reading achievement in the United States at the state level (Lance, 2004) and national level (McQuillan, 1998).

Our recent study (Krashen et al., forthcoming) of the *Progress in International Reading Literacy Study* (PIRLS) 2006 examination given to 10-year olds in 40 countries provides strong confirmation of the importance of libraries. Countries included in the analysis were: Austria, Belgium (both French and Flemish), Bulgaria, Canada (five provinces analysed separately), Taiwan, Denmark, France, Georgia, Germany, Hong Kong, Hungary, Iceland, Indonesia, Iran, Israel, Italy, Kuwait, Latvia, Lithuania, Republic of Macedonia, Republic of Moldova, Morocco, Netherlands, New Zealand, Norway, Poland, Romania, Russian Federation, Singapore, Slovak Republic, Slovenia, South Africa, Spain, Sweden, Trinidad and Tobago. Most countries tested about 4,000 students from about 150 schools.

The reading test consisted of five literary passages and five informational passages followed by multiple-choice and open-ended questions. The tests were originally written in English and then translated into 45 languages. We selected a few factors that theory predicted would be important predictors of reading achievement. Table 2.5 presents the results in terms of a multiple regression analysis, a statistical tool that allows us to see the impact of each factor, uninfluenced by the others.

SES is socio-economic class, defined here as a combination of education, life expectancy and wealth. In agreement with many other studies, we found that SES had a profound impact on performance on the reading test: higher SES meant better performance. SSR in Table 2.5 stands for the percentage of students in each country who participated in sustained silent reading programmes in school: students in countries that utilized more sustained silent reading tended to do better in reading. This result fell just short of the usual standard for statistical significance, but the positive relationship between SSR and reading proficiency is consistent with the results of in-school self-selected reading programmes, as mentioned earlier (Krashen, 2004).

'Library' in Table 2.5 means the percentage of schools in each country with school libraries containing more than 500 books. 'Library' is a very strong predictor of reading scores, nearly as strong as the effect of poverty (compare the betas in Table 2.5). Not only is the effect of libraries in this study consistent with other reports, it is independent of the effect of socio-economic class.

The final predictor is the amount of formal instruction in reading that children receive in each country. The beta is negative: more time devoted to instruction is associated with *lower* reading scores. This predictor fell just short of statistical significance. It may be the case that a little reading instruction is beneficial, but after a point it is ineffective and counterproductive.

The r2 is .63. This means that if we know the level of poverty of a country, the percentage of children who are in sustained silent reading programmes, the percentage of schools with libraries with more than 500 volumes, and the amount of time devoted to formal reading instruction, we have 63% of the information we need to predict that country's reading scores. This is impressive.

Table 2.5 Multiple regression analysis

Predictor	Beta	P
SES	.42	0.003
SSR	.19	0.09
Library	.34	.005
Instruction	−.19	0.07
r2 = .63		

Note: p = probability that the result could have occurred by chance. p = .005 means that the odds are five in a thousand chance this result could have occurred by chance (highly unlikely). Normal procedure is to consider p = .05 or less to be 'statistically significant'.

Notice that all four predictors are related to reading. High SES generally means easy access to books outside of school, more SSR time means of course more reading, access to libraries is associated with more reading (Krashen, 2004) and more time devoted to reading instruction could mean less time devoted to actual reading. The finding that the impact of the school library was nearly as strong as the impact of SES suggests that the library can, to at least some extent, make up for the effects of low SES on reading: several studies confirm that children of poverty have little access to books at home or in their community (Krashen, 2004); the school library may be the only source of books for these children.

The negative relationship between instruction and reading proficiency could be a result of schools offering more instruction to those who need it most. The result is, however, also consistent with reports showing little or no effect of intensive reading instruction on tests that require children to understand what they read (Garan, 2002; Krashen, 2009). What we can conclude is that the research shows that the library is a better investment than heavy skills-based reading teaching.

Conclusions

The case for self-selected, free reading can only be described as astonishing, and new data emerges regularly, confirming previous discoveries and adding new ones.

Despite all this, reading is constantly under attack: in the United States, school and public libraries are constantly being closed and school librarians are assigned to other tasks, despite the pious pronouncements of politicians about the importance of reading. Those most affected are children of poverty, who have few other sources of books.

In addition, materials and curriculum based on skill-building are not only surviving, they are expanding, despite negative research results (Krashen, 2010), the presence of a very pleasant alternative and the consistently bored reactions of students. In fact, for most people, the skill-building hypothesis is not a hypothesis, it is an axiom.

References

Arendash, G., Mori, T., Cao, C., Mamcarz, M., Runfeldt, M., Dickson, A., Rezai-Zadeh, K., Tan, J., Citron, B., Lin, X., Echeverria, V. and Potter, H. (2009), 'Caffeine reverses cognitive impairment and decreases brain amyloid-β levels in aged Alzheimer's disease mice', *Journal of Alzheimer's Disease*, 17(3), 661–80.

Bell, T. (2001), *Extensive Reading: Speed and Comprehension. The Reading Matrix, 1.* Accessible at www.readingmatrix.com/archives/archives_vol1_no1.html

Bradshaw, T. and Nichols, B. (2004), *Reading at Risk: A Survey of Literary Reading in America.* Washington DC: National Endowment for the Arts Research Division Report #46.

Brassell, D. (2003), 'Sixteen books went home tonight: Fifteen were introduced by the teacher', *The California Reader*, 36(3), 33–9.

Cho, K. S. (2010), 'A decade of reading research in Korea: A progress report', *International Journal of Foreign Language Teaching*, 5(2), 15–17 (ijflt.com).

Filback, R. and Krashen, S. (2002), 'The impact of reading the bible and studying the bible on biblical knowledge', *Knowledge Quest*, 31(2), 50–1.

Galluccia, M., Antuono, P., Ongaro, F., Forloni, P., Albani, D., Amicia, G. and Reginia, C. (2009), 'Physical activity, socialization and reading in the elderly over the age of seventy: What is the relation with cognitive decline? Evidence from "The Treviso Longeva (TRELONG) study"', *Archives of Gerontology and Geriatrics*, 48(3), 284–6.

Garan, E. (2002), *Resisting Reading Mandates*. Portsmouth, NH: Heinemann.

Geda, Y. E. (2009), 'Cognitive activities are associated with decreased risk of mild cognitive impairment: The Mayo Clinic population-based study of aging', AAN 2009.

Hsu, Y. Y. and Lee, S. Y. (2005), 'Does extensive reading also benefit junior college students in vocabulary acquisition and reading ability?' *The Proceedings of the 22*nd *International Conference in English Teaching and Learning*, pp. 116–27. Taipei: Crane Publishing Company.

Kim, J. and Krashen, S. (2000), 'Another home run', *California English*, 6(2), 25.

Krashen, S. (2003), 'The (lack of) experimental evidence supporting the use of accelerated reader', *Journal of Children's Literature,* 29(2) 9, 16–30.

— (2004), *The Power of Reading*. Portsmouth: Heinemann and Westport: Libraries Unlimited.

— (2005), 'Accelerated reader: Evidence still lacking', *Knowledge Quest,* 33(3), 48–9.

— (2007), 'Extensive reading in English as a foreign language by adolescents and young adults: A meta-analysis', *International Journal of Foreign Language Teaching,* 3(2), 23–9.

— (2009), 'Does intensive reading instruction contribute to reading comprehension?', *Knowledge Quest,* 37(4), 72–4.

— (2010), 'Comments on the LEARN Act' (available as pdf-download from sdkrashen. com and from http://sites.google.com/site/sdkrashen/home).

Krashen, S., Lee, S. Y. and McQuillan, J. (forthcoming), 'Is the library important? Multivariate studies at the national and international level', *Journal of Language and Literacy*. Available at www.coe.uga.edu/jolle/index.html

Lance, K. (2004), 'The impact of school library media centers on academic achievement', in C. Kuhlthau (ed.), *School Library Media Annual*. Westport, CT: Libraries Unlimited, pp. 188–97.

Lee, S. Y. (2005), 'The robustness of extensive reading: Evidence from two studies', *International Journal of Foreign Language Teaching,* 1(3), 13–19.

— (2006), 'A one-year study of SSR: University level EFL students in Taiwan', *International Journal of Foreign Language Education,* 2(1), 6–8.

Lee, S. Y., Hsieh, M. I. and Wang, F. Y. (2009), 'English acquisition through storytelling: A corpus-based analysis of and comparison between school texts and storybooks'. *The Proceedings of the 2009 International Conference on Applied Linguistics & Language Teaching*. National Taiwan University of Science and Technology. Taipei: Crane Publishing Co., pp. 312–22.

Lituanas, P. M., Jacobs, G. M. and Renandya, W. A. (1999), 'A study of extensive reading with remedial reading students', in Y. M. Cheah and S. M. Ng (eds), *Language Instructional Issues in Asian Classrooms*. Newark, DE: International Development in Asia Committee, International Reading Association, pp. 89–104.

Liu, C. K. (2007), 'A reading program that keeps winning', in *Selected Papers from the Sixteenth International Symposium on English Teaching. English Teachers' Association/ ROC*. Taipei: Crane Publishing Company.

Mason, B. (2010), 'Research on hearing stories and free reading in Japan: A progress report', *International Journal of Foreign Language Teaching,* 5(2), 8–10 (ijflt.com).

Mason, B. and Krashen, S. (1997), 'Extensive reading in English as a foreign language', *System*, 25, 91–102.

McQuillan, J. (1998), *The Literacy Crisis: False Claims and Real Solutions*. Portsmouth, NH: Heinemann Publishing Company.

Mullis, I., Martin, M., Kennedy, A. and Foy, P. (2006), 'PIRLS 2006 international report'. Boston: International Study Center, Boston University.

Sheu, S. P.-H. (2004), 'Extensive reading with EFL learners at beginning level', *TESL Reporter*, 36(2), 8–26.

Sims, J. (1996), 'A new perspective: Extensive reading for pleasure'. *The Proceedings of the Fifth International Symposium on English Teaching*, pp. 137–44. Taipei: Crane Publishing Company.

Smith, F. (2006), *Reading without Nonsense* (4th edn). New York: Teachers College Press.

Smith, K. (2006), 'A comparison of "pure" extensive reading with intensive reading and extensive reading with supplementary activities', *International Journal of Foreign Language Teaching* (IJFLT) 2(2), 12–15.

— (2007), 'The effect of adding SSR to regular instruction'. In *Selected Papers from the Sixteenth International Symposium on English Teaching*. English Teachers' Association/ ROC, Taipei: Crane Publishing Company.

Stanovich, K. and Cunningham, A. (1992), 'Studying the consequences of literacy within a literate society: The cognitive correlates of print exposure', *Memory and Cognition*, 20(1), 51–68.

— (1993), 'Where does knowledge come from? Specific associations between print exposure and information acquisition', *Journal of Educational Psychology*, 85(2), 211–29.

Trelease, J. (2006), *The Read-Aloud Handbook* (6th edn). New York: Penguin.

Ujiie, J. and Krashen, S. (2002), 'Home run books and reading enjoyment', *Knowledge Quest*, 31(1), 36–7.

Veghese, J., Lipton, R., Katz, M., Hall, C., Derby, C., Kuslansky, G., Armbrose, A., Silwinski, M. and Buschke, H. (2003), 'Leisure activities and the risk of dementia in the elderly', *New English Journal of Medicine*, 348, 2508–16.

Von Sprecken, D., Kim, J. and Krashen, S. (2000), 'The home run book: Can one positive reading experience create a reader?', *California School Library Journal*, 23(2), 8–9.

Wang, F. Y. and Lee, S. Y. (2007), 'Storytelling is the bridge', *International Journal of Foreign Language Teaching*, 3(2), 30–5 (ijflt.com).

West, R., Stanovich, K. and Mitchell, H. (1993), 'Reading in the real world and its correlates', *Reading Research Quarterly*, 28, 35–50.

Yuan, Y. P. and Nash, T. (1992), 'Reading subskills and quantity reading'. Selected papers from *The Eighth Conference on English Teaching and Learning in the Republic of China*, pp. 291–304. Taipei: Crane.

Zill, N. and Winglee, M. (1990), *Who Reads Literature?* Cabin John, MD: Seven Locks Press.

3

Efficient Use of Literature in Second Language Education: Free Reading and Listening to Stories

Beniko Mason

This chapter describes studies that investigated the effects and efficiency of comprehension-based methodology in second language acquisition in Japan. The results of these studies consistently show that the combination of free reading and listening to stories is not only an effective means of foreign language acquisition, but is also highly efficient.

The critics of the Comprehension Hypothesis (as presented for example in Krashen, 1985) have long held the belief that comprehension-based methods are inefficient. Even though they have conceded that they are more effective than the traditionally used methods and that comprehensible input is necessary for language acquisition, they still claim that the combination of both traditional and comprehension approaches must be used in classrooms. The following presents studies that investigated exactly this point: whether comprehension-based methods are more efficient than the traditional methods and also more efficient than the combination of the two methodologies.

Study 1: Mason, B. and Krashen, S. (1997). Extensive reading in English as a foreign language

The first experiment in this study confirmed that pleasure reading could change reluctant EFL students to willing-to-read students at university level in Japan. These students had failed in their English studies before, and were called Sai-Rishu (retaker) students. They did self-selected reading for one semester and learned to enjoy reading in English. They began the semester far behind the traditionally taught control group on a cloze test, but nearly caught up with them by the end of the semester showing that the method is not only effective but also efficient, let alone motivating. The effect size of the difference between the groups on the pretests was .72, but on the post-test it was only .25.

Table 3.1 Extensive reading vs intensive reading on cloze test

Class	N	Pretest mean (SD)	Post-test mean (SD)	Gain
ER: response in Japanese	40	29.45 (8.31)	45.52 (8.28)	16.08
ER: response in English	36	28.03 (9.02)	46.89 (6.58)	18.86
Cloze exercise class	38	30.13 (8.07)	44.29 (9.16)	14.16

In the second experiment, groups that did extensive reading outperformed traditionally taught groups at both university and junior college levels on the same cloze test (N=128). The effect sizes between the groups increased from .18 (pretest) to .62 (post-test) for the university group and from .11 to .84 for the junior college group; at the beginning the difference between the groups was small but at the end the difference between the experimental and control groups was substantial. The data also showed that students' writing improved because of self-selected reading.

The third experiment in this series compared the effects of self-selected reading and cloze exercises, a form-focused approach, as well as the effect of writing book summaries in Japanese versus writing in English.

All groups gained on a cloze test after one academic year, with the English summary group doing significantly better than the cloze exercise group. Both reading groups did better than the cloze group on a test of reading comprehension. On a writing test (read a story and write a summary, rated by two raters), the Japanese writing group actually did best, a surprising result (see Table 3.1).

Study 2: Mason, B. (2004). The effect of adding supplementary writing to an extensive reading programme

This study investigated whether adding supplementary writing to an extensive reading programme would increase its effectiveness for the development of grammatical accuracy when the treatment lasted for three semesters. As in a previous study (see Study 1 above), all three groups did extensive reading, averaging 2,300 pages in three semesters. One group wrote summaries of what they read in their first language, Japanese, another wrote summaries in English and a third group wrote summaries in English that were corrected. All groups improved in written accuracy (number of error-free clauses per 100 words), and there were no significant differences among the groups.

Table 3.2 presents the effect sizes between the groups. Note that the group that wrote in Japanese was superior to all other groups in five out of six comparisons. (A plus sign indicates that the first group of each pair was superior.) The conclusion was that adding supplementary summary writing did not lead to greater accuracy and that it was therefore inefficient.

The results of this study were consistent with those of many others showing that increasing output did not increase second language proficiency (Krashen, 2003), as well as Truscott's conclusion that error correction is of limited value (Truscott, 1996).

Table 3.2 Effect sizes for Mason (2004)

Test	Comparison pairs		
	JSG: ESG	ESG: Correction	JSG: Correction
Cloze	+0.12	– 0.02	+ 0.15
Reading/TOEIC	+ 0.10	– 0.17	– 0.08
Error-free clauses	+0.39	0.00	+ 0.39

Note: JSG= Japanese summary group, ESG = English summary group,
Correction = English Summary plus Correction.

Of course, one can always claim that more or different kinds of output are necessary, and that more and different kinds of correction will work, but the burden of proof is clearly on those who make these claims.

Study 3: Mason, B. (2005). Vocabulary acquisition through storytelling: Story listening versus list learning

It has been demonstrated that vocabulary acquisition is possible from listening to stories (Elley, 1989), but it has also been argued that this source of vocabulary is insufficient and inefficient, that students need direct instruction as well (Nation, 1990). In this study, I attempted to confirm that listening to stories lead to the acquisition of vocabulary, and also attempted to determine how efficient this acquisition was, that is, how it compared to direct instruction.

Participants were first year college English majors in Japan. All students participated in both treatments. In the story-listening treatment, participants first took a pretest on 30 words (write a definition in Japanese). They then listened to a story, 'The North Wind and the Sun', that contained the 30 words. The words on the sheet were written on the blackboard in front of the class. While the teacher told the story she pointed to the words on the board so that students could tell which word was used to tell the story. The story took about 20 minutes. After listening to the story, the participants retook the vocabulary test. A week later, the participants took an unexpected follow-up test on the same words presented in a different order.

The second treatment was given a week later, with a different list of 30 words. They were given the Japanese definitions of the words and were told to try to learn the words in the next 20 minutes, using any techniques they wanted to use. Students were allowed to work together. Subjects then took a post-test and a follow-up post-test one week later.

As shown in Table 3.3, the list method used in the second treatment was very successful on a test given immediately after studying the words, but there was a large drop in retention (63% forgotten) on the delayed test. Far fewer words were forgotten after the storytelling treatment (25%). Analysis of Covariance revealed that the adjusted means for the follow-up post-test were not significantly different (list-learning = 14.6, storytelling = 13.2 $F = 1.5, p = .23$).

Table 3.3 Descriptive statistics of the story and list methods

Variables	N	Mean	S.D.	Gain	Lost
LIST PRE	35	3.9	2.6		
LIST POST	35	28.5	2.6	24.6	
LIST DELAYED	34	12.8	4.4	8.9	15.7
STORY PRE	38	8.3	2.8		
STORY POST	38	17.2	4.7	8.9	
STORY DELAYED	27	15.0	3.2	6.7	2.2

Study 4: Mason, B. and Krashen, S. (2004). Is form-focused vocabulary instruction worth while?

In this study, we compared vocabulary growth in English as a foreign language through hearing a story with a combination of a story and supplementary activities designed to focus students specifically on learning the new words in the story. One group of college students heard a story with unfamiliar words (as in the design of the previous study), which took 15 minutes, and another (the 'Story-Plus' group) heard a story and did supplementary form-focused activities, which took a total of 85 minutes.

The Story-Plus group was significantly better on all measures, including on a surprise follow-up test given five weeks later, learning about twice as many words as the Story-Only group. But the Story-Only group was as or more efficient: if we count time for testing, the Story-Only group acquired .15 words per minute (15 minutes for listening to a story and 5 minutes each taking the pre- and post-tests) and the Story-Plus group acquired .13 words per minute, nearly identical results. Not counting testing time, the Story-Only group looks even better, acquiring .25 words per minute.

The finding that story-listening is as effective as or more effective than traditional methods is encouraging. Stories are far more pleasant and engaging than traditional instruction, and students can gain other aspects of language from stories, as well as knowledge.

Study Series 5: Mason, B., Vanata, M., Jander, K., Borsch, R. and Krashen, S. (2009). The effects and efficiency of hearing stories on vocabulary acquisition by students of German as a second foreign language in Japan

The studies in this series were replications of the studies done in Mason (2005) and Mason and Krashen (2004) using German as a second foreign language by Japanese students. The subjects in these experiments had not studied German in their secondary schools and they did not read or hear German outside of school except for homework on grammar. Although the language used was their second foreign language, which was not as familiar to them as English was, the results were similar to the results in the previous studies.

The first experiment of the three included in this paper confirmed that hearing a story resulted in a higher acquisition/learning rate than the list method for beginning students of German as a foreign language. The second and third experiments confirmed that supplementary focus-on-form activities were not worthwhile for vocabulary acquisition/learning.

The next study in this series demonstrated that the strong version of the comprehension theory, the combination of reading and listening, results in more efficient language acquisition than the combination of weak versions of the traditional approach and the input approach.

Study 6: Mason, B. (2007). The efficiency of self-selected reading and hearing stories on adult second language acquisition

One group consisting of Health Science majors listened to a fairy/folk tale for 30 to 40 minutes in English every week in class told by the teacher and read graded readers at home (total of 18 hours of class time in one semester). The other group, English majors, took six other English classes using an audio-lingual, form-based approach (total of 126 hours of class time in 1 semester) besides the same kind of reading class that the Health Science students took.

Both groups improved after one semester, the Health Science students' gains per hour of class time were far greater; they were, in other words, more efficient. Table 3.4 presents improvements in accuracy as the ratio of error-free phrases to total phrases written. Again, the English majors made larger gains, but were less efficient.

Another criticism for comprehension-based methods is that such easy and pleasant ways of acquiring language will not prepare students for academic proficiency, and that students need to be prepared for the TOEFL test. The goal of the next study was to investigate whether self-selected reading alone will improve TOEFL scores.

Study 7: Mason, B. (2006). Free voluntary reading and autonomy in second language acquisition: Improving TOEFL scores from reading alone

Previous research strongly suggests that reading is good preparation for the TOEFL. One case study (Constantino, 1995) and two multivariate correlational studies (Gradman et al., 1991; Constantino et al. 1997) have shown that the amount of recreational reading students do is a strong predictor of TOEFL performance.

Table 3.4 Percentage of error-free phrases

	Pretest	Post-test	Gain	Efficiency
English	47% (9.8/20.9)	55%(28.2/51.6)	8%	.06 (8/126)
Health Science	35% (6.2/17.6)	40% (13/32.9)	5%	.28 (5/18)

Showing that just engaging in independent reading improves scores on the TOEFL examination would have strong implications for both theory and practice. On the level of theory, it would confirm that language acquisition is possible from comprehensible input (in this case reading) alone. On the level of practice, it would tell us whether independent study is a viable and practical means of preparing for the TOEFL examination, especially if we can compare students' progress with those who prepare for the TOEFL examination in more traditional ways.

The subjects (N=6) in this study were well-educated, experienced language students, were highly motivated and volunteered to engage in a reading programme during the vacation time or when they were not attending English classes. Each chose somewhat different reading material, according to their own interests, with favourite authors including Sidney Sheldon, Paulo Coelho, Judy Blume and Bertice Berry. In addition, several continued to read graded readers, familiar to them because of classes they had taken previously.

Subjects read for between one to four months, and took alternate forms of the TOEFL test before and after doing the reading. The average gain was 3.5 points per week on the overall test, and improvement was seen in all three components, listening (2.2 points), grammar (3.6 points), and reading (4.6 points). This gain is about the same as one sees with a full time TOEFL preparation class given in the United States and is consistent with the previous studies showing that reading is an excellent predictor of TOEFL performance.

Study 8: Mason, B. (2011). Impressive gains on the TOEIC after one year of comprehensible input, with no output or grammar study

In this paper, I reported on a case that provides additional evidence for the 'reading hypothesis' and also provides a clear direction for those who need to improve quickly. Mr Tanaka was a 42-year-old man who worked in the radiology department in a local hospital in Osaka, Japan. After his graduation from vocational college, he had not studied English for 20 years.

Mr Tanaka took the TOEIC examination in January 2009, after reading graded readers for 6 months (2,590 pages), scoring 475 (255 in listening, and 220 in reading). He took it again 1 year later in January 2010, scoring 655 (330 in listening, and 325 in reading). He thus gained 180 points in one year.

Between January 2009 and January 2010, Mr Tanaka read 6,456 pages, which took 217 hours. He also enrolled in a story-listening class (30 hours): thus his total input time was 247 hours. He improved .73 points on the TOEIC for each hour spent reading or listening (180 points improvement/247 hours). He informed me also that he had spent 70 hours of vocabulary study on his own. If we include the 70 additional hours of vocabulary study, his total investment in English was 317 hours and his rate of improvement was .57 points per hour.

Comparison with junior college English majors in Osaka, Japan who spent 500 hours of classroom instruction (0.27), and with international students in a

Table 3.5 Points gained per hour

	Mr Tanaka	English majors	TOEFL prep
TOEIC	0.73	0.27	
TOEFL	0.25		0.13

Note: English majors: from Pendergast (2010)
TOEFL prep: from Swinton (1983), discussed in Mason (2006).

TOEFL preparation course in an Intensive English Programme in the United States (0.13), showed that Mr Tanaka's progress was much faster with almost no cost (see Table 3.5).

Summary and conclusion

This chapter has described studies that investigated the effects and efficiency of comprehension-based methodology in second language acquisition in Japan with Japanese university students and one older acquirer. What can be concluded from this series of studies is that comprehensible input-based methods, that is free reading (self-selected reading / extensive reading) and story listening or the combination of both are not only an effective means of foreign language acquisition, but are also highly efficient despite the concerns expressed by some others.

References

Constantino, R. (1995), 'The effect of pleasure reading: Passing the TOEFL test doesn't have to hurt', *Mosaic*, 3(1), 15–17.

Constantino, R., Lee, S. Y., Cho, K. S. and Krashen, S. (1997), 'Free voluntary reading as a predictor of TOEFL scores', *Applied Language Learning*, 8, 111–18.

Elley, W. (1989), 'Vocabulary acquisition from listening to stories', *Reading Research Quarterly*, 24(2), 174–87.

Gradman, H. and Hanania, E. (1991), 'Language learning background factors and ESL proficiency', *Modern Language Journal*, 75, 39–51.

Krashen, S. (1985), *The Input Hypothesis: Issues and Implications*. Torrance, CA: Laredo Publishing Company Inc.

— (2003), *Explorations in Language Acquisition and Use*. Portsmouth, NH: Heinemann Publishing.

Mason, B. (2004), 'The effect of adding supplementary writing to an extensive reading program', *The International Journal of Foreign Language Teaching*, 1(1), 2–16.

— (2005), 'Vocabulary acquisition through storytelling', *TexTESOL III Newsletter*, February, 3–5.

— (2006), 'Free voluntary reading and autonomy in second language acquisition: Improving TOEFL scores from reading alone', *The International Journal of Foreign Language Teaching*, 2(1), 2–5.

— (2007), 'The efficiency of self-selected reading and hearing stories on adult second language acquisition', in *Selected Papers from the Sixteenth International Symposium*

    on English Teaching. English Teachers' Association – ROC. Taipei: Crane Publishing,
        pp. 630–3.
— (2011), 'Impressive gains on the TOEIC after one year of comprehensible input, with no
        output or grammar study', *The International Journal of Foreign Language Teaching*, 7(1).
Mason, B. and Krashen, S. (1997), 'Extensive reading in English as a foreign language',
        System, 25(1), 91–102.
— (2004), 'Is form-focused vocabulary instruction worth while?' *RELC Journal*, 35(2),
        179–85.
Mason, B., Vanata, M., Jander, K., Borsch, R. and Krashen, S. (2009), 'The effects and
        efficiency of hearing stories on vocabulary acquisition by students of German as a
        second foreign language in Japan', *The Indonesian Journal of English Language Teaching*,
        5(1), 1–14.
Nation, P. S. (1990), *Teaching and Learning Vocabulary*. New York: Heinle and Heinle.
Pendergast, T. (2010), 'English language proficiency gains in an integrated, self-access
        program class of 2005 Part 2: The ETS test battery', *Shitennoji University Junior College
        Journal*, 49, 355–69.
Swinton, S. S. (1983), *TOEFL Research Reports, Report 14*. Princeton, NJ: Educational
        Testing Service.
Truscott, J. (1996), 'The case against grammar correction in L2 writing classes', *Language
        Learning*, 46, 327–69.

4

Extensive Reading of Picturebooks in Primary EFL

Annika Kolb

Extensive reading at primary school?

Stories and picturebooks play a widely accepted role in the teaching of English as a foreign language in primary schools (Ellis et al., 2002; Enever et al., 2006). Journals and methodology books on primary EFL feature a wealth of teaching suggestions on the use of stories and picturebooks in the foreign language classroom. However, these teaching suggestions – and my observations in German primary EFL classrooms – follow a common procedure: it is nearly always the teacher who presents the story to the children while the understanding of the text is supported through mime and gestures, the illustrations in the book and possibly additional explanations. This is succeeded by follow-up activities in which the children work on certain aspects of the text. Hardly ever do the children get the chance to explore an unknown text on their own or to read a picturebook by themselves.

One of the reasons for this is the fact that many primary teachers still have reservations about the role of written language in the EFL classroom. While statements on the matter in various curricula are contradictory and a consistent scheme for the introduction of written language in primary EFL is lacking, 'leaving teachers to find out by trial and error what approach best serves their learners in coping with written English' (Diehr, 2010, p. 52), many teachers rather hesitantly include written language in their teaching. Reading activities are often restricted to isolated phrases and short sentences and mainly consist in understanding task instructions. The fear that the confrontation with written language right from the beginning would confuse the children and interfere with the pronunciation is wide-spread.

In contrast, research into the use of written language in primary EFL has shown very promising results, revealing that written language can considerably support young learners' language learning (Diehr, 2010; Diehr et al., 2010; Edelenbos et al., 2006). Furthermore, after the disappointing results of German students in international studies, reading competence has shifted into the focus of attention in the German context and its promotion has been declared a challenge for every school subject (e.g. Artelt et al., 2010). The need to foster students' reading motivation in order to increase their reading competence is often emphasized.

These objectives lie at the heart of the extensive reading approach which tries to foster a reading culture among students. It can be characterized as follows: 'Pupils are given the time, encouragement and materials to read pleasurably, at their own level, as many books as they can, without the pressures of testing or marks' (Davis, 1995, p. 329). Although most of the studies on extensive reading refer to secondary school or adult learners, there is also some evidence that young language learners benefit from this approach (Elley, 1991; Lugossy, 2006): 'Extensive reading is appropriate at all stages of language learning, it is never too early (...) to learn to read in a second language' (Day et al., 1998, p. xiv).

The present chapter describes a case study on extensive reading with English picturebooks in a German primary EFL classroom. It aimed to find out to what extent the students were able to understand English picturebooks on their own, what comprehension strategies they developed and what effects the project had on their reading competence.

The picturebook project

To explore the potential of this approach for the German primary EFL classroom, the project was designed according to the characteristics of extensive reading (Day et al., 1998, pp. 7–9; Grabe, 2009, pp. 311–13):

- *Students read a large number of texts*: in our project, a Year 4 grade was given a selection of nine English picturebooks (there were two–three copies of each title available). The 23 children in the class were 9–10 years old and had been learning English for 3.5 years. Over the course of three weeks the children had the opportunity to explore the books in pairs or small groups. The not particularly large number was chosen in order not to overtax the children at their first experiences of this kind, but still gave them the opportunity to choose among books and read several texts.
- *Reading is individual and silent*: in extensive reading programmes, there is usually time allocated for sustained silent reading. In this respect, the project did not follow the extensive reading approach in a strict sense, but allowed the students to work in pairs or small groups. This was due to research results which have shown that young language learners benefit considerably from sharing their views and figuring out the meaning of a text together (Reichart-Wallrabenstein, 2004). Furthermore, the reading was not always silent: it was supported through audio recordings of some of the texts, so the children could read along while they were listening to the book.
- *Students choose texts according to their own interests*: the selection of picturebooks included a variety of topics and different styles of illustration as well as varying amounts of texts to cater for different language competence levels.
- *Real-world reading*: in extensive reading programmes, the students read for pleasure and information, the focus is on the content of the books and the overall understanding of the stories.

- *Little or no follow-up activities*: extensive reading means reading as an end in itself, the text is considered in its own right and does not merely serve as a springboard for further language learning activities. Follow-up activities in extensive reading programmes focus on personal statements and comments on the reading. In the project, the children were given a reading log to document their reading activities and express subjective reactions to the texts.

In line with the objectives that are pursued in extensive reading programmes, the picturebook project aimed at improving students' competences in the following areas:

- *Reading motivation and confidence*: according to numerous research studies, extensive reading helps develop a positive attitude towards reading (e.g. Elley, 1991; Grabe, 2009; Krashen, 2004, 2007). It is put forward that having read and understood a whole book in English considerably fosters the students' confidence and contributes to the development of a reading habit.
- *Reading competence*: extensive reading has proved to promote reading abilities, for example overall comprehension skills and reading strategies (see research overview in Day et al., 1998, pp. 33–9 and Krashen, 2007).
- *Language competence*: extensive reading also promotes general language competence, for example passive vocabulary, language awareness, improvement in writing skills, confidence and fluency in speaking (Biebricher, 2008; Day et al., 1998, pp. 35–9; Krashen, 2004, 2007).

To realize this approach in a primary EFL classroom, the use of picturebooks seemed particularly suitable since the interplay between text and pictures can help overcome linguistic difficulties:

(u)sing the powerful visual representations as tools to move beyond the initially tedious process of decoding a foreign language, into a world of images and meanings created individually, allows the child to engage immediately with the visual text. (Enever, 2006, p. 67)

Data collection

The exploration of the extensive reading approach in a German primary-school classroom tried to find answers to the following research questions:

- How do the students cope with the task of reading a picturebook on their own?
- What strategies do they develop for understanding the stories?
- What effects does the project have on the students' reading competence?

To this end, interviews with nine students before and after the project as well as with the teacher were conducted. The study also used the students' reading logs, classroom video recordings and student self-assessment questionnaires on reading competence before and after the project. These data were analysed using a qualitative content analysis approach.

Exploring picturebooks – some findings

Comprehension strategies

In the picturebook project, the students worked in pairs or small groups with the books. They were asked to read and follow the story and to document their reading in the reading logs. For some picturebooks, there were also audio versions of the text available, so that the students could listen to the CD and read along. Based on the student interviews, the classroom videos and the self-assessment questionnaires, I would like to shed some light onto the reading process. How do the students go about the task of reading and understanding a book on their own? For this I will first report strategies that could be observed in the classroom videos and that students mention in the interviews. In a second step, I will present the results of the self-assessment questionnaires regarding the students' use of strategy. Since the oral input from the CD provided additional support and therefore the task went beyond a mere reading task, the term 'comprehension strategies' instead of 'reading strategies' is employed (Hudson 2007, p. 300).

Observing the reading process

The following strategies that students used to figure out meaning could be identified in the data:

- Use of pictures

Not surprisingly, the students often turn to the illustrations as a support for understanding the story. The videos show that when they turn the page, very often they first look at the pictures. Frequently, the illustrations help them understand key words in the story. This support through the pictures is also explained in the interviews. Cheryl states: 'Well, first, we read the book. And then, through the pictures, we filled in the words that we didn't understand.'[1] Marina says: 'I did try to read first, and when I didn't understand a page at all, I looked at the pictures a little bit. And then you realize what it is about.' These quotes show that while the pictures are of great help, the students still focus very much on the text and do not try to understand the story by the pictures alone.

- Prediction

Apart from supporting the understanding of key words and the plot of the story, the illustrations in the picturebooks also play an important role for the strategy of prediction. At various points, the pictures prompt the students to predict the continuation of the story, using them as the basis for making suggestions about what could happen next. Oxana explicitly refers to prediction as a strategy for understanding when she says: 'Well, first I have a look at the book, at the pictures. And then I think it could be about this or that'. She claims that she has learned this approach from the project and had not used it before.

- Use of the audio recording

The classroom videos reveal that, when available, the students closely follow the recordings of the text in the books. Thus, they are able to link the oral presentation and the written form of the story. In the interviews, many students point out that listening to the spoken version of the text supported their understanding. In this context, they report different procedures:

> Patrick: For me it is easier if I first listen to the CD, then I know better what's it about. First, I listen to the CD, then I know what it is about, because I have understood a lot of words. Then I read the story, and I understand more words.

While Patrick makes use of the audio version to come to a global understanding of the story before he starts reading, other students use the written and the oral version of the text simultaneously.

- Reading aloud

Another interesting aspect observed in the videos is that reading aloud is a very common strategy. The students try to read out the texts to each other or join in the audio recordings.

That many children also use this strategy when there is no spoken version of the text proved to be problematic. In these cases they struggle with the pronunciation of unknown words. For many children reading a book seems to mean reading it aloud – this probably reflects a widespread routine in schools. Although poor oral reading skills can go along with good reading comprehension results and therefore the wrong pronunciation does not automatically hinder the comprehension of a word (Rymarczyk et al., 2010), this strategy did prevent the students from understanding the texts when they tried to read the book to each other with one partner lacking the opportunity to see the written form.

Whereas as a strategy to enhance the understanding of the story reading aloud is not always helpful, the classroom observations show that at various points it leads to an increased language awareness, above all concerning the pronunciation and the phoneme-grapheme correspondence in English. While listening to the recordings and reading along in the picturebooks, the students frequently compare their attempts at pronunciation with the audio version. They build hypotheses about the pronunciation of words and then compare it with the recording. Along these lines, Cheryl states in the interview that she has learned in the project: 'That you pronounce the letters s-h as the sound [ʃ]. In English, you write completely differently from how you speak.'

- Group work

In line with earlier research results on the topic (Reichart-Wallrabenstein, 2004), the work in small groups proved to be quite effective for figuring out the meaning of the texts. The students compare their understanding of the text or help each other with unknown words. Cheryl says: 'What we did was that everybody read one sentence and then everybody said how they understood the sentence. That's how we did it.' Moritz talks about the cooperation with his partner: 'And sometimes he understood it and I didn't, sometimes he didn't understand it and then I understood it and so on.' Here, the adaptation of the extensive reading approach which usually calls for individual reading seems to be justified.

- Guessing from context

A very prominent strategy for understanding the English text that the children mention in the interviews is guessing from context. When the interviewer asks him what he did when he didn't understand a word, Tobias says for example: 'I read the sentence again, and I tried to connect it with the words that I did understand and to figure out what it could mean.' That the students use this strategy quite frequently can also be seen in the reading logs. Many examples show that they have understood the overall story but are wrong about some details of the books.

- Reading for gist

The students also become aware that for understanding the stories, they do not have to understand every single word. When asked what he has learned from the project, Luis explains:

> For example, skimming the text. Dario went down with his finger and then, oddly, I continued reading one line below. But in the end, we still knew what the story was about.

This strategy also becomes evident in the reading logs: most of the students were able to summarize the plot of the stories, but did not always go into great detail.

Self-assessment of comprehension strategies

In the self-assessment questionnaires the students were asked to rate on a three-level scale to what extent several comprehension strategies helped them with their reading. With one exception, all strategies were rated equally high or higher after the project than before.

Figure 4.1 focuses on the strategies which feature an increase or a decrease after the project. In accordance with the results of the video analyses and the student interviews, the children report that their reading comprehension is particularly fostered through prediction, the use of pictures, guessing words from context and the use of picture dictionaries. Therefore the project has either enhanced the students' strategy use, or increased their awareness of the benefit of certain strategies for understanding. The only strategy which exhibits a decrease in the children's rating is being read aloud to by a partner. This result is in line with the observations of the reading process, which revealed considerable difficulties when children tried to read the stories aloud to

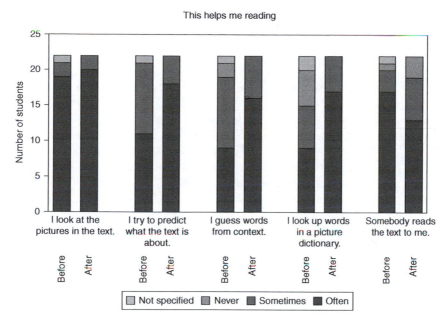

Figure 4.1 Self-assessment of reading strategies before and after the project

a partner. Here, the students became aware of the problematic contribution of this strategy for their understanding.

Enhancing reading competence

Since the study did not include a reading comprehension test it does not give direct information about the effects of the picturebook project on the students' reading competence. Yet, it includes the children's self-assessment of their competence in the questionnaires and the interviews. The presentation of these results follows Burwitz-Melzer's (2007) model of reading competence in a foreign language. She argues for a comprehensive model of reading competence and distinguishes between motivation competences, cognitive and affective competences, intercultural competences, the ability to respond to texts and reflective competences.

- Motivational competences

In many student interviews an increase in reading confidence can be identified:

> Cheryl: I have learnt that books in English aren't as difficult as I had always thought. That they are easy. Because I had always thought that they are very difficult, oh my god, I can't do that. But now I know that I can do it.

Similarly Jennifer comments: 'I had always thought, oh no, in English you can't understand a word, but we understood lots of things.' Many students report that they were proud of having faced the challenge and understood the stories on their own. They were very positive about the books and enjoyed reading.

- Cognitive and affective competences

The self-assessment of students' reading competence reveals considerable increases in their abilities to make meaning of texts. Figure 4.2 compares the students' self-assessment before (upper bar) and after (lower bar) the picturebook project.

According to the students' statements, especially their ability to read and understand English sentences (matching sentences and pictures, understanding task instructions), to find information in a text, to answer questions on a text and to read English picturebooks has increased. These results are confirmed in the interviews, for example when Cheryl says after the project: 'Now I can also read the books. And understand them, even longer sentences. Before, I couldn't do that. Because we had never done anything like that before.'

- Responding to texts

In Burwitz-Melzer's model, responding to texts is an important part of reading competence. The project tried to take account of this through the reading logs in which the students were asked to comment and give their opinion on the books. The children's reading logs included drawings with English captions which show that the students seem to have enjoyed the book. They also show that most children were

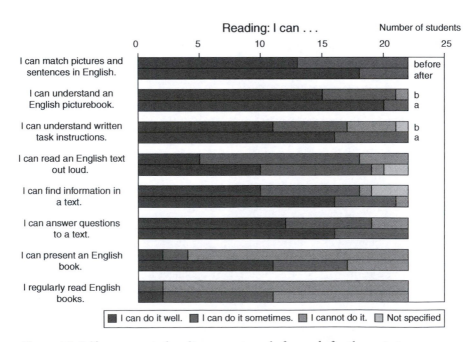

Figure 4.2 Self-assessment of reading competence before and after the project

able to understand and give an account of the main plot of the stories as well as state their opinion on the books. This opportunity to give personal statements was highly valued by the students. Cheryl points out that she especially liked this aspect of the reading logs:

> Because there, you could write about how you yourself have experienced it [the book, A.K.], how you yourself have perceived it. You didn't have to write, like copying from the board, but you were allowed to write yourself, in your own words.

- Reflective competences

Another area of reading competence is the ability to reflect on one's learning process. This was impressively demonstrated in the interviews in which the students proved very able to reflect on their learning experiences and to describe the procedures they used when working with the books. This sample quote from the student interviews shows that their awareness of competence in a certain field was heightened and they were able to perceive learning gains:

> Lars: I learnt that, well, I did not know that I could read English that fast. (…) I can read faster. Because before, I had thought that I was reading very slowly, but then – surprisingly I could understand it and read it fast.

This often underestimated ability of primary-school children to reflect on their learning (Kolb, 2007) can provide the basis for the discussion of reading strategies and learning outcomes in class in order to further enhance the students' reading competence.

Conclusion

The small qualitative study shows that primary-school children are able to work with English picturebooks on their own. In the process of engaging with the texts, they make use of a variety of comprehension strategies and their awareness of their strategy use is increased.

While the study cannot answer the question whether the children's reading competence has in fact increased the students themselves report a considerable rise in reading motivation, confidence and reading competence.

These results point at the potential for this approach for primary EFL. Extensive reading in primary school gives students the opportunity to experience written language as a means of communication and allows for first authentic and autonomous reading experiences. The approach can develop and expand the students' repertoire of reading strategies, especially when their experiences during the reading phases are exchanged and reflected upon in class. This would also give teachers the opportunity to put across that reading a text does not necessarily mean reading aloud.

The frequently voiced concern that picturebooks that are written for very young L1 readers are not interesting for older L2 primary school children was not confirmed. Tobias says:

> Well, I think, it always depends on how often you have already read an English book. Certainly, there are also students in Year 9 who have never read an English book. And they would surely start with such a small book as well.

For the children the linguistic challenge seems to be at the heart of the experience.

Note

1 All students' quotes are translated from German.

References

Artelt, C. and Dörfler, T. (2010), 'Förderung von Lesekompetenz als Aufgabe aller Fächer. Forschungsergebnisse und Anregungen für die Praxis', in Bayerisches Staatsministerium für Unterricht und Kultus und Staatsinstitut für Schulqualität und Bildungsforschung (eds), *ProLesen. Auf dem Weg zur Leseschule – Leseförderung in den gesellschaftswissenschaftlichen Fächern*. Donauwörth: Auer, pp. 13–36.

Biebricher, C. (2008), *Lesen in der Fremdsprache. Eine Studie zu Effekten extensiven Lesens*. Tübingen: Narr.

Burwitz-Melzer, E. (2007), 'Ein Lesekompetenzmodell für den fremdsprachlichen Literaturunterricht', in L. Bredella and W. Hallet (eds), *Literaturunterricht, Kompetenzen und Bildung*. Trier: Wissenschaftlicher Verlag, pp. 127–57.

Davis, C. (1995), 'Extensive reading – an expensive extravagance?', *ELT Journal*, 49(4), 329–36.

Day, R. and Bamford, J. (1998), *Extensive Reading in the Second Language Classroom*. Cambridge: Cambridge University Press.

Diehr, B. (2010), 'Research into reading in the primary school: A fresh look at the use of written English with young learners of English as a foreign language', in B. Diehr and R. Rymarczyk (eds), *Researching Literacy in a Foreign Language among Primary School Learners*. Frankfurt a. M.: Peter Lang, pp. 51–68.

Diehr, B. and Rymarczyk, J. (eds) (2010), *Researching Literacy in a Foreign Language among Primary School Learners*. Frankfurt a. M.: Peter Lang.

Edelenbos, P., Kubanek, A. and Johnstone, R. (2006), *The Main Pedagogical Principles Underlying the Teaching of Young Learners*. Strasbourg: Council of Europe.

Elley, W. (1991), 'Acquiring literacy in a second language: The effect of book-based programmes', *Language Learning*, 41, 375–411.

Ellis, G. and Brewster, J. (2002), *Tell it Again! The New Storytelling Handbook for Primary Teachers*. Harlow: Pearson.

Enever, J. (2006), 'The use of picture books in the development of critical visual and written literacy in English as a foreign language', in J. Enever and G. Schmid-Schönbein (eds), *Picture Books and Young Learners of English*. Berlin: Langenscheidt, pp. 59–70.

Enever, J. and Schmid-Schönbein, G. (eds) (2006), *Picture Books and Young Learners of English*. Münchener Arbeiten zur Fremdsprachen-Forschung. München: Langenscheidt.

Grabe, W. (2009), *Reading in a Second Language. Moving from Theory to Practice*. Cambridge: Cambridge University Press.

Hudson, T. (2007), *Teaching Second Language Reading*. Oxford: Oxford University Press.

Kolb, A. (2007), *Portfolioarbeit. Wie Grundschulkinder ihr Sprachenlernen reflektieren*. Tübingen: Narr.

Krashen, S. (2004), *The Power of Reading. Insights from the Research*. Westport, CT: Libraries Unlimited.

— (2007), 'Extensive reading in English as a foreign language by adolescents and young adults: A meta-analysis', *International Journal of Foreign Language Teaching*, 3(2), 23–9.

Lugossy, R. (2006), 'Browsing and borrowing your way to motivation through picture books', in J. Enever and G. Schmid-Schönbein (eds), *Picture Books and Young Learners of English*, Berlin: Langenscheidt, pp. 23–34.

Reichart-Wallrabenstein, M. (2004), *Kinder und Schrift im Englischunterricht der Grundschule: Eine Theorie- und Empiriegeleitete Studie zur Diskussion um die Integration von Schriftlichkeit*. Berlin: dissertation.de.

Rymarczyk, J. and Musall, A. (2010), 'Reading skills of first graders who learn to read and write in German and English', in B. Diehr and R. Rymarczyk (eds), *Researching Literacy in a Foreign Language among Primary School Learners*. Frankfurt a. M.: Peter Lang, pp. 69–88.

5

Free Space: An Extensive Reading Project in a Flemish School

Johan Strobbe

This chapter is about an extensive reading project in a secondary school in Brugge (Bruges), Belgium, where I am a teacher of EFL. The students involved in the project had to read a number of English language young adult novels and create a reading portfolio. The focus was mainly on reading pleasure, not on in-depth analyses of texts or on finding information about authors, literary trends or movements. The activities surrounding the novels were not only meant to be fun, they were also designed to promote foreign language learning and improve the students' communicative skills. This chapter is an account of this small-scale action-research project, with 16 participants, drawing on the ideas of extensive reading.

First, I will explain the idea behind the project. Secondly, I will expound on the procedure and on the assignments the students had to complete. Finally, I will formulate some conclusions and explain what could be done differently.

Idea behind the project

When I started an extensive reading project with my students in 2007 I had no intention of drawing hard-and-fast conclusions from it. My only aim was to provide reading pleasure and to actively involve my students in literature and language learning. The aim was not the study of literature. The project fitted in with an initiative of the Flemish Ministry of Education originally called *vrije ruimte* (free space). It was later renamed *seminarie* (seminar) and was intended to give secondary schools more freedom – or 'space' – to include more creative and fewer cognitive activities in their curriculum.

In my school in Brugge, 16–17-year-old students were introduced to the art of flower arranging or acrylic painting, they learned how to entertain elderly people in a nursing home, they joined the school choir or . . . they read novels. Reading is not self-evident for adolescents. Research seems to suggest that reading novels is not that popular with teenagers. Only 18% of Flemish 15-year-olds mention reading as one of their hobbies and a lot of them have given up reading altogether (de Saedeleer, 2010). Motivating my students to read several novels in a foreign language would be a huge challenge. At least, that is what I thought. But as I am fully convinced of the power of extensive reading, I definitely wanted to take on that challenge. So I persuaded the principal of my school to organize a project on young adult literature with a double lesson every other week for a whole school year.

The official Flemish curricula require that teachers of EFL teach four different reading strategies: skimming, scanning, intensive reading and extensive reading. Many teachers of English feel that the curriculum is very demanding and often find themselves pressed for time. A lot of time is spent on intensive reading, basically of non-fictional texts, and on skimming and scanning short texts. Hence, extensive reading, which inherently requires more time, is often not practised. I must admit that it used to be the Cinderella of reading strategies in my classroom as well. But with the introduction of the seminars I saw an opportunity to put that right. In addition, in my ordinary lessons on literature I discuss the literary canon, Literature, with a capital L. I believe that authors like Chaucer and Shakespeare are still relevant today and that my students have the right to understand and enjoy them despite the challenging vocabulary – the funny old words– and the unfamiliar language. However, I also want to introduce my students to the huge reservoir of brilliant contemporary teenage fiction. I find it very surprising that young adult novels are so often ignored in English coursebooks for secondary schools, because teenagers seem to enjoy literature in which the protagonists are their own age. They can identify with those characters. Moreover, they recognize the themes that young adult fiction touches upon – often adolescence or the coming of age– and that are often too sensitive to be included in EFL coursebooks: bullying, drug abuse, teenage gangs, sexual abuse, migration, etc. As a teacher I saw an opportunity here to work towards the 'cross-curricular' objectives on hygiene and health, citizenship and so forth.[1]

Why teenage fiction?

Apart from the fact that the themes addressed in young adult literature are recognizable for adolescents, it also often includes various linguistic varieties. It often incorporates interesting features of spoken language that are absent in the more traditional coursebooks. That is why, in my view, it is essential to step away from the literary canon at times and provide students with a more realistic picture of English as actually spoken today. Through the dialogues in modern teenage novels and through the thoughts of the main characters they experience the 'authentic' language of their peers. However, there may be a drawback here. Some of the language used may be above the students' comprehension level so that they quickly become discouraged. One way of addressing this problem is, of course, carefully selecting the books and making sure that they match student abilities. What I also do as a first step in my English classes is select extracts and make them accessible by leaving out the lexically sophisticated descriptive parts. I just provide the dialogues. Often these dialogues contain very little difficult vocabulary and the new language is mostly understood from the context. For example, one novel I discuss in my EFL classroom and which I also introduced to the students in the course of the project was Narinder Dhami's *Bend It Like Beckham*. At one point in the novel Jess, the main character in the book, talks with Tony, who has just told her that he is gay. Part of the dialogue goes like this:

Jess: My sister thinks you're mad about me.
Tony: I am. I just don't want to marry you.
Jess: I wonder what all those tossers would say if they knew.
Tony: Jess, you're not going to tell anyone?
Jess: Of course not. It's OK, Tony. I mean, it's OK with me. (Based on Dhami, 2002)

This conversation contains little or no difficult vocabulary for 16–17-year-olds. The only word my students did not know was *tossers*, but it was clear to them from the context that it is an offensive word. After having read and discussed the dialogues we read the extract from the book, with the descriptive parts. In this way the new language was introduced incrementally and did not spoil the reading pleasure. What is more, the extract contains one of the key scenes in the novel and some of my students wanted to know how the story continued or felt motivated to read the whole novel. It should be noted concerning the difficulty of literature that Flemish teachers sometimes tend to underestimate their students' ability to cope with authentic literature. I know quite a few 13–14-year-olds who are in their second year of learning English who would not wait for the Dutch translation of the *Twilight* series and read – and understood – the books in their original English version.

I would also like to note that I am not an advocate of the theory that considers young adult literature basically as a stepping stone towards the more 'serious' or adult literature. This stepping stone theory may be true, but it seems to suggest that teenage fiction is not a fully fledged genre in its own right. However, teen fiction can function as a sort of lead-in to discuss 'canonized' literature in class. Young adult literature and the canon can thus be taught in tandem. In the reading list I used in the project I included, for instance, two teenage novels by Jan Mark that can be used as an introduction to Shakespeare. In *Heathrow Nights* (Mark, 2000), for instance, Russell, the main character, and two of his friends wreck a school performance of *Hamlet*. As a consequence he is banned from going on the half-term school trip. In addition, he seems to have a lot in common with Hamlet, with whom he begins to identify: his father died, his mother remarried rather hastily and he hates his stepdad. A lot of this is recognizable to young readers and it may convince them of the fact that *Hamlet* is not just compulsory (and boring) school reading but that the plot is closer to their world than they might have thought at first. In *Stratford Boys* (Mark, 2003), Jan Mark takes us back to late-sixteenth-century Stratford, where the young Shakespeare – Will in the book – is growing up. This book is not an easy read, but it can serve as a perfect introduction to a performance of one of Shakespeare's plays, particularly *A Midsummer Night's Dream*.

Procedure of the project

In my first seminar I worked with 16 students, 12 girls and 4 boys. This actually confirmed what research has established, namely that teenage girls are more avid readers than boys (De Gendt, 2005). I started the seminar by handing out a reading list. The list contained titles of young adult novels, and only young adult novels.[2] This was actually the only restriction I had imposed, since one of the principles of extensive reading is that learners read what they want to read (Bamford et al., 2004, p. 2). I had made sure, however, that the list was extensive, containing over 120 titles to suit all tastes. The first seminar took place in the school's language lab where we had access to the internet. I had prepared a questionnaire, which I had called 'A rally through the reading list'. It contained questions like:

- The most prestigious award for children's literature is the Carnegie Medal. Which author(s) from the list have won that award?
- Which book(s) from the list is (are) written in a diary form?
- Which books address the following themes: a, (political) refugees, b, anorexia, c, drugs, d, football, e, William Shakespeare, f, growing up?
- Which of the books is: a, an historical novel, b, a fantasy novel, c, a detective story, d, a collection of different stories?
- Which book, do you think, has the nicest cover? (Have a look at www.amazon. co.uk)

The last question was 'Which book(s) from the list would you like to read? Explain briefly why'. In that seminar the students could read synopses on sites like Amazon, study covers, compare reviews, visit author websites, etc. The purpose of this seminar was, of course, that they could already get an idea of the storylines and the themes of (some of) the books and thus make a motivated, conscious choice. And as a teacher I had to respect that choice. In short, I wanted to get my students ready to read. I also thought it important that the books were 'physically' present in the room. I had taken books from the school library and I had also brought some of my own copies. In this way, the students could literally grab them, browse through them, get curious and start to talk about them. To finish the seminar the students could pick the novel(s) they had chosen to read and take it (them) home.

In the next two seminars I gave my students the opportunity to read. They went to the school library, the self-study area or some of the cozier rooms in the school and read, read and read some more: for pleasure, at their own level and according to one of the principles of extensive reading: 'Learners choose what they want to read' (Bamford et al., 2004, p. 2). This was reading largely in the sense of Krashen's free voluntary reading, 'not assigned reading, [. . .] not followed by book reports or comprehension questions, but [. . .] done for its own sake' (Krashen, 1989, p. 89). However, I did give my students two assignments. First, they had to complete two worksheets per book (see below). Secondly, I asked them to prepare a short talk about the novel they had read. They had to say something about the plot (without giving too much away) and share some of their reading experiences. I also asked them to read a short, well-chosen extract and thus motivate their fellow-students to read that novel too. This worked really well. It happened quite often that students chose to read a book that a fellow-student had recommended in those first seminars. At a later stage in the project students who had read the same book formed groups – small 'reading circles' – to talk about their reading experiences: what they liked about the book, what they did not understand, what themes and motifs they had found, etc. Again, this worked really well. I have experienced that young adults often like to talk about their reading habits and experiences. And it probably helped that this happened outside the existing English course and that they seemed to worry less about making lexical or grammatical mistakes.

Despite one of the principles of extensive reading that stipulates reading is its own reward (Bamford et al., 2004, p. 3), I had to grade the students' performance in the project. I needed assignments – on paper – that could justify the students' grade on the school report. One of the dangers here is that follow-up activities and tasks often spoil the reading pleasure. Students mostly find it demotivating to have to write a book report or answer comprehension questions. For the activities and task sheets I wanted my students to complete I borrowed many ideas from the literature on extensive reading.[3] In total I provided 14 worksheets. Among the activities I used was posting a review on Amazon, designing a 'Wanted' poster for one of the characters, writing a diary entry of one of the characters, keeping a reading journal, making a story scrap book, etc. One of the assignments that proved to be very rewarding was the 'quotes project'. In that task the students were invited to use post-it notes to mark passages while reading which they thought were important, provocative, surprising, dramatic, etc. After having read the entire novel they had to select five quotes from these passages and one 'quintessential' quote that captured the essence or true meaning of the novel for them. Then they had to explain why they had chosen these quotes and how they fitted in the novel: did they add to the development of the character or the plot?

All these assignments were designed to foster the students' creativity. One of the most creative tasks they could choose was one in which they were asked to work a scene from a novel into a play. This invited them to go back to the text and again explore the meaning of the scene. It also involved building a makeshift stage, deciding where the props had to be put, finding costumes, etc. They also had to prepare a script making sure that the actors knew exactly not only what they should say, but also where they should stand and how they were supposed to move around the stage. One of the books my students particularly liked to perform scenes from was *Junk* (Burgess, 1997). In actual fact, this novel has been adapted for the stage (Retallack, 1999). Consequently, another worthwhile activity was comparing the students' version with the official version.

While acting out key scenes from novels they had read was great fun, the students probably enjoyed creating their portfolio most. Since a portfolio is by definition a personal piece of work I had given very little instruction as to the content of it. At the end of the project the students had to hand in a beautifully edited portfolio with an attractive cover and containing a table of contents, a bibliography, the task sheets they had completed in the course of the project and a general reflection. In the final seminar of the project I asked my students to answer questions such as: Do you think you have become a better reader now that we have finished the project? Do you feel that your

English has improved? What does your portfolio reveal about you as a reader? Which assignment did you enjoy most? Which, do you think, is your best task sheet and how does it compare with your other task sheets?

Apart from these compulsory parts of the portfolio most students also included drawings, cartoons, photographs, newspaper cuttings about newly published teenage fiction, etc. Some also added screenshots of reviews they had read or posted themselves on the internet. Most teachers will agree that correcting and assessing student assignments can be a tiring and tedious chore. Going through these portfolios, however, was a real pleasure. Most students had built up positive attitudes and habits towards reading. It was obvious that most of them had become even more eager readers. In addition, the portfolios clearly showed the students' progress. The task sheets completed towards the end of the project were markedly better than the ones done at the beginning. The range of vocabulary in the reflections was wider, and there were fewer grammatical or spelling mistakes. Moreover, as to the content the reflections showed more depth. While in the first reflection the students focused almost solely on the themes of the novels, in the later task sheets they also wrote about style and language. And as they had read more they were able to compare novels in the same genre.

Some conclusions

It is not possible to know if the project has succeeded in motivating my students to become lifelong readers. However, it was obvious that most of the students participating in the project truly enjoyed it. While I had expected them to read 4 or 5 novels, most of them read 12 to 15, thus living up to one of the principles of extensive reading: 'learners read as much as possible' (Bamford et al., 2004, p. 2). It appeared that once they had experienced that they can indeed read an English novel, they kept reading them. This seems to contradict what research has established, namely that young adults do not like reading. I believe that secondary-school teachers can motivate and challenge their students to read provided they take some conditions into account. One important aspect in reading promotion – and in the concept of extensive reading – is that students read what they want to read. It is absolutely essential that teachers provide their students with a long list, including different genres. In addition, they should be open to suggestions and ideas from their students. In the course of the project I have added quite a few titles to the reading list. Most of these were suggested by my students. It is good to realize that no reading list is definitive.

The procedure and the conclusions described above may perhaps sound all too positive. Indeed, we should add a short comment here. The students involved in the project had chosen to take part voluntarily. The school had organized several projects – ranging from acrylic painting to a course in Adobe Photoshop – and the students could register for the programme they liked most. Consequently, the students who opted for the teenage fiction project were probably avid readers already, albeit of books in their mother tongue. However, this does not alter the fact that most of them made considerable progress in the course of the programme. They became better readers and their language skills improved. The language learning benefits were no doubt the result of the quantity of reading and the nature of the follow-up activities and task sheets. Again, this confirms Krashen's axiom that free voluntary reading does not only expand the reader's vocabulary, but that it also promotes better spelling and writing skills (Krashen, 1993, p. 23).

Despite the very positive impression I have about the project I would probably change a few things if I were to repeat it. I would definitely add non-fiction to the reading list. Some students simply do not like reading literary texts. Including non-fictional texts, for instance travel stories from *Discovery Channel* or *National Geographic*, might incite those students to take to an extensive reading programme for the simple reason that students are more likely to read material they are interested in. Also, today there is a wide range of outstanding graphic novels available. Moreover, a lot of these are adaptations of classic literary works. Students who need visual support and find reading an 'ordinary' novel a tough, almost unfeasible job might like to read these. Today I would also include more collections of short stories since they are perfect to be read on tablets, laptops and all sorts of e-readers. In short, I would provide an even more extensive list of reading material to appeal to as many students as possible.

Today I also see more alternatives to the task sheets I had provided. At the time I invited my students to post their own reviews on sites like Amazon, but now I would certainly include more IT in the assignments. I have since discovered more interesting sites which the students can browse and which they can use to add their own review. In my regular English course I have invited my students to join *Goodreads* (www. goodreads.com/) and to rate books there and send in reviews. This works really well. It is a writing assignment with a clear purpose and students like to see their work published and to find out if or how other readers reacted to their reviews. Other assignments involving IT are, for instance, recorded audio podcasts (*bookcasts*), Wikis, etc. Today's students – the digital natives – would no doubt like these assignments and they would definitely foster positive attitudes towards foreign language learning, and hopefully towards reading more in particular.

Some of the so-called digital natives prefer to read newspapers, magazines and books on their iPads. I have spent my adolescence without the internet and as a digital immigrant – and voracious reader – I will probably always prefer paper books. I love to touch and smell them. And for me there is simply no substitute for the pleasure of storing books on the bookshelf after I have finished them. Pleasure, it is one of the key concepts of extensive reading. It is with pleasure that I look back on the reading project of 2007.

Notes

1　Next to the core curricular objectives, Flemish schools that want government recognition and funding should meet a number of cross-curricular objectives. These have to do with citizenship, hygiene, learning to learn, IT, etc.

2　The list included authors such as Tim Bowler, David Almond, Melvin Burgess, Kevin Brooks, Mark Haddon, David Klass, Michael Morpurgo, Philip Pullman, etc.

3   I drew much of my inspiration from Bamford and Day (2004). Another recommended
     read is Day, Bassett et al. (2011). I also exchanged ideas with my colleagues, especially
     Lieve Deprez, Sylvie Engels and pedagogical advisor Johan Delbaere.

Bibliography

Burgess, M. (1997), *Junk*. London: Penguin.
Dhami, N. (2002), *Bend It Like Beckham*. London: Hodder Children's Books.
Mark, J. (2000), *Heathrow Nights*. London: Hodder.
— (2003), *Stratford Boys*. London: Hodder.
Retallack, J. (1999), *Junk by Melvin Burgess, Adapted for the Stage*. London: Methuen.

References

Bamford, J. and Day, R. R. (2004), *Extensive Reading Activities for Teaching Language*.
     Cambridge: Cambridge University Press. [Cambridge Handbooks for Language
     Teachers]
Day, R., Bassett, J., Bowler, B., Parminter, S., Bullard, N., Furr, M., Prentice, N., Mahmood,
     M., Stewart, D. and Robb, T. (2011), *Bringing Extensive Reading into the Classroom*.
     Oxford: Oxford University Press.
De Gendt, T. (2005), 'Lezen is voor mietjes'. *De Morgen*, 25 August, 25.
de Saedeleer, M. (2010), 'Waar is het leesplezier gebleven?' *De Morgen*, 9 December, 17.
Krashen, S. (1989), *Language Acquisition and Language Education: Extensions and
     Applications*. New York: Prentice Hall International. [Language Teaching Methodology
     Series]
— (1993), *The Power of Reading: Insights from the Research*. Englewood: Libraries
     Unlimited.

Part Two

Visual Literacy with Picturebooks and Graphic Novels in ELT

6

Approaching Literary and Language Competence: Picturebooks and Graphic Novels in the EFL Classroom

Eva Burwitz-Melzer

Defining the claim: Literacy, literary literacy and visual literacy

The teaching of literature in the FL classroom was greeted as one of the central achievements in the teaching of languages and cultures in the 1990s and at the beginning of the new millennium. However, the changes in educational policy brought about by PISA and similar studies have created a new situation at least in the German school context: today, literature has become an 'endangered species' due to the interests of Chambers of Commerce and output-oriented Ministries of Education. Language teachers today often find little time to indulge in the difficult business of teaching novels, poetry, plays and short stories. The *Common European Framework* and the German national educational standards with their pragmatic orientation to everyday and business-related communication have reduced the reading of literary texts in schools to a minimum. However important it may be to teach language learners the competence of reading with the aim of understanding all everyday written products in countries of the target language, it should be our aim not just to promote literacy, but rather *literary* literacy (Versaci, 2008, p. 94). Teaching literary literacy means to connect reading to our students' lives and worlds and make them lifelong readers – in their mother tongue as well as in the L2. When Perloff in 1997 in the *Chronicle of Higher Education* argued that the profession of literary studies had become too specialized, she suggested that teachers as a remedy should concentrate on making students aware of the importance of literature for their daily lives. Perloff made proposals for literary programmes that were as controversial in the United States as similar proposals have been in Germany for some years (Perloff, cit. in Versaci, 2008, p. 94). If we consider the teaching of literary texts 'a dwindling pie' (ibid.) since output orientation gradually ousts them out of the curriculum, teachers of literature need strong arguments for sticking to poems and stories, picturebooks and graphic novels.

An important argument in this context claims that '. . . literary literacy is informed by the idea that a love of reading is an end in itself; after all, a life without stories is a much poorer life' (Versaci, 2008, p. 94). This issue of helping our students become lifelong readers by linking literature to their daily lives and world knowledge is not an issue which is only important for L1 learners – it also applies to L2 learners and can be enhanced and adapted from kindergarten onward through all grades and school types. Beyond that, literary literacy fosters holistic learning of a new language while offering excitement, fun and many new ideas to young people. Another strong argument for literary literacy in teaching a second language is, of course, that the discussion of ambivalent topics like cultural and intercultural issues is necessary to develop sufficient social skills to survive peacefully in today's world. However meaningful the careful evaluation of skills and sub-skills may be, however lucid the demands of standards may be, the allotment to levels like A1 or C2 does not in itself make a language speaker successful in his or her striving for communication with members of other cultures; these levels do not say anything about empathy, sensitivity or intercultural understanding. Understanding the other, however, is one of the main problems we encounter when we learn or teach a foreign language, and it cannot be solved by teaching reading as a merely informative skill.

Developing language competence and the understanding of the other through authentic literary texts can be based on all kinds of genres and text forms: prose (short stories, novelettes and novels), poetry and drama, picturebooks, comics and graphic novels as well as films. The latter text forms open up a new focus on literacy: today it is no longer restricted to the classical fictional texts but involves visual art forms as well.

The New London Group developed the concept of *multiliteracies* in the 1990s while discussing the problems of teaching literacy. They argued that traditional literary education was restricted to print, whereas they wanted to include non-print material into the canon as well:

> A pedagogy of multiliteracies, by contrast, focuses on modes of representation much broader than language alone. These differ according to culture and context, and have specific cognitive, cultural, and social effects. In some cultural contexts – in an Aboriginal community or in a multimedia environment, for instance – the visual mode of representation may be much more powerful and closely related to language than "mere literacy" would ever be able to allow. Multiliteracies also create a different kind of pedagogy, one in which language and other modes of meaning are dynamic representational resources, constantly being remade by their users as they work to achieve their various cultural purposes. (New London Group, 1996, p. 10)

This issue has been debated over the past years, since prejudices about literary texts that involve visual modes have been strong. Picturebooks are usually regarded as less satisfactory for learners beyond the elementary stage, because they seem to offer only entertainment for the very young. Yet a closer look will show that today picturebooks exist for all ages, that they are a demanding art form involving readers on all competence levels.

Similarly, many prejudices prevail about comics and comic books. Comic books for a long time were regarded as 'trash' and therefore harmful to young people, recalling the arguments of critics like Nyberg or Wertham, who in the 1950s suspected that juvenile delinquency was caused by comics because young imprisoned criminals who had been interviewed for Wertham's study had admitted to reading comics (cit. in Versaci, 2008, p. 95).

US studies from the last 25 years, however, have shown that the 'mixing of words and images is a great way to foster comprehension and memory skills' (Carter, 2008, p. 48). Among researchers investigating this field, one should mention the studies of Maria (1990) who established that with some training in visualization and effective prompting, 4th graders were able to enrich their comprehension of a story based on the artwork and were more willing to participate in discussions of the story. Other key research in this area is that of Gunning who observed that 'Creating images serves three functions: fostering understanding, retaining information and monitoring for meaning' (2005, p. 301). In fact, the Dual Coding Theory (DCT) which states that schemata can be stored both verbally and visually still has a major impact on cognitive psychology and therefore also on language learning (Clark et al., 1991; Paivio, 1991). Contemporary research in the United States suggests that comics and graphic novels may have a beneficial effect on reluctant readers and also enhance the reading of good learners. The longitudinal study of Smith and Wilhelm (2002) has demonstrated that young men who are reluctant readers can be trained to read more by using graphic novels in the classroom. Michael Bitz's *Comic Book Project* (2004) shows that K-8 students were able to develop their literary skills by creating comic books themselves. In the project the students 'brainstormed, outlined, sketched, wrote and designed original comic books . . .' It proves that children 'discover meaningful dimensions of their worlds when they can explore them through creative arts, including comic books' (Bitz, 2004, pp. 574–5).

Quoting more than 60 years of research into comics, Krashen (2004) and Xu (2005) argue in favour of reading comics in the classroom. While Krashen states that the relationship between comics and pupils is almost as old as the comic superheroes are themselves (Krashen, 2004, p. 97), Xu deplores that the number of teachers using comics is still quite low (Xu, 2005, p. 2).

Connecting the terms literacy, literary literacy and visual literacy, one can come to some first conclusions: literary art forms which involve pictures and sequential art like comics address younger and older readers from the very start of their learning and still reach teenagers and young adults on an advanced level. Dual text encoding may help the student to learn a foreign language, since the visual representations make pupils see what they read and foster their memory of words and concepts. Additionally, for those learning a foreign or a second language the use of dual texts, graphic and verbal, may lead to a better understanding of the other culture, its values and its traditions. The choice of texts that combine written and visual modes may be a good way to activate those male and female learners who are

- interested in modern visual art forms
- or inexperienced with literature,

- or easily daunted by literary challenges like longer written texts,
- or who simply want a change in the choice of literary texts.

Language teachers at schools and teacher educators at universities therefore need to re-plan their curricula involving visual literacy into their concepts of teaching language and culture. Teaching concepts, teaching objectives, the competences taught, the texts discussed, the methods used and the curriculum for teacher training have to be changed accordingly. Therefore, a 'visual turn' in pedagogy, language learning classes and literary curricula in German schools is needed.

Some characteristics of picturebooks and graphic novels

Picturebooks

In picturebooks and graphic novels both text systems are intricately linked and work together. The ways in which they do so depend on the complex text-picture relationship in the individual picturebook or graphic novel.

> Picturebooks intended for young children which communicate information or tell stories through a series of many pictures combined with relatively slight text or no text at all – are unlike any other form of verbal or visual art. (Nodelman, 1988, p. vii)

Nodelman describes picturebooks for young learners, but the second quotation makes no such distinction:

> A picturebook is text, illustrations, total design; an item of manufacture and a commercial product; a social, cultural, historical document; and, foremost, an experience for a child. As art form it hinges on the interdependence of pictures and words, on the simultaneous display of two facing pages, and on the drama of the turning of the page. On its own terms its possibilities are limitless. (Bader, 1976, p. 1)

What then are the characteristics of fictional picturebooks?

- Picturebooks usually present one story or several closely connected stories;
- they may involve all kinds of topics and literary genres;
- their two text systems both have an aesthetic function;
- the two text systems interact in many different ways. Some critics talk about a whole system of relationships with symmetry, enhancement, counterpoint, deviation and contradiction (Nikolajeva et al., 2001), some simply summarize these relationships as 'irony' (Nodelman, 1988, p. 221) or a 'double orientation' (Lewis, 2001, p. 68);

- the two modes are self-referential in that they constantly refer back to themselves making the reader conscious of their language and their illustrations;
- they are ambivalent in meaning because of *Leerstellen* in the verbal and visual mode that is there are gaps which require the reader to imagine what happened;
- picturebooks are complex products of a culture and reflect their cultural background. Intertextual relationships are frequent.

Little Beauty by Anthony Browne may serve as an example here. It tells the story of a singular friendship between a gorilla and a little cat, alluding to the story of King Kong with a new and fabulous twist in the end.

Browne depicts the first scenes in a layout pattern typical for him: the text is on the left-hand page and a large visual plate on the right-hand side. Text and picture are in a contradictory relationship: 'Once upon a time there was a special gorilla who had been taught to use the sign language. If there was anything he wanted he could ask his keepers for it by using his hands to sign. It seemed that he had everything he needed.' This fairy tale start is juxtaposed by the pictures, particularly the gorilla's disinterested and empty look at the TV set in front of him. The opulent scenery with a grandfather's chair, lovely William Morris tapestry, hamburger, presumably a soy hamburger since gorillas are herbivorous, the cup of tea and the TV set shows that the gorilla indeed is very well looked after, yet it only SEEMS AS IF he has everything he needs. It is an artificial life, putting the gorilla in a position close to man – he is even able to communicate with his keepers in a complicated sign language. 'But he was SAD.' The very simple technique to enlarge key words underlines their meaning – even to young readers.

Since the gorilla is lonely, his keepers decide to give him a small companion – a beautiful little cat and the gorilla immediately accepts the cat as a dear friend. The pictures of the gorilla on these right-hand pages are reciprocal in that they show sadness and happiness in a very obvious juxtaposition. Some pictures do not even need words or only very few of them, like the one that shows the gorilla and his little friend portrayed in a sketchy way with bold strokes – their surroundings blended out.

Doom enters the small paradise with a film on TV, a gorilla standing on top of a skyscraper attacking a plane. The nocturnal TV scene showing the upset friends watching the film and simultaneously the scene they watch, focuses in on a close-up of the angry gorilla in red, who hammers violently on the TV set. The announcement that Little Beauty will be taken from him to protect her from possible aggression is mirrored by a fearful expression on the gorilla's face. The focus is shifted to the cat alone for the first time. While her friend is watching her sceptically, she starts using the sign language, which he must have taught her (it seems to be an intellectual relationship, too). The last double page brings relief at last, since Little Beauty takes responsibility for the broken TV set, and proves that she is not helpless at all, but very well equipped to look after herself. Browne freshens up the old King Kong story adding a surprising twist to the old motif of being almost tamed, tricked and killed by civilization.

Graphic novels

Scott McCloud, who sees the origins of the sequential art of comics in South American codices, in the tapestry of Bayeux and Egyptian hieroglyphs, stresses the fact that comics are:

> *com.ics* (komiks) n. plural in form, used with a singular verb. 1. Juxtaposed pictorial and other images in deliberate sequence, intended to convey information and /or to produce an aesthetic response in the viewer. (McCloud, 1994, p. 9)

Art Spiegelman expands on that when he ironically 'defines' the medium: 'A graphic novel is a comic book you need a bookmark for.'

Spiegelman's description above all refers to the length as a distinguishing feature of the graphic novel. Graphic novels like comic books and comic strips all belong to the family of comics, that is to the family of sequential arts (Eisner), yet they are longer than the usual 32 pages standard comic book. Usually, a graphic novel is a collection of comics that offers some form of continuity: it may be a single story, yet it may also be a collection of only loosely related comic strips. This umbrella definition leaves the question of genres undecided – on purpose. A graphic novel may belong to the fantasy genre like *Coraline* by Neil Gaiman, it may be a fictional biography like *Maus* by Art Spiegelman or *Ethel and Ernest* by Raymond Briggs. A graphic novel may depict various anonymous people in a big city, like William Eisner's *The Building*, telling emotional or socially critical stories. It may describe chapters in the lives of famous people like *Houdini: The Handcuff King* by Jason Lutes and Nick Bertozzi or refer to recent political developments like *Waltz with Bashir*, the Lebanon war story by Ari Folman and David Polonsky. Some graphic novels are very much influenced by the Japanese tradition of mangas, some graphic novels are pictorial stories of literary classics. Graphic novels for younger readers also include the classical Superhero stories. Despite the fairly vague definitions and the somewhat fuzzy delimitations of the medium, the term 'graphic novel' today is an established one, used by commercial publishers as well as in literary criticism.

Neil Gaiman's graphic novel *Coraline* (see Figure 6.1) will be used here as an example to illustrate the potential of the medium. It followed his prize-winning novelette with the same title and preceded the film, which was released in 2009. For the graphic novel, the plot of the novelette was slightly adapted. The main protagonist is Coraline, who has moved to a new home with her family. She is an only child with working parents. In the first couple of days in the new home she lives through some exciting fantastic adventures in a kind of parallel world, which will challenge her view of her family and herself as a member of it. The plot bears definite traits of a coming-of-age story showing Coraline maturing from a rather sulky child to a teenager. There are 13 chapters of irregular length, which will help teachers to portion the graphic novel for classroom usage.

The illustrations are in an elaborate, realistic style that uses one to ten panels per page. The layout differs from page to page, adding momentum and action whenever the plot needs this. The panels are mostly framed and have different sizes and different shapes. The perspectives vary widely. In most cases the sequence of the panels is clear.

Figure 6.1 *Coraline* by Neil Gaiman and Craig Russell © (2008). Reprinted by permission of Bloomsbury Publishing Plc.

The verbal text uses the traditional patterns of comics: the characters' direct speech is written in speech balloons, the narrator's text is in light brown and set in rectangular or circular captions; there are thought balloons in bubbles or without frames. Readers are familiar with these conventions, but in a classroom where visual literacy is one of the competences to be acquired, it may be useful to make students aware of these different tools and to discuss the elaborated 'camera angles', the rapid succession of similar panels to indicate action and the special design to indicate a parallel world.

Picturebooks and graphic novels – blurred boundaries

When comparing the definitions and a typology of picturebooks and graphic novels it becomes clear that these two genres are very close to each other. They are so close, indeed, that it is sometimes very difficult to decide whether a book belongs to one group or the other. The next example therefore will look at a publication that is a picturebook and a graphic novel at the same time, though it does not offer a dual text but is restricted to illustrations. This structural variation occurs quite often in picturebooks as well as in graphic novels, and sometimes teachers are misled into thinking that a book that only offers pictures is the easiest text type to use in a foreign language classroom. The following example will show that this is not the case – quite the contrary, picturebooks and graphic novels which are restricted to the graphic mode demand elaborate verbalization. If the author does not provide words, the reader will have to do so, and this is often very difficult.

The example I would like to add here is Shaun Tan's book *The Arrival* (2008), which describes the migration of a father and later on his family to a foreign country. The book consists of sepia-coloured illustrations that sometimes are giant double spreads covering two pages and very often are minute squares, between 9 or 12 and up to 30 per page. These illustrations give the book the appearance of an old photo album, of family stories told again and again by grandparents.

The story is divided into six chapters that describe the stages of the family's immigration to a new country. The untitled chapters show the archetypal process of emigration of the first generation, the parents and then of the rest of the family. Embedded in this linear narrative of migration are several stories of people the protagonist meets in the course of events. They have all undergone similar experiences that forced them to migrate: political persecution, imprisonment, ethnic cleansing, war and the destruction of their homes. The welcome in the new country is a warm one, yet Tan's pictures convey just as well the feeling of being a stranger in a foreign country, not knowing how to communicate in the new language, not even knowing the animals, the food and the most common everyday rituals. It is due to this depiction of the feeling of being the 'other', the one who has yet to learn how to cope with the new situation, that makes this book important for students in the EFL classroom. The illustrations evoke many details of former generations of American and Australian immigrants, and thus Shaun Tan has created a book about the archetypal experience of being a stranger willing to integrate into the new surroundings. The wordlessness of the book adds to the feeling of being estranged. Only at the very end, successful communication is achieved by the daughter of the family who herself now welcomes a complete stranger to the new home.

Competences and learning objectives

The three examples have made it clear that, although there are many differences between picturebooks and graphic novels, there are also many common aspects. One of the features they share '. . . is the notion of the "readerly gap" – the highly imaginative space that lies hidden between the words and the pictures/panels, or in the mysterious syntax of the pictures/panels themselves, or between the voices of the narrators in the stories' (Styles et al., 1996, p. 2). This imaginative space allows for a special and highly individual reception of the verbal and visual mode, the reader's construction of meaning, which is central according to receptionist theory. Picturebooks and graphic novels thus lend themselves to the construction of individual meanings of a text, demanding discussion and comparison of these different meanings in the classroom.

Before illustrating learning opportunities for different groups of learners with two examples for teaching units, I will point out the most important competences that may be fostered by talking about picturebooks and graphic novels in the EFL classroom.

Of course, picturebooks as well as graphic novels help to develop most of the traditional language competences since they require discussion, ask for repeated and detailed reading and may also lead to creative or analytical written tasks in order to come to terms with the complex features of graphic and visual modes and their 'readerly gaps'. Moreover, protagonists and actions in the stories may demand explanation or negotiating of values through discussions and small reports.

The second group of competences focuses on the fostering of literary and visual literacy. Dealing with picturebooks and graphic novels in the foreign language classroom helps young students to learn how to read or to listen to a literary text and to decode a verbal and a visual mode and understand their interaction. Younger as well as more advanced students learn how to analyse and interpret illustrations and text, more advanced learners become familiar with different genres and text types, as well as with rhetorical and stylistic devices.

Social and political learning objectives form a third group of competences that may be developed by the use of picturebooks and graphic novels. They may motivate learners to identify with different characters, to use empathy and train the changing of perspectives, as well as the acceptance of different opinions. It is to this group of aims that Martha Nussbaum refers when she talks about 'the political promise of literature':

> It is for this reason that literature is so urgently important for the citizen, as an expansion of sympathies that real life cannot cultivate sufficiently. It is the political promise of literature that it can transport us, while remaining ourselves, into the life of another, revealing similarities but also profound differences between the life and thought of that other and myself and making them comprehensible, or at least nearly comprehensible. (Nussbaum, 1998, p. 111)

This leads directly to the next group of competences which may be called intercultural: picturebooks and graphic novels offer glances into target cultures and stimulate readers to decode cultural symbols that differ from those in their home cultures. This may help to make learners aware of stereotypes, and to diminish prejudice. In a multicultural classroom picturebooks and graphic novels invite comparisons between different cultures.

A last group of learning objectives, which should not be forgotten in this context, is concerned with the enhancement of use of the new media. Picturebooks and graphic novels may challenge pupils to use the WWW to gain information about author and text, about the foreign culture and to chat about the text with other readers.

Two examples for the classroom

Shortcut by David Macaulay: A paper chase in ten chapters

David Macaulay, the author of *Shortcut* (1995), is an internationally acclaimed writer of children's books. His books, like *Black and White*, have won several prizes and have been translated into many languages. The book *Shortcut* (see Figure 6.2) tells the story of Albert, the farmer, and his mare June who go to the market to sell

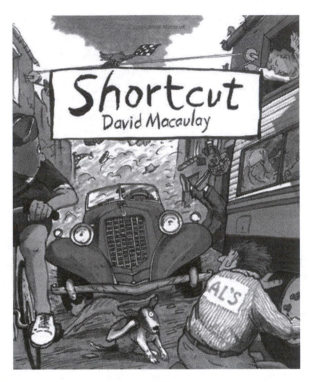

Figure 6.2 *Shortcut* by David Macaulay © (1995). Reprinted by permission of Houghton Mifflin Harcourt Publishing Company. All rights reserved.

watermelons. But then the story is not so simple as it might appear on the surface. It has a multiple-cause-and-effect plot in ten chapters, which less skilled readers will find difficult to understand when reading it from page to page in a linear way. Macaulay makes us take the long road – we have to leaf through this book again and again on a cyclical paper chase to pick up the verbal and the visual clues, to link cause to effect and understand the intricately intertwined five storylines woven into one narrative. Only very attentive readers who are willing to decode the book on a careful hunt for minute information will be successful. Therefore *Shortcut* may be used to practise intensive reading with children and teenagers and make them aware of the process of decoding.

The story of Albert and June is narrated in short and simple sentences.

Albert and June are up early. It is market day. Once a week they take their ripest melons into town. As they cross the bridge, Albert and June always make a wish. To save time, they will take the shortcut. Albert removes his coat and helps June up the hill. When they reach the top, Albert gets his coat and they are off again. In a little while they stop to eat at the Railway Café. June is very hungry. She stretches to reach some tasty clover. After lunch, they continue toward town, crooning their favourite songs. A rope blocks their path – but not for long. Their melons are very popular, and the wagon is soon empty. Once again, Albert and June get their wish. They are home before dark. (Macaulay, 1995, unpaginated)

Parallel to this story, four other stories unravel: the one about Patty and her pet pig, which disappears in a mysterious way, and only reappears at the end of the book. And the story of Professor Tweet who studies bird behaviour in a balloon. He is suddenly set free and has to save his life by an audacious manoeuvre. Then there is Sybil and her daredevil car race to the market, which is stopped by a policeman. And sheer luck happens to Bob the dreamer who falls over board . . . and finds a treasure!

The picture-text relationship is one that can be described by enhancement, yet also by irony. The text often remains short, tongue-in-cheek – but the illustrations convey a more detailed message. 'Sybil is off to market' only expresses that she is on her way, the picture, however, gives important information about her means of transport, her speed and how the world surrounding her reacts to her car race. 'Though she follows the sign, it is still a long, long way. By the time she arrives, Albert is out of melons and she is out of luck.' The two pages accompanying this text give away one of the many confusions in the picturebook. Albert's jacket hanging over the sign covers up the arrow that shows the real direction of the shortcut. Sybil, who doesn't know the way, follows the wrong arrow – and, as a result, is too late for the market but just in time for the policeman who caught her speeding. As ever so often in this book, the real surprise comes after the turning of the page.

This beautiful and clever picturebook is a perfect training-ground for visual literacy and tongue-in-cheek irony. Students will probably have fun finding all the clues in the pictures, re-tracing the narrative steps again and again. It is obvious that such a picturebook demands careful readings and well-planned discussions and tasks. The characters are presented in six funny snapshots, building up suspense before the story proper starts. Why is the old lady crying, why is Bob's head under water and why does Sybil's appear on a police photo? Teachers might lead their students' attention to the cover of the book, which shows an arrow. Where does it lead? How does it tie in with the title?

Following these pre-reading questions should be a first reading of the book, which pupils in grade six or seven (4th or 5th year of EFL learning) can do on their own. The simple sentences are not difficult to understand, the illustrations offer additional information. The division into chapters helps teachers to divide the reading tasks into reasonable chunks. After Chapters 2, 3 or 4, questions will arise: 'What's going to happen?' followed by a short discussion about the next step in the story of Patty and Pearl or of Professor Tweet.

Having gone through the book once, the teacher might like to start a discussion about its Chinese box structure, one plot unfolding out of the other and all intertwined. It will be a good partner task to ask pupils to unravel the many clues in the picture: 'Where exactly and how often do we see the signpost with the "shortcut" – what is wrong with it, why does Sybil take the wrong way?' – 'Where have we seen the rope from Professor Tweet's balloon first, and where do all the coins come from that Bob finds in the river under the bridge? Are they really all from Professor Tweet's balloon?'

A careful selection of paper chase questions will guide pupils through the book on their search for information. They will have to present their results and discuss them later in class.

As a next step, the stories may be unravelled, that is told one by one in different groups. What about Albert and June – how do they live? Do they go to market every day? What about Patty and her pig? Why is she so determined to find her again, which tracks does she follow? What do they do in the end?

In a creative phase following this structural analysis, pupils may choose one strand of the story and write a little bit more about it. Describe Albert's and June's life on Sundays, comment on Sybil's attempt to sell her car and tell her buyer her reasons for selling it, etc. Pupils might like to accomplish this task on their own or in small groups, adding collages, photos or drawings to illustrate their stories.

A reflection phase at the end will help the class to sum up what they have learned about this picturebook in particular and picturebooks in general; they should be able to link what they have learned to their world-knowledge and name new (picturebook) topics they are interested in. Probably the picturebook experience will lead to a strong interest in visual literacy, which should be kept alive with an occasional example of a new picturebook, comic, cartoon or a graphic novel.

Houdini. The Handcuff King by Jason Lutes and Nick Bertozzi

In *Houdini. The Handcuff King* (2007), Jason Lutes and Nick Bertozzi introduce the readers to one day in the life of Harry Houdini, who was born as Erik Weisz in Budapest and emigrated to the United States in 1874 to become a world-famous magician and escapist. He was able not only to escape from handcuffs but also from straitjackets, ropes, police stations, even coffins that had been buried. Harry Houdini is a personification of the American success story, and this graphic novel tells the reader why. Not only was he a very disciplined and agile artist, an obsessed and ingenious plotter, but also a very creative promoter who knew how to seize the public's attention well before the age of TV and the internet.

The graphic novel gives us a good impression of the escapist's practice with its 90 pages of black, white and light-blue panels strictly framed in a rather conventional manner reminiscent of woodcuts of the 1920s. Some of the panels offer spectacular panoramas of the city or the audience waiting for Houdini. The strict layout of the pages and the sparse colouring add to the tension, which is built up until the final stunt. The special treat of this graphic novel is that it gives away one of Houdini's tricks. The readers can now understand how it worked.

The graphic novel contains a lot of cultural features, describing the life of a world-famous star a hundred years ago. It describes the problem of anti-Semitism in the United States at the beginning of the twentieth century, and the – to modern standards – strange but successful methods of advertising and promotion. The story also tells us that the audience was never quite sure whether Houdini was in league with demons or supernatural powers. It was a time when scientists presented stunning news about X-rays, germs, genes and radio waves, and still unknown species in far away parts of the world – no one knew what was possible or not. Houdini, however, stressed the fact that he had earned his fame by creativity and agility, discipline and ingenuity. Since the language level of this graphic novel is not too difficult, the book makes good reading for 10th or 11th graders.

Dealing with this novel in the classroom means exploring the different layers of text and illustrations, cultural and historical facts. The short biography can be read in one teaching unit; for inexperienced learning groups, however, a step-by-step reading process is advisable to concentrate on text and panels; a division of the text in several parts is recommendable.

It may be a good idea to start reading *Houdini* with a glance at a modern illusionist like David Copperfield and what makes it so attractive to watch his performances. Is it glamour? The excitement that something might go wrong with his tricks and somebody may be hurt after all? Or is it the wish to detect the secrets behind his show? Questions like these will lead into a discussion that reveals what modern audiences watching a magician's performance might expect, and they will thus pave the way into the reading of the graphic novel about Houdini.

A glance at the first pages (*1. Morning Practice*) introduces Houdini's most important tools for practice: handcuffs, the pick he uses to open the lock and a watch to control the time. Within these first pages we learn about his trick that involves his wife and makes her an accomplice in his stunt at the end of the book. Classroom discussion should carefully cover Houdini's practice, and the role his wife plays in it. Their close relationship, Bess' partnership and her key role in his stunts are prerequisites for Houdini's success and survival. A careful look at the panels, their different perspectives and their focus will show how the reader's attention is consequently shifted from Houdini, who concentrates on his practice alone, to his wife. Onomatopoeic details like the 'tick, tick' of the clock should be discovered by the students.

The next pages (*2. Meeting Staff and Journalists*) show the escapist's daily routine of jogging, checking on his promotion staff, practising the final jump and talking to the press. Classroom discussion should concentrate on some details like the anti-Semitic remarks of the police officers (pp. 13–14) and Harry Houdini's ironic dealing with their prejudice.

In the next pages (*3. Departure from Hotel*), Houdini steps out of the hotel and meets his audience, a vast mass of people who are longing to see this celebrity. Here, the change of perspective to Houdini's own view of the audience (pp. 31–2) is particularly interesting and should be included in the classroom discussion. This part ends with a bird's eye view of Harvard Bridge showing the immense crowd that has assembled to see Houdini dive into the water. Here, at the latest, it is advisable to ask students what will happen next, because suspense is building up. Will Houdini be successful? Will he manage to free himself? What might go wrong now?

The last and fourth part shows the solution of how his trick works. We see his wife on her way to the Bridge, taking the pick out of her sleeve and putting it into her mouth. Houdini slowly takes off his clothes, is inspected by the police and then we see his wife. Houdini and his wife, as the only two white figures in the crowd of black and light-blue people, exchange a farewell kiss. The reader may guess what happened during this kiss!

Only with her help is he equipped to perform his trick. When the final stunt – Houdini's jump, fully handcuffed, into the ice-cold water – is shown, the rapid succession of views of Houdini in large black panels sinking deeper and deeper into the river, still handcuffed, and the audience who hold their breath and look at their watches, makes the reader wince – till he or she knows that the trick works and everything turns out well. Discussion in the classroom should dwell on the trick itself, because the understanding of it is crucial to the meaning of the book. But also, a careful look at the panels must be included. It is remarkable how views of the audience and glances into the water at Houdini alternate with each other in this part, creating suspense.

After the graphic novel has been read and discussed, some additional, creative tasks or research questions may be added to round off the teaching sequence. The filling in of thought or speech bubbles is one of the ways of giving students a deeper understanding of the action in the text, of characters and of ambiguities. What is Harry thinking before the hotel doors are opened to him when he leaves for his jump from the bridge? What does he think when he steps out of the hotel and meets the mass of people there? What is his wife thinking when she is on her way to him with the pick in her mouth? Is it 'ethical' to deceive an audience that is willing to be deceived? There are enough panels in the text that do not have thought or speech bubbles. It is easy to photocopy these pages and let the students fill in what the characters feel, think or say. Literary literacy, but also intercultural and social competences may be fostered by such tasks.

Other tasks may involve characters who do not appear in the book at all, but who can be easily imagined. Take, for example a reporter from a magazine or daily newspaper. How does he inform his audience about the jump? What information does he select, what does he omit? If there is a photo reporter with him, what does he choose as a motif? Students might write a short article and draw some panels showing their view of the stunt, including audience and magician and police as well as Houdini and his staff. Here writing competences, but also visual competences are fostered.

Yet another set of tasks may ask the learner to look at historical details. The internet still holds an abundance of material on Harry Houdini, many sources are provided by the *New York Times* which has a special Houdini section of newspaper articles, or the Houdini Museum, NY, which offers some video films of his stunts, interviews and even of his funeral. If one 'googles' the famous illusionist, further material can be found on *youtube*, among them an original film of a straightjacket escape (www.youtube.com/watch?v=mUbytEgTXZQ). The teaching objective here is to prepare a presentation on Houdini as a collage with primary sources – images and texts.

Consequences for teacher education

The examples may have illustrated the point that literary literacy and visual literacy are two very challenging topics, which should be integrated into foreign language classrooms. Yet, teacher education, up to now, has not really given a lot of attention to this 'visual turn', that is the upcoming generation of teachers does not yet really know how to use multimodal texts and how to integrate visual elements into the curriculum.

Therefore, it makes sense to offer visual literacy as one element in the agenda of teacher education, introducing students at universities to the basics of reading multimodal literature. More picturebooks and graphic novels should be collected in academic libraries and seminar classrooms.

Bibliography

Briggs, R. (1998), *Ethel and Ernest*. London: Jonathan Cape.

Browne, A. (2008), *Little Beauty*. London: Walker Books.

Eisner, W. (1988), *The Building*. Princeton, WI: Kitchen Sink Press.

Folman, A. and Polonsky, D. (2008), *Waltz with Bashir. A Lebanon War Story* (1st US edn). New York: Metropolitan Books.

Gaiman, N. and Russell, P. C. (2008), *Coraline.* London: Bloomsbury.

Lutes, J. and Bertozzi, N. (2007), *Houdini. The Handcuff King* (1st edn). New York: Hyperion.

Macaulay, D. (1990), *Black and White*. Boston: Houghton Mifflin.

— (1995), *Shortcut*. Boston: Houghton.

Spiegelman, A. (2009), *Maus. A Survivor's Tale* (reprint). London: Penguin Books.

Tan, S. (2007), *The Arrival* (1st edn). New York: Arthur A. Levine Books.

References

Bader, B. (1976), *American Picturebooks from Noah's Ark to the Beast Wthin*. New York: Macmillan and London: Collier Macmillan.

Bitz, M. (2004), 'The Comic Book Project: Forging alternative pathways to literacy', *Journal of Adolescent and Adult Literacy*, 47(7), 574–86.

Carter, J. B. (2008), 'Comics, the canon, and the classroom', in N. Frey and D. Fisher (eds), *Teaching Visual Literacy*. Thousand Oaks, CA: Corwin Press, pp. 47–60.

Clark, J. M. and Paivio, A. (1991), 'Dual Coding Theory and education', *Educational Psychology Review*, 3(3), 149–70.

Gunning, T. G. (2005), *Creating Literacy Instruction for All Students* (5th edn). Boston: Allyn and Bacon.

Krashen, S. D. (2004), *The Power of Reading* (2nd edn). Portsmouth, NH: Heinemann.

Lewis, D. (2001), *Reading Contemporary Picturebooks. Picturing Text*. London: RoutledgeFalmer.

Maria, K. (1990), *Reading Comprehension Instruction: Issues and Strategies.* Parkton, MD: York.

McCloud, S. (1994), *Understanding Comics. The Invisible Art*. New York: Harper Perennial.

New London Group (1996), 'A pedagogy of multiliteracies: Designing social futures', *Harvard Educational Review*, 66(1), 64.

Nikolajeva, M. and Scott, C. (2001), *How Picturebooks Work*. New York and London: Garland.

Nodelman, P. (1988, 2nd edn, 1996), *Words About Pictures: The Narrative Art of Children's Picturebooks*. Athens, GA and London: University of Georgia Press.

Nussbaum, M. (1998), *Cultivating Humanity: A Classical Defense of Reform in Liberal Education*. Cambridge, MA: Harvard University Press.

Paivio, A. (1991), *Images in Mind: The Evolution of a Theory*. New York and London: Harvester Wheatsheaf.

Smith, M. W. and Wilhelm, J. D. (2002), *Reading Don't Fix No Chevys*. Portsmouth, NH: Heinemann.

Styles, M. and Watson, V. (eds) (1996), *Talking Pictures: Pictorial Texts and Young Readers*. London: Hodders and Stoughton.

Versaci, R. (2008), 'Literary literacy and the role of the comic book: or, "You teach a class on what"?', in N. Frey and D. Fisher (eds), *Teaching Visual Literacy Using Comic Books, Graphic Novels, Anime, Cartoons, and More to Develop Comprehension and Thinking Skills*. Thousand Oaks, CA: Corwin Press, pp. 91–112.

Xu, S. H. (2005), *Trading Cards and Comic Strips: Popular Culture Texts and Literacy Learning in Grades K-8*. Newark, DE: International Reading Association.

7

Picturebook: Object of Discovery

Sandie Mourão

This chapter discusses the peritextual features of picturebooks, defining peritext and giving examples. With reference to empirical research, I share data collected during the repeated read-alouds of three picturebooks, *Just like Jasper* (Inkpen et al., 1990), *Good Night Gorilla* (Rathmann, 1996) and *Rosie's Walk* (Hutchins, 1968), which demonstrates how preschool students responded to the peritextual features of these picturebooks. I conclude that in showing the whole picturebook and enabling students to share thoughts and ideas in their L1 they expanded their L2 language and literacy skills as well as enhanced their cognitive and aesthetic development. I propose that language teachers should be more aware of how to use the picturebook as an object of discovery.

The picturebook as object

Picturebooks are multimodal objects containing two semiotic modes – a visual and a verbal, which when put together create a composite text (Kress et al., 1996). However, a picturebook is not just the visual and the verbal together creating multilayered meaning. What makes a picturebook so very different from other books, with or without pictures, is the special attention given to the way it is put together, created and designed. Bader (1976) highlights design as a third element in the making of a picturebook and Marantz (1977) describes the picturebook as being conceived of as 'a unit, a totality that integrates all the designated parts in a sequence in which the relationships among them – the cover, endpapers, typography, pictures – are crucial to the understanding of the book' (p. 14). In picturebooks the features that are overlooked in adult literature, considered to be peripheral to the body of a work, are put to deliberate use 'integrated into a single organic entity whose parts are in harmony with each other and the whole' (Shulevitz, 1985, p. 54).

Picturebook peritext

Genette (1997) coined the term 'paratext' for what I am discussing in this chapter, and in agreement with Shulevitz, says that it is the paratext that enables a text to become a book and to be offered as such to its readers. Genette divides paratext into epitext and peritext. Epitext includes all outside elements, which help us know more about a text: these may include, films of the book, letters, interviews, reviews, resource materials, a chat with a colleague in the staff room and so on. Peritext consists of all the features which frame a text, such as prefaces, covers, titles and so on. Children's publishing has become highly adept at using illustrators, authors, editors and book designers together to exploit the peritext, bringing a wholeness to picturebooks. Special attention has been paid to the ways in which the possible use of the dust jacket, front and back covers, endpapers, half-title and title pages, copyright and dedication pages all work together with illustrations and words. Illustrations in particular, *overflow* the narrative (Díaz Armas, 2006), as the peritextual features are often used by the illustrator to provide narrative information making the picturebook a unified end product and one that should be considered carefully from cover to cover.

Picturebook anatomy

It is useful to consider picturebook anatomy before continuing and if you have a picturebook at hand, you may want to look at it as we proceed.

A picturebook has a cover: this can be a hardcover or a paperback one. In hardcover editions there is often a jacket or dust cover, which wraps around the hardcover to protect it. Upon opening a hardcover picturebook, the first sheets of paper we see are the end papers, parts of the binding, glued to the cover and the pages of the book and literally holding the book as object together. Some paperback editions also include the end papers, as they can be a 'visual bridge' between the cover and the first pages, like 'background music, they evoke a suitable mood while moving into the front matter' (Shulevitz, 1985, p. 115).

Books are printed using large sheets of paper, which are cut to produce a signature of 8 book leaves, making 16 pages. Picturebooks are normally made of 2 signatures and are therefore designed to fit into 32 pages, occasionally there are just 24 or as many as 48. These pages are divided into front matter, the body of the book and back matter. The front matter can include the following:

- A half title page, showing the title;
- A title page, showing the full title, the author and illustrator's names, the publisher's name;
- A copyright page, which contains copyright notice, date and place of publication and important information in small print;
- A dedication, which can be on a separate page or not.
- All these pages can also contain illustrations. In most picturebooks you will find between three and seven pages of front matter. Occasionally the copyright page is placed as back matter.

Picturebook peritext in research and resource materials

Published research that looks at the use of peritextual features in picturebooks is sparse, however recently the number has increased. Sipe et al. (2006) have created a typology to represent how endpapers contribute to the aesthetics of a picturebook, which differs from a typology created by Ramos (2007) and Bosch et al. (2011). Consejo (2011) describes the different functions of the peritextual features within picturebooks, and chastises librarians for placing library stickers on endpapers and the illustrations we see on half title, copyright and title pages, the latter referred to as prologue and epilogue illustrations (Bjorvand, 2011).

In relation to how children respond to the peritextual features of picturebooks, Sipe (2000; 2008) and Pantaleo (2003) have described how they make predictions about characters, plot and setting during the shared reading of picturebooks. Sipe in particular relates how children responded to picturebooks as made objects or cultural products.

Has the picturebook peritext been considered in ELT yet? Empirical research is non-existent. But there are some references to using these features in resource materials. Peritext is referred to in a set of online materials, which accompanied *The Magic Pencil Exhibition*. These materials focused on using the covers of a number of quality picturebooks and can still be accessed online (see link below). Mourão (2009) gives specific examples of how to use the peritext of picturebooks, which belong to *Primary Brit Lit* packs. The British Council has produced a number of online resource packs for using picturebooks to promote diversity through children's literature. These materials offer step-by-step instructions of how to go 'through' the book. They have acknowledged the peritext and support teachers in bringing these features to the children's attention.

Picturebook peritexts in action

In my empirical research in a teaching English as a foreign language context, I have found that children pay particular attention to the peritextual elements of a picturebook, especially when they are given the opportunity to use them to predict and confirm meaning, as well as to put to use any words they know in English. I shall briefly describe my study before sharing some of the responses and reactions I observed and finish with some conclusions about how the students used their L1 to support later L2 use through these features.

A brief description of the study

The aim of the study is to understand how illustrations in picturebooks provide affordances for language development in a foreign language context, a context that favours and focuses on the verbal text and its acquisition (Ellis et al., 2002; Linse, 2007). Following the interpretative paradigm of naturalistic, qualitative enquiry, preschool students, whose first language was Portuguese (L1), were observed learning English as a foreign language (L2) and interacting with English picturebooks of different word-picture dynamics, with or without a repetitive verbal text.

Data was collected from January to June 2009. Three Portuguese pre-schools who had English lessons twice a week for the duration of 30 minutes were selected as convenience samples and a total of 64 children, between 56 and 79 months, were observed interacting with the picturebooks during these lessons. The observations occurred in two stages. First, during teacher-led repeated read alouds (RRAs) over seven consecutive English lessons, where spontaneous responses were encouraged. Here the teacher mediated between the book and the students, reading the verbal text, occasionally prompting predictions, and fielding responses to the illustrations and verbal text as they arose. Initiation, response, and feedback exchanges (Sinclair et al., 1975) were avoided. The second stage of observations took place during out of class, small group retells, after the seventh read-aloud. Here the students were encouraged to retell the picturebook to their English class puppet, thus participating in re-enactments (Holdaway, 1979). Each instance was audio recorded and filmed. The corpus consists of transcriptions from three different picturebooks.

The peritextual features of *Good Night Gorilla*

Good Night Gorilla is an entertaining picturebook about a Gorilla who steals the zookeeper's keys. He opens his cage, and that of several other animals, and they all follow the zookeeper home and settle down for the night in his bedroom. The zookeeper's wife notices them all and takes them back to the zoo, except for the gorilla and a mouse, who return with her, crawl into her bed and fall asleep.

The front and back covers of *Good Night Gorilla* (see Figure 7.1) were particularly useful as they presented all the animals, the zookeeper and the setting of the zoo at night. Students confidently labelled animals they knew like elephant, giraffe and lion and even monkey. See Figure 7.2 for the sequence of utterances, which introduced

Figure 7.1 Front and back covers of *Good Night Gorilla* by Peggy Rathmann © (1994). Used by permission of G.P. Putnam's Spms. A Division of Penguin Young Readers Group, a Member of Penguin Group (USA) Inc., 345 Hudson Street, New York, NY 10014. All rights reserved.

João	*Oh a monkey*
??	Monkey
Teacher	*Actually it isn't a* monkey
Maria	*Gorilla*
Teacher	A gorilla. well done it's a gorilla. that's right

Figure 7.2 School 01 – sequence of utterances during RRA1 of *Good Night Gorilla* on front cover (italic font denotes L1).

'gorilla' in the L2 during discussion around the front cover of *Good Night Gorilla* in RRA1.

There were also some animals which were difficult to identify or unfamiliar, like the hyena or the armadillo. None of the groups knew what an armadillo was in their L1, so this caused some speculation, which also took place in the L1, however over the RRAs students managed to use both the L1 and L2 labels for this animal. I can confidently say that both '*tatu*' and 'armadillo' became part of their extended lexical repertoires. This use of the front and back covers is typical in ELT and not to be belittled in its importance in providing the affordances for students to remember or encounter new words, using their L1 as a bridge between the known and the unknown (Read, 2006).

The peritextual features of *Just like Jasper*

Just like Jasper is the story about Jasper, a black and white cat, who goes to a toyshop to spend his birthday money. He looks at many different toys and eventually chooses a toy cat, who looks just like him, hence the title *Just like Jasper*! The peritextual features were especially important in supporting the narrative. There are illustrations and coloured fonts on the front and back covers, two prologue illustrations in the front matter and the copyright page with an epilogue illustration as part of the back matter.

Students used the covers (see Figure 7.3) to predict what the story was about, but in particular here on returning to the covers during the RRAs they commented on the brightly coloured letters of the title, finding letters that appeared in their names and recognizing 'Jasper' when the word appeared later on the title page and in the body of the book. This is standard, but very important, behaviour for sharing a picturebook with emergent readers (Clay, 1967; Sulzby, 1985).

The three pages leading up to the main body of the text are key to helping us understand why Jasper has a coin to spend in the toyshop. There are two prologue illustrations: the first shows Jasper holding an envelope (see Figure 7.4). Upon seeing this illustration the students speculated about what they thought was in the envelope. Figure 7.5 is an excerpt of what ensued with one group when they first encountered this page.

This excerpt is an example of the students making sense of the world through personal spontaneous responses in their L1, reacting in a way that was not possible for them in the L2. It was however an important conversation, reflecting 'the drawing of the story to oneself' (Sipe, 2008, p. 152), with each child suggesting something in relation to his own personal experience of receiving letters at home, which even included receiving fines! None of the L1 utterances was rephrased into English in this

Nick Butterworth and Mick Inkpen

Figure 7.3 Front cover of *Just like Jasper* by Mick Inkpen and Nick Butterworth © (1990). Used by permission of Hodder Children's Books.

Figure 7.4 Page iii of *Just like Jasper* by Mick Inkpen and Nick Butterworth © (1990). Used by permission of Hodder Children's Books.

Fábio	*It's a letter and it will have lots of animals*
Teacher	*Lots of animals inside? I don't know. what do we normally find inside envelopes?*
Julio	*We don't know*
Jorge	*Postcards*
Paulo	*Written things* [running his hand in horizontal lines imitating lines of writing]
Maria	*Maybe it's a sweet.*
Maria	*Maybe it's a fine*
Jorge	*Cards*
Maria	*My parents have received two fines* [holding up two fingers]
Julio	*An invitation*
Teacher	*An invitation very nice. invitations come in the post too. let's see what's inside. do you think it's a fine?*
??	*No*
Teacher	*Maybe it's an invitation? or a letter or a card? let's see* [turns page] *Ahhh*

Figure 7.5 School 01 – sequence of utterances during RRA1 *Just like Jasper* on page iii (italic font denotes L1).

Figure 7.6 Page iv and title page of *Just like Jasper* by Mick Inkpen and Nick Butterworth © (1990). Used by permission of Hodder Children's Books.

excerpt as the envelope in fact contained a coin. However, once the students saw the coin in the next prologue illustration (see Figure 7.6), their spontaneous labelling of '*Moeda!*' was rephrased into 'Money', which appeared later in the verbal text. Once again, discussion around the coin in the envelope also involved the sharing of personal experiences, with children remarking that it was either lucky or made of chocolate. Students described parents receiving coins in envelopes and one child said he had been given a large coin from his mother's school. When asked what they thought Jasper might do with his money many children were quick to speculate in their L1, using their previous knowledge of the world. Gradually they were led towards considering that Jasper might spend his money in a toyshop.

During the RRAs these prologue illustrations were eventually identified in the L2, using content words that had been picked up from the consistent spontaneous labelling of the illustrations and rephrasing. The sequence of events depicted in these illustrations – Jasper receiving an envelope, opening the envelope and finding a coin – really was a visual prologue to the narrative, which continued through the body of the picturebook. Figure 7.7 shows an excerpt from children in School 02 using these illustrations as part of the narrative to their story.

Notice in this excerpt, which is the sixth time the children had encountered this picturebook, that the L1 has almost disappeared, replaced by descriptions of the pages in the L2. These descriptions can be considered co-created narratives and include non-verbal utterances, which we can see in Ricardo's use of a money sign by rubbing his thumb over two finger tips (Armstrong et al., 2003).

The peritextual features of this picturebook gave the students the opportunity to create meaning around the visual narrative, and to use L2 words and formulaic expressions they had acquired during the read-aloud sessions. However, these aspects of the picturebook also provided reasons for the students to put to use previously learned L2 expressions. The copyright page in *Just like Jasper* (Figure 7.8), found at the back of the book contained an epilogue illustration which implied a happy ending, showing Jasper the cat holding his toy cat. This illustration brought different responses from the groups of children depending on what L2 expressions and lexical sets they had been playing with prior to the sharing of this picturebook.

School 01 had been learning how to say the activities they engage in at school, 'playing' was one of these words and by RRA 7, the children were using the word 'playing' as a holophrase, as you can see from Figure 7.9 below.

School 02 created a different narrative around this epilogue illustration. They had played with emotion words in English and so over the read-aloud sessions they gradually introduced the word 'happy' to the final page in the book, it became very much part of the story, as you can see from Figure 7.10 below.

Joel	Just like Jasper
?	*A coin*
Teacher	Jasper's got an []
Nélia	⌈Envelope
Carla	⌊Envelope
Teacher	Envelope. well done Carla [turns page] and in the envelope he's got[]
Ricardo	*it's money* [makes the money gesture with his fingers]
Teacher	Money good. he's got some money. some birthday money
Raul	Just like Jasper [reading title page]

Figure 7.7 School 02 – sequence of utterances during RRA 6 of *Just like Jasper* on pages iii and iv (italic font denotes L1).

Other titles by Nick Butterworth and Mick Inkpen:

The Nativity Play
Nice and Nasty
Sports Day
The School Trip
Jasper's Beanstalk

and by Mick Inkpen:

One Bear at Bedtime
The Blue Balloon
Threadbear
Kipper
Kipper's Toybox

Copyright © Nick Butterworth and Mick Inkpen 1989

The rights of Nick Butterworth and Mick Inkpen to be identified
as the Author of the Work have been asserted by them in
accordance with the Copyright, Designs and Patents Act 1988

First published 1989 by Hodder and Stoughton.
This edition published 1997 by Hodder Children's Books
a division of Hodder Headline plc
338 Euston Road
London NW1 3BH

10 9 8 7

British Library Cataloguing in Publication Data
A catalogue record of this book is available from the British Library

ISBN 0 340 52582 7

Printed in Hong Kong

All rights reserved

Figure 7.8 Copyright page of *Just like Jasper* by Mick Inkpen and Nick Butterworth
© (1990). Used by permission of Hodder Children's Books.

??	Can just like jasper
Fabio	*Two cats* [showing two fingers]
Tania	Playing.
??	Playing
Teacher	Yes he's playing isn't he?
Tania	Playing

Figure 7.9 School 01 – sequence of utterances during RRA 7 of *Just like Jasper* on the
copyright page (italic font denotes L1).

Teacher	Here's Jasper and the little cat. and they're []
Ricardo	*Me me.* happy
??	Happy
Joel	*He found the toy cat*

Figure 7.10 School 02 – sequence of utterances during RRA 7 of *Just like Jasper* on the
copyright page (italic font denotes L1).

Sipe (2008) describes supporting children's response to the peritext as helping
develop 'critical and inferential thinking, and visual interpretation skills' (p. 15) in
addition to being 'critical in developing children's sense of visual aesthetics [and]
contributing to their abilities in literacy' (p.16). To demonstrate, I'd like to share a
cameo taken from the RRA sessions with *Rosie's Walk*.

The peritextual features of *Rosie's Walk*

In *Rosie's Walk* the pictures and words contradict each other and give two different stories. The words tell us about a hen going for a walk around a farm and the pictures show us that she is being followed by an accident-prone fox, who is trying to catch her.

The title page of *Rosie's Walk* represents a map of the farm that Rosie walks around. However, the map connection can only be made once the story has been shared, during subsequent RRAs. The students in my study spent a lot of time looking at this spread: they wondered where the fox was, they labelled the farm buildings and the animals they could see, they even questioned where the yard was in relation to everything. They compared the illustration to a map, and during both the RRAs and the retells gave frenzied descriptions of where Rosie had gone, giving alternatives, including shortcuts. These animated discussions were both in the L1 and the L2, but I still consider them to be valid participations in the retell showing a conscious awareness of the sequence of events in the story. The example I want to share with you comes from a retell in School 01.

In Figure 7.11 we can see that Fabricio was a natural imitator and this short extract is a wonderful example of how he was able to memorize bits of the verbal text from *Rosie's Walk* and use them to describe Rosie's journey. This is especially interesting as very few children actually managed to pick up the verbal text, which is not repetitive and accompanied Rosie's plodding journey, which children did not respond to at all – they were far more interested in the entertaining antics of the fox.

The next example highlights a discussion around the publisher's logo and the author/illustrator, which occurred in repeated read-aloud 6, while using the children's library copy instead of a big book *Scholastic* edition, which had a very discrete logo. This small version was a *Picture Puffins* 1970 edition. It is probable that the children had noticed the logo while browsing through the book in their library but during RRA 6 the conversation reproduced in Figure 7.12 ensued.

Notice how Laura was quick to remember the term 'logo' ('*marca*') and that Rui had recalled that a person, or sometimes two, was responsible for writing and illustrating a picturebook. This had all been discussed before with other picturebooks and Rui's logic that the author and illustrator should have a logo too is a good one! The author's name had been read out in every RRA, however it was only in session 6 that these children began to question it. They all knew that I was English and their concept of nationality was still emerging, but David was quick to compare Pat Hutchins with me and ask if she was English too, which led to the questions about names in different languages. It is Ricardo who wants to connect to Pat Hutchins and hear her name in his own language. This is a very rich excerpt and one that took place entirely in the

| Dario | *She follows this route* [points to hen hutch traces a route from verso to recto and pauses at the beehives] |
| Fabrício | [Points to the pond in recto] whats di pond. around di yard. de rooo uuuund [waves over the spread] |

Figure 7.11 School 01 – sequence of utterances during retell on *Rosie's Walk*.

Raul	*Why is there a bird there?*
Laura	*It's the logo*
Teacher	*It's the logo. remember ther e was a bird on the other book. remember?* Meg and Mog. *it's the same thing. it's the logo of the people who make the books. the publishers*
Rui	*And the people who do the writing and the drawing?*
Bela	*Where is their logo?*
Teacher	*It isn't the lady's logo, it's the logo of the people who make the book. it's their symbol. and here is the name of the lady who wrote the book* [pointing to Pat Hutchins' name on the cover]
Bela	*So say it*
Teacher	Pat Hutchins. Pat Hutchins [turn page to half title page] Rosie's Walk
David	⌈*Is he English too?*
Teacher	⌊[*Turn page to title page*]
Laura	⌈Rosie's Walk
Teacher	⌊*She is English yes. she's a woman* [turn page to dedication page]
Edgar	*She's got an English name?*
Teacher	Yes Pat Hutchins *is an English name*
Raul	*And in Portuguese?*

Figure 7.12 School 03 – sequence of utterances during RRA 6 of *Rosie's Walk*, on front cover to dedication page (italic font denotes L1).

L1. However, it shows that the students are developing an understanding of the book as object, and beginning to understand that authors, illustrators and publishers are involved in its making. Anecdotal evidence from the preschool teacher confirmed that these children went on to discuss logos in the Portuguese books in their library, as well as look for dedications, which they became particularly interested in.

Dedications exist in most picturebooks, though not always on a page of their own. In *Rosie's Walk*, the dedication page contains a prologue illustration of flowers alongside the dedication, 'For Wendy and Stephen'. On reading the dedications in the picturebooks it highlights that the picturebook creator has made the book for someone. All students in this study took the idea on board and the dedication page became part of their RRA experience as well as their retells. In School 01 the students confirmed in the L1 that they had understood what the page represented, Figure 7.13 shows Maria and Marta doing just this.

In School 02, the students actually joined in, chorusing the dedication in English as it was read during the RRAs. Several students in the study made reference to the dedication in their retells, either in the L1, or by saying, 'For Wendy and Stephen'. Whatever approach they used it showed that they considered this page in the picturebook as part of the narrative sequence. But most of all it shows they had understood the concept behind the dedication page.

Maria	*It is for some children*
Marta	*It's written there it's for two children*

Figure 7.13 School 01 – sequence of utterances during RRA 2 of *Rosie's Walk*, on the dedication page (italic font denotes L1).

Concluding comments

To recapitulate, I have provided you with evidence from my study that making use of the peritextual features in picturebooks supported these students' analysis of narrative meaning, one of the categories outlined in Sipe's theory of literary understanding (2000; 2008). It enabled them to develop on a cognitive level by predicting characters, plot and setting and promoting critical and inferential thinking and interpretation skills. Children also used the illustrations to extend their sense of visual aesthetics, which contributed to developing visual understanding and visual literacy.

Peritextual features also gave these students the opportunity to use what they knew both in their L1 and the L2. The L1 provided a first step towards using the L2, for they shared information and experience and labelled and described things they were interested in, which in turn was rephrased into the L2 and gradually appropriated by the students during the RRAs. There were also occasions when these students were able to use L2 words they already knew. This opportunity was not afforded by the words, but by the illustrations and the way in which the book worked as a whole.

Lastly, by using the peritextual features in these picturebooks, these students were able to talk about picturebooks and together improve their understanding of who is involved in creating these beautiful objects.

Lo (2008) states that 'any exclusive focus on the linguistic narrows the communication experience in the classroom' (p. 79). Literacy in the L2 is not just learning to read and write, we need to move beyond just learning the language in the words to include the language that can come from the illustrations and that which is about illustrations. Initially younger students may need their L1 to do this, but older students will be confident to do so using the L2. We are not focusing on a predetermined language learning objective, instead language and learning is being shaped by social interaction and providing for a constructed meaning through language given by the different communication modes within the picturebook.

'The picturebook is a unique literary experience, where meaning is generated simultaneously from written text, visual image and overall design' (Serafini, 2009, p. 10), we should be more aware of how picturebooks reveal their message and present them to our students as an object with a message to be discovered, together.

Additional resources

British Council Teaching English –www.teachingenglish.org.uk/teaching-kids/promoting-diversity-through-children's-literature
BritLit Resource Kit – www.teachingenglish.org.uk/britlit
Magic Pencil Exhibition story support materials – www.teachingenglish.org.uk/teaching-kids/magic-pencil
Picturebooks in ELT blog – http://picturebooksinelt.blogspot.com/

Bibliography

Hutchins, P. (1968), *Rosie's Walk*. London: Walker Books.
Inkpen, M. and Butterworth, N. (1990), *Just like Jasper*. London: Hodder Children's Books.
Rathman, P. (1994), *Good Night Gorilla!* New York: Penguin.

References

Armstrong, N. and Wagner, M. (2003), *Field Guide to Gestures: How to Identify and Interpret Virtually Every Gesture Known to Man*. Philadelphia: Quirk Books.

Bader, B. (1976), *American Picturebooks from Noah's Ark to The Beast Within*. New York: Macmillan Publishing Company.

Bjorvand, A.-M. (2011), 'Peritexts in Astrid Lindgren's picturebooks', Paper presented at the *History and Theory of the Picturebook Conference*, Tübingen, Germany, September 2011.

Bosch, E. and Duran, T. (2011), 'Before and after the picturebook frame: A typology of endpapers', *New Review of Children's Literature and Librarianship*, 17(2), 122–43.

Clay, M. M. (1967), 'The reading behaviour of five-year old children: A research report', *New Zealand Journal of Educational Studies*, 2, 11–13.

Consejo, E. (2011), 'Peritextos del s. XXI. Las guardas en el discurso Literario infantile', *Revista OCNOS*, n. 7, 111–22.

Díaz Armas, J. (2006), 'El contrato de lectura en el álbum: paratextos y desbordamiento narrativo', *Revista: Primeras noticias*, Número 222, 33–40.

Ellis, G. and Brewster, J. (2002), *Tell it Again! The New Storytelling Handbook for Primary Teachers*. Harlow: Pearson Education Limited.

Genette, G. (1997), *Paratexts: Thresholds of Interpretation*. Cambridge: Cambridge University Press.

Holdaway, D. (1979), *The Foundations of Literacy*. Gosford, N-S. W. Ashton: Scholastic.

Kress, G. and van Leeuwen, T. (1996), *Reading Images: the Grammar of Visual Design*. London: Routledge.

Linse, C. T. (2007), 'Predictable books in the children's EFL classroom', *ELT Journal*, 61(1), 46–54.

Lo, M. M. (2008), 'Multilteracies in teaching young learners of English', in W. Arnold, K. Powell and H. Mol (eds), *Literacy in the Language Classroom: The Role of the YL Professional in Developing Reading and Writing Skills in Young Learners*. Canterbury: IATEFL.

Marantz, K. (1977), 'The picturebook as art object: A call for balanced reviewing', *The Wilson Library Bulletin*, 148–51.

Mourão, S. (2009), 'Using stories in the primary classroom', in L. Denhamand and N. Figueras (eds), *BritLit: Using Literature in EFL Classrooms*. Barcelona: APAC, pp. 19–33.

Pantaleo, S. (2003), '"Godzilla lives in New York": Grade 1 students and the peritextual features of picturebooks', *Journal of Children's Literature*, 29, 66–77.

Ramos, A. M. (2007), *Livros de Palmo e Meio: Reflexões sobre Literatura para a Infância*. Lisboa: Editorial Caminho, SA.

Read, C. (2006), 'Supporting teachers in supporting learners', in J. Enever and G. Schmid-Shonbein (eds), *Picture Books and Young Learners of English*. München: Langenscheidt ELT GmbH.

Serafini, F. (2009), 'Understanding visual images in picturebooks', in J. Evans (ed.), *Talking Beyond the Page: Reading and Responding to Picturebooks*. Abingdon: Routledge.

Shulevitz, U. (1985), *Writing with Pictures: How to Write and Illustrate Children's Books*. New York: Watson-Guptill Publications.

Sinclair, J. and Coulthard, M. (1975), *Towards an Analysis of Discourse: The English Used by Teachers and Pupils*. Oxford: Oxford University Press.

Sipe, L. (2000), 'The construction of literary understanding by first and second graders in oral response to picture storybook read-alouds', *Reading Research Quarterly*, 35(2), 252–75.

— (2008), *Storytime: Young Children's Literary Understanding in the Classroom*. New York: Teachers College Press.

Sipe, L. and McGuire, C. (2009), 'Picturebook endpapers. Resources for literary and aesthetic interpretation', in J. Evans (ed.), *Talking Beyond the Page: Reading and Responding to Picturebooks*. Abingdon: Routledge.

Sulzby, E. (1985), 'Children's emergent reading of favourite storybooks: A developmental study', *Reading Research Quarterly*, 20(4), 458–81.

8

Fairy Tales with a Difference: Creating a Continuum from Primary to Secondary ELT

Janice Bland

Introduction

This chapter will consider two picturebook fairy tales that can be read with young EFL students, for example following the transition from the primary to secondary EFL classroom. Picturebooks are characterized by a provocative tension between the different modes: the images, layout and verbal text (see also Burwitz-Melzer and Mourão in this volume). In postmodern fairy tales there is also the tension or collision between the pretext and the contemporary reworking of the story. The pretexts for the selected picturebooks in this chapter are *The Three Little Pigs* and *Goldilocks and the Three Bears*. The relationship between text and pretext creates 'information gaps' in the content, which the perceptive reader and community of readers in the classroom can fill: 'All in all, these new books encourage a critical, active stance that celebrates a diversity of response rather than univocal interpretation' (Sipe et al., 2008, p. 5). The second language reader is often a couple of years older than the typical mother-tongue reader of the same book. Due to their more developed cognitive skills, L2 students can gain confidence in being perceptive and confident 'gap' readers despite their limited English. Additionally, due to the multilayered nature of postmodern literature, these texts often address a wide range of readers. It is of great consequence for the EFL-literature classroom, though scarcely known in the EFL teaching context worldwide, that postmodern picturebooks 'engage with polymorphous cultural forms and (. . .) address an older audience' (Stephens, 2008, p. 89). Jill May has made the same point, referring to children's literature more generally:

> Most authors, however, do not purposely tell their audience how to respond. And they don't label their stories as ones written for a particular audience. (. . .) After all, children's books are read by adults and children, so the books do not have one audience. As texts with dual (or multiple) audiences, children's stories hold more than one meaning. The theme, or central idea, may be perceived in different ways. (May, 1995, p. 55)

Information gaps and postmodern texts

The metaphor of the 'gap' is significant for literature teaching in the EFL classroom to children and young adults, echoing the well-established 'information gap' of the language classroom. Too many questions designed to display command of language (display questions) lead to bored and restless students. Even in the primary school, genuine questions based on an information gap are preferable wherever possible. Ask a genuine question (which of course has to be linguistically manageable), and a class of young learners is attentive, thoughtful and highly motivated to supply an answer. It is, according to contemporary literary scholarship, contentious whether we can demand a single 'correct' interpretation and absolute meaning when dealing with open and ambiguous literature. I suggest we need to empower young readers, encourage them to invest processing effort and fill the gaps within and between texts with their own meanings. This requires mental effort, and, moreover, 'is not a comfortable pedagogy for it removes certainty from the teacher and the learner. The teacher is not the final arbiter of knowledge or does not determine *the* meaning of the text' (Hall, 1998, p. 187, emphasis in the original). A cooperative act of discussion discovers far more about a literary text than a single reader could alone, so that 'by pooling our thoughts we extend our individual ability to think' (Chambers, 2011, p. 110).

Much of schooling is a pursuit of closure. Teachers seek answers to questions and students seek to predict and satisfy the teachers' expectations. However, postmodern texts do not necessarily satisfy expectations at the close, nor do they allow all questions to be answered. But they often stimulate a dynamic approach to literary discussion and a joint attempt at meaning making, as we all have a desire to complete the patterns we perceive. Coles and Hall describe postmodernism as an often-disputed area of literary and cultural study:

> One feature likely to be undisputed though is its rejection of unity, homogeneity, totality, and closure. But it is often these concepts which underpin the school teaching of texts, especially in primary schools where teacher questioning is often designed to elicit from pupils *the* meaning of a book. To step back from this position involves rejecting the pursuit of 'true' meanings. It requires the teacher to cede to pupils a degree of authority over the text. The postmodern perspective is a questioning one. It does provide an alternative discourse, a different way of thinking, that can be appropriated for a critical examination of texts. (Coles et al., 2001, p. 114, emphasis in the original)

Meaning making with Wiesner's *The Three Pigs*

An excellent example of an excessive postmodern fairy-tale picturebook is David Wiesner's *The Three Pigs* (Caldecott Medal Winner). At least some students in a 5th or 6th grade EFL-literature classroom will know and remember the well-known canonized version of *The Three Little Pigs*, and be able to retell the tale to their peers. The title page of Wiesner's very unusual story shows an extreme close-up of three pigs, realistically drawn, that appear anything other than 'little'. Children's responses to this picturebook have shown how they are extremely interested in the details and meanings of the illustrations. A 6-year-old student in a case study in the United States, remarking on the size of the pigs, suggests a new title for the book: *The Three Grownup Pigs*. The class goes on to discuss the illustration on the title page:

Norman: They're, they look like *real* three pigs. And in the other stories, the other pigs didn't look a lot like real pigs.

Morgan: They're pigs like animal pigs and the other ones are like people pigs.

Teacher: There are animal or people pigs, oh, what do you mean by people pigs?

Steven: Like they walk on their two feet. They talk.

Mandy: And they wear clothes. (Sipe, 2008, p. 225)

If children in grade one are already interested in distinguishing anthropomorphized characters in their books from more realistic animal characters, then clearly we can expect an interesting discussion on characterization with older EFL students. For Wiesner's *The Three Pigs* very much implies multiple audiences, in that it can delight and cognitively engage sophisticated readers, too.

There are at least three intertexts to *The Three Pigs*, each forming an inner or embedded storyworld. Apart from the well-known fairy tale, the nursery rhyme *Hey Diddle Diddle* makes an appearance and a traditional tale with a dragon-slaying prince also plays a role. The three pigs quickly learn to move from story to story, whereby their travels between the stories form an embedding or framing storyworld. They are amazed to discover that their physical appearance also changes to fit in with the particular illustration style of each story. When they are in the framing storyworld, apparently outside the stories, they are extremely realistically drawn; in the story of the dragon they become romanticized sepia line drawings. However, when in the nursery rhyme, they are crudely flat and cartoon-like, which the pigs appear not to like at all. 'See the colors they are. They're turning like marker colors' a child comments in the case study (Sipe, 2008, p. 225). This is an excellent opportunity for a wider discussion of the different kinds and quality of illustrations in picturebooks, and a comparison with the over-simplified outlines and flat, saturated colours of the generic animals and household objects that are typical for EFL textbooks for primary-school children.

Krashen differentiates context as overdetermining, underdetermining and partly determining (Krashen, 1999, pp. 12–14). The pictures in EFL textbooks for young learners are nearly always overdetermining, stylized, stereotyped and crude illustrations, limiting a creative response. People, objects, and settings, such as families, toys, food, furniture, pets and landscapes, are mostly reduced, simplified and drastically 'tidied up'. An imaginative response is blocked, as the pictures are almost universally bright, yet reduced to sameness. Complex, naturalistic, untidy, ambiguous and thus partly determining contextualization is strictly avoided. The more challenging partly determining context, found in complex picturebook illustrations, requires a creative participatory reading, compels imaginative learner input in order to bridge the gaps and finally promotes acceptance of ambivalent response.

The most excessive characteristic of *The Three Pigs*, however, is the use of space in deconstructing, extending and finally reinventing the story. This is done in the framing storyworld, by the energetic pigs themselves. The subversion of the story begins as an accident, when the wolf, instead of merely blowing the straw house down, blows the first pig right out of the story and towards the reader into a liminal space beyond (Figure 8.1).

This is known as 'ascending' metalepsis (Pier, 2005, p. 304), and has the effect of bringing the character very close to the reader. This closeness is compounded in the picturebook narrative by the hyper-realistic illustration style of the pigs when they are in the framing storyworld, and the extreme close-up detailed further below (see Figure 8.2).

The journey of the three pigs continues in ever more fantastic ways. When all three pigs are outside the story, they fold one of the pages of the story they have left into a paper plane and fly away. They leave their framing world and land in other stories, known as 'descending' metalepsis. In the new story the illustration style becomes less life-like, the reader is distanced from the pigs once again. The wolf, for unexplained reasons, cannot escape the embedded story and therefore cannot draw close to the reader. He is seen to be puzzled by the events, especially when the pigs fold up the very page he is on for their flight. He appears to be imprisoned by the page, his paws push

Figure 8.1 Recto page from *The Three Pigs* by David Wiesner © (2001). Reprinted by permission of Clarion Books, an imprint of Houghton Mifflin Harcourt Publishing Company. All rights reserved.

Figure 8.2 Verso page from *The Three Pigs* by David Wiesner © (2001). Reprinted by permission of Clarion Books, an imprint of Houghton Mifflin Harcourt Publishing Company. All rights reserved.

against the edges, but he is unable to escape. We can only guess his thoughts, however. He never becomes 'real' and he has no speech balloons. The story text continues relentlessly 'he blew the house in . . . and ate the pig up', but the pigs have disappeared and the wolf is left with no dinner and in total confusion. For some students, this may be the first experience of a book where the pictures so blatantly contradict the verbal text. This can be explained as irony, for the text is saying one thing but the pictures mean something else. There is plenty to talk and write about in the EFL-literature classroom, a book as complex as this one needs to be revisited from different angles. There are numerous opportunities for creating the dialogues between the confused, amazed and puzzled characters, so very much happens in the pictures and with very little verbal comment. The wolf's story is entirely blank, and could be recreated by the lower secondary-school EFL readers creating their own comic strip from the point of view of the wolf.

The graphic language has connections not only to comics (with the pigs' brief speech balloons), but also to film. Wiesner employs cinematic devices such as salience (highlighting details) and extreme close-ups. There is an example of an extreme close-up on the page just before the pigs discover the 'Hey Diddle Diddle' rhyme.

The enormous head of one of the pigs fills the page and invades the reader/viewer's space and seems to contact the reader: 'I think . . . someone's out there' (Figure 8.2). Wiesner uses salience to highlight the pigs' flight to freedom across an almost entirely blank double spread. They are in the wide, empty spaces between the stories. What does a completely white page in the middle of a picturebook suggest to the students? Freedom? Emptiness? Opportunity? Adventure? Outer space? Nothingness? Death? Rebirth? The possibilities of interpretation in such ambiguity are, of course, endless. Asking students to create their own titles for pages such as these is a task that requires thought and interpretation, and can lead to interesting comparisons when they defend their chosen titles.

The three pigs' flight to freedom on the paper aeroplane continues across four double spreads, with minimal speech bubbles: merely 'Wheeeeeee!' and, as they come in to land, 'Uh-oh'. This is an excellent opportunity for creative writing to the children's own pictures: drawing and describing the largely unseen flight of the three pigs. They may fly around a clock tower, under a bridge, up into the clouds, over a mountain, down a waterfall, across a river, along a railway track and through a tunnel. They may fly in and out of the children's favourite storyworlds, with speech bubbles and possibly with quotations from other books. They may fly across the ocean to meet animals from other continents. As Wiesner's four double spreads show very little, the children must invest their own creativity and imagination to cross this excessive and yet, with ingenuity, eminently bridgeable gap. It is the postmodern playfulness of *The Three Pigs* that entices the reader to become powerfully involved:

> The reader/viewer has a clear mandate; think about this story, relate this story to other reading experiences, manipulate the story so it makes sense. Do not be shy, be a coauthor. Feel free to play with the story, add to it and alter it! (. . .) By pushing, shoving, and folding pages of their story, they (the three pigs) discover new worlds with alternative realities and a freedom to go beyond their intended destiny. But these pigs, like others before them, eventually realise that there is no place like home. Empowered with newfound knowledge and friends, they rebuild their story-land, making it a better place to live in. (Goldstone, 2008, p. 120)

Finally the pigs feel homesick for their well-crafted house of bricks and decide to return home. They reassemble the very letters of the traditional story to write their own ending, which includes the dragon and the cat escaped from the 'Hey Diddle Diddle' rhyme: 'And they all lived happily ever after'.

And they all lived happily ever after

A happy ending is the norm in children's literature (there are exceptions): 'Wise authors know from fairy tales that a happy ending is not necessarily something to be dismissed as superficial – at least not for children, who deserve to be encouraged in their hopes of coming to terms with the challenges before them' (Tabbert et al., 1995, p. 5). In much children's literature a certain metanarrative that is, according to John Stephens, 'socially and emotionally satisfying' for children, is still largely accepted: 'the notion that truth and justice will – or morally should – prevail' (Stephens, 2010, p. 209). This metanarrative does not exist for a great deal of serious adult literature; consequently adult literature, even when simplified in a graded reader, is less encouraging for pre-adult readers. It is a metanarrative that also scarcely exists for many young people in their daily lives, as the hopelessness, sense of disenfranchisement and apparent lack of any stake in society that partly lay behind the youth rioting in major English cities in August 2011 clearly indicates. 'Illiteracy is a life sentence' and 'School shatters your dreams before you get anywhere' are at the time of writing frequently quoted statements in the British media (Sergeant, 2011). Reynolds refers to the radical freshness of children's fictions: 'Many children's books offer quirky or critical or alternative visions of the world designed to promote that ultimate response of childhood, "Why?" "Why are things as they are?" "Why can't they be different?" ' (Reynolds, 2010, p. 3). Jack Zipes writes on the literary versus the oral fairy tale:

> As in the oral tradition, its original impulse of hope for better living conditions has not vanished in the literary tradition, although many of the signs have been manipulated in the name of male authoritarian forces. As long as the fairy tale continues to awaken our wonderment and enable us to project counterworlds to our present society, it will serve a meaningful social and aesthetic function, not just for compensation but for revelation: The worlds portrayed by the best of our fairy tales are like magic spells of enchantment that actually free us. Instead of petrifying our minds, they arouse our imagination and compel us to realise how we can fight terror and cunningly insert ourselves into our daily struggles, turning the course of the world's events in our favour. (Zipes, 2007, p. 31)

Engaged reading with Browne's *Me and You*

Engaged reading with young EFL students can be approached with Anthony Brown's *Me and You* (Kate Greenaway Medal short-listed), a postmodern version of *Goldilocks and the Three Bears*. The verbal text is brief and deliberately in rather stereotypical middle-class *Janet and John* style, narrated by the little bear, beginning: 'This is our house. There's Daddy Bear, Mummy Bear and me.' *Janet and John* was a series of readers used for learning to read in nearly all UK primary schools, as well as in America and New Zealand, from the 1950s to the early 1970s.

> It hardly mattered whether the families were New Zealand or American or British (...). They all looked much the same – mother, father, two closely spaced children – and they all carried the same message: this is the only right way to live. (Else, 2008, p. 231)

The novice readers learning with *Janet and John* (80% of all primary-school children in the United Kingdom in the 60s) had no choice but to compare their own probably less wealthy, less comfortable lives with that of Janet and John, and quite possibly find their lives wanting. For today's children, however, there could be a far wider choice of reading material that does not pretend to give answers but encourages children to ask questions. As the complexity is in the pictures of *Me and You*, not in the verbal text, the book need not overchallenge EFL readers.

The pictures of the nicely dressed bear family and their very pleasant detached house are on the right-hand pages (recto). This is the privileged position, by publishing convention the first page of a book is always on a recto page. There is a note of irony that appears in the verbal text when the bear family goes out for a walk while their porridge cools down:

> Daddy talked about *his* work and Mummy talked about *her* work. I just messed about.
>
> On the way back, Daddy talked about the car and Mummy talked about the house. I just messed about.
>
> When we got home, the front door was open. Daddy said that Mummy must have left it open, and Mummy said it must have been Daddy. I didn't say anything. (Browne, 2011, unpaginated)

The lines above are accompanied by three pictures of the affluent bear family, with their noses in the air. The left-hand pages (verso) are devoted to Goldilocks, who is very far from the conventional fairy-tale princess. Her story is narrated in pictures only, with no verbal text. Whereas the bears have full-page images in colour to show the neatness and comfort of their well-ordered home and family life, Goldilocks' story is told in much smaller pictures – four or six images crowd each page – with very little colour. Her clothes are nondescript, neither smart nor colourful, but her long, unkempt hair has a warm red-gold glow. We can read from the pictures that tell Goldilocks' story that she is standing beside her mother, who appears to be gazing hopelessly at the meat on display at the local butcher's shop, when a balloon floats past. Goldilocks chases the balloon without success, through many colourless streets, which appear forbidding with their high walls, railings and broken windows. Goldilocks cannot find her way back to her mother, but discovers the very respectable house of the bears, with the door left open.

What happens next follows the traditional fairy-tale pattern (involving three bowls of porridge, three chairs and three beds) until the angry bears chase Goldilocks out of their comfortable home. We see her long journey back through the grey streets, through heavy rain, wind, graffiti shaped like a tornado and even snow, and still with no sign of her mother. However, there is an almost fairy-tale ending. Goldilocks spies her mother at last and runs to meet her. The final page shows a full-colour embrace of mother and daughter, the warm red-gold of their hair ending the melancholy story on a bright note.

There are 60 pictures in this 32-page picturebook. The pictures can be described by EFL students at all levels, including elementary, for example: 'First Goldilocks tries the big bowl of porridge, then she tries the medium-sized bowl of porridge, next she tries the little bowl of porridge, and eats it all up'. Somewhat beyond the beginner level, however, narrative devices can be brought into the booktalk: how, for example, the colour and size as well as the content of the images add layers of meaning to the story, suggesting poverty versus wealth. What does this add to the traditional story? Focalization can be discussed – we see the events from the point of view of the focalizer character – in *Me and You* the focalization varies from Goldilocks (verso pages) to the little bear (recto pages). The genres of realism and fantasy can be investigated. Goldilocks' story is portrayed realistically, mostly in grey and sepia tones with a dark emphasis on inner-city shabbiness. The bears, who clearly live in the same city, inhabit a bright fairy-tale world of middle-class comfort, which seems like an island of fantasy in the drab neighbourhood. They meet briefly when Goldilocks is discovered in little bear's bed, but are unable to communicate. Little bear narrates: 'The girl leaped out of bed, ran downstairs and out of the door. I wonder what happened to her?' (Browne, 2011). The little bear is a quiet member of his family, nonetheless as narrator he appears literate and able to tell a story; Goldilocks, in contrast, is voiceless, she never speaks. What meaning does this convey to the reader? Is this connected to the contrast in their social standing and education? To what extent is poverty 'voiceless'?

It would be interesting to discuss the significance of the title *Me and You*. As the little bear is the narrator, he is 'me' and Goldilocks is 'you'. Is Goldilocks as a child of poverty 'othered' by the narrative, and the middle-class bear narrator represented as the norm? This picturebook teaches the importance of focalization as a narrative practice. Goldilocks too is a focalizer, her story is portrayed in vivid detail in the images, her fearful but courageous bearing shown in her body language and facial expressions. Consequently, though downtrodden in appearance, she is not represented as other, but as the protagonist of her own story, and wins the reader's sympathy and respect. A shabby silent distressed girl as equal protagonist to the middle-class male may well be empowering for many readers of this picturebook in the 5th or 6th grade who are themselves vulnerable, for 'critics have argued that never seeing someone like themselves in a leading role may affect readers' expectations about life. The effect on young readers, in particular, may be considerable' (Mikkelsen et al., 2001, p. 77).

Picturebooks have been named the ideal primary texts of childhood (Styles et al., 2009, p. 120); picturebooks can introduce a playful process involving imagination and experimentation in the EFL classroom. With careful teacher scaffolding, negotiation of both meaning and interpretation can be practised, so that when the students 'experience that they are able to express themselves within the new language context, the feeling of success leads to motivation and more self-confidence, which are essential requirements for foreign language acquisition' (Ramke, 2012, p. 10). I have shown in this chapter the empowering as well as thoughtful meaning making that can be engendered in the EFL classroom by postmodern picturebook fairy tales, 'with a difference'.

Bibliography

Browne, A. (2011), *Me and You*. London: Corgi Books.
Wiesner, D. (2001), *The Three Pigs*. New York: Clarion Books.

References

Chambers, A. (2011), *Tell Me: The Reading Environment*. Woodchester: Thimble Press.

Coles, M. and Hall, C. (2001), 'Breaking the line: New literacies, postmodernism and the teaching of printed texts', *Reading Literacy and Language*, 11, 111–14.

Else, A. (2008), 'Up the garden path: Janet and John revisited', in P. Griffith, P. Hughes and A. Loney (eds), *A Book in the Hand: Essays on the History of the Book in New Zealand*. Auckland: Auckland University Press. Accessed 05.09.11 at www.nzetc.org/tm/scholarly/tei-GriHand-t1-g1-t15.html

Goldstone, B. (2008), 'The paradox of space in postmodern picturebooks', in L. Sipe and S. Pantaleo (eds), *Postmodern Picturebooks: Play, Parody, and Self-Referentiality*. New York: Routledge, pp. 117–29.

Hall, K. (1998), 'Critical literacy and the case for it in the early years of school', *Language, Culture and Curriculum*, 11(2), 183–94.

Krashen, S. (1999), *The Arguments Against Whole Language & Why They Are Wrong*. Portsmouth: Heinemann.

May, J. (1995), *Children's Literature and Critical Theory*. New York: Oxford University Press.

Mikkelsen, N. and Pinsent, P. (2001), 'Bias', in V. Watson (ed.), *The Cambridge Guide to Children's Books in English*. Cambridge: Cambridge University Press, pp. 75–8.

Pier, J. (2005), 'Metalepsis', in D. Herman, M. Jahn and M.-L. Ryan (eds), *Routledge Encyclopedia of Narrative Theory*. Oxford: Routledge, pp. 303–4.

Ramke, K. (2011), *From Picturebooks to Graphic Novels: Why and How to Employ Multimodal Texts in the Lower Secondary EFL Classroom*. Unpublished MEd thesis, Hildesheim University.

Reynolds, K. (2010), *Radical Children's Literature*. Basingstoke: Palgrave Macmillan.

Sergeant, H. (2011), 'These rioters are Tony Blair's children', *The Spectator*, 13.08.11. Accessed 14.08.11 at www.spectator.co.uk/spectator/thisweek/7157318/web-exclusive-these-rioters-are-tony-blairs-children.thtml

Sipe, L. (2008), 'First graders interpret David Wiesner's *The Three Pigs*: A case study', in L. Sipe and S. Pantaleo (eds), *Postmodern Picturebooks: Play, Parody, and Self-Referentiality*. New York: Routledge, pp. 222–37.

Sipe, L. and Pantaleo, S. (2008), *Postmodern Picturebooks: Play, Parody, and Self-Referentiality*. New York: Routledge.

Stephens, J. (2008), 'They are always surprised at what people throw away', in L. Sipe and S. Pantaleo (eds), *Postmodern Picturebooks: Play, Parody, and Self-Referentiality*. New York: Routledge, pp. 89–102.

— (2010), 'Metanarrative', in D. Rudd (ed.), *The Routledge Companion to Children's Literature*. Abingdon: Routledge, pp. 209–10.

Styles, M. and Noble, K. (2009), 'Thinking in action: Analysing children's multimodal responses to multimodal picturebooks', in J. Evans (ed.), *Talking Beyond the Page: Reading and Responding to Picturebooks*. New York: Routledge, pp. 118–33.

Tabbert, R. and Wardetzky, K. (1995), 'On the success of children's books and fairy tales: A comparative view of impact theory and reception research', *The Lion and the Unicorn*, 19(1), 1–19.

Zipes, J. (2007), *When Dreams Came True: Classical Fairy Tales and Their Tradition* (2nd edn). New York: Routledge.

Part Three

Intercultural Encounters with Children's Literature

9

Otherness in Children's Literature.
Perspectives for the EFL Classroom

Christiane Lütge

Introduction

This chapter explores one of the most prominent features throughout children's literature, that is the experience of 'otherness' in different contexts such as distant settings, magical worlds or transcultural encounters. Opportunities for encountering difference and for creatively engaging with diversity are numerous in children's literature and allow for playful and yet differentiated approaches towards the understanding of otherness. Children's literature often challenges and transcends the binary opposition of 'self' and 'other', thus providing an enormous educational potential that can be exploited for the foreign language classroom. Examples such as David Almond's *Skellig* as well as J. K. Rowling's *Harry Potter* series lend themselves to rewarding variations on the topic of intercultural learning.

Otherness in second language education

In an age of standardized testing the teaching of literature in contexts of second language education is facing new challenges. The same applies to inter- and transcultural learning with its emphasis on understanding otherness. The Common European Framework supports the notion that a language learner needs to possess the ability to learn about and to relate to otherness. Enhancing children's self-esteem and their positive attitude towards otherness is vital and is therefore explicitly addressed:

> In an intercultural approach, it is a central objective of language education to pro-
> mote the favourable development of the learner's whole personality and sense of
> identity in response to the enriching experience of otherness in language and cul-
> ture. (Council of Europe, 2000, p. 1)

The connection with teaching literature in the EFL classroom comes in through the role it has been ascribed in the context of inter- and transcultural learning. Since the early

1990s, the potential of literature for cultural learning has been emphasized. Teaching foreign literature with its representation of linguistic and cultural otherness can be a perfect starting point for reflections on the perspectivity of individual viewpoints. When students compare and contrast their own values and worldviews to those of literary texts, they may need to change and coordinate perspectives, a prerequisite for developing intercultural competence (Bredella, 2008). Developing both language competence and an understanding of 'the other' through authentic literary texts is the big goal in second language education, which addresses the needs of the 'intercultural speaker' (Kramsch, 1993) and follows the principles of 'Intercultural Communicative Competence' (Byram, 1997). Intercultural learning as a new paradigm for teaching literature has resulted in an increasing number of postcolonial and minority texts in the foreign language classroom, because these often dramatize intercultural conflicts and reveal causes for misunderstanding and misrecognition of others (Bredella, 2000, p. 378).

One may argue that the teaching of literature in second language education has been recently somewhat overburdened in the attempt to take into account the normative affordances of the Common European Framework. Other dimensions of literariness that cannot easily be broken down into competences involve emotional, cultural or aesthetic aspects. According to David Russell, teaching literature should endow the student

> with such opportunities [as] enable him to better understand himself as a person, as a member of a human community not circumscribed by a narrow extent of time and space, and as the possessor of a continually developed heritage of literature that can help give direction to his aesthetic and moral life. (Russell, 1970, p. 241)

In fact, aesthetic reading as focusing on what the reader experiences during the reading event (Rosenblatt, 2005) has a strong bearing on the development of literary literacy and identity formation processes that relate the student's 'self' with potential 'others' through literary encounters – whether explicitly intercultural in plot and narrative structures or focusing on other facets of 'otherness'. Understanding otherness, in terms of culture, gender, class and creed – to name but a few aspects – is a complex process with fuzzy edges and does not lend itself to easy categorizations. In fact, it would be potentially reductive to approach the notion of otherness in second language education only in terms of ethnic-cultural otherness, thus redichotomizing perceptions of 'us and them'. In order to account for the enriching experience of otherness in language and culture stipulated by the CEF, various encounters with otherness in literature – at different age levels – should be considered.

Encounters with otherness in children's and young adult literature

Children's literature abounds in encounters with otherness: alien creatures, wizards, monsters, miraculous or supernatural or at least highly peculiar characters make their appearance in secret gardens, secondary worlds or exotic settings. Encounters with otherness in this context offer disturbances with and within the presented setting, but they also enable the student to enjoy the unexpected – be it nonsense, magic or fantasy.

According to Cunningham, one way in which fantasy encourages young adults to consider new horizons in their own thinking is the common device of talking animals or magical creatures and races. This convention is found in fantasy stories as wide-ranging as the *Harry Potter* series, *The Chronicles of Narnia*, *The Lord of the Rings*, *His Dark Materials* and *Howl's Moving Castle* (Cunningham, 2010). One of the hallmarks of these stories is their ability to engage and enchant the heart, as Cunningham puts it, but in spite of all supernatural ingredients there are still links with our everyday world, and the line between the human and the superhuman is often fluid. More importantly, though, especially with a view to the notion of otherness in second language education:

> These stories open the mind and heart to the possibility of embracing those we find very different from ourselves. Fantasy teaches its readers not to be fooled by outward appearance. Instead they are encouraged to discern the heart and dis-cover what possibilities might reside just beneath the surface. (Cunningham, 2010, p. 121)

Dealing with difference – whatever that may be for children and young adults – is central to many traditional and modern texts. Pullman discusses the idea of 'otherness within the self' – reminding one of Julia Kristeva's conception of the *Strangers to Ourselves* (1991) – in a comment about the *His Dark Materials* trilogy:

> Lyra and Will and the other characters are meant to be human beings like us, and the story is about a universal human experience, namely growing up. The 'fan-tasy' parts of the story were there as a picture of aspects of human nature, not as something alien and strange. For example, readers have told me that the daemons, which at first seem so utterly fantastic, soon become so familiar and essential a part of each character that they, the readers, feel as if they've got a daemon themselves. And my point is that they have, that we all have. It's an aspect of our personality that we often overlook, but it's there. That's what I mean by realism: I was using the fantastical elements to say something that I thought was true about us and about our lives. (Quoted in Dickerson et al., 2006, p. 202)

In much of children's literature there is the initiation of a young hero or heroine who has to come to terms with a challenging unknown or parallel world and interacts with 'others' – human, non-human or supernatural – that display special features and challenge or accompany the child's quest or journey. Aberrations from an alleged 'norm' are normal, even the encounter with a grinning Cheshire cat that features so prominently among the many strange creatures in children's literature: ' "Please would you tell me", said Alice, a little timidly, for she was not quite sure whether it was good manners for her to speak first, "why your cat grins like that?" ' (Carroll, 1966, p. 49).

Encounters with otherness that call into question what is perceived as taken for granted, thus playing with the reader's expectations and offering new perspectives on – sometimes – old certainties, are essential for the 'enriching experience of otherness' to develop. What is more, in children's literature the notion of otherness is not necessarily focused on the experience of ethnic-national otherness but relates to a multitude of 'othernesses', including aspects of gender, class and creed but also experiences with challenging situations and magical creatures. It is important to consider here that the development both of the child's reading and socialization process has a strong bearing on identity formation – the power of reading (Krashen, 2004) plays a significant role also for EFL contexts. The experience of an individual self and processes of 'othering' – along whatever lines they may take place – is vital for this development. In fact, the multitude of 'othernesses' through children's – and young adults' eyes – (be they bothersome parents or siblings, grinning Cheshire cats, scary wizards, ignorant muggles, bewitching angels, new neighbours or classmates) opens up new ways of addressing questions of identity formation and gives rise to questions like:

- Who or what is 'the other' and is this a static or rather a dynamic category subject to developments within the student's general and reading socialization?
- What do depictions of 'otherness' in children's literature reveal about their constructedness by their mainly adult authors?
- How can this topic be made use of for intercultural learning in second language education?

The potential of children's and young adult literature for the EFL classroom covering a multitude of aspects of otherness should not be underestimated.

David Almond's *Skellig*

Skellig is a novel by David Almond, for which he was awarded the Carnegie medal in 1998 and the Whitbread Children's Book of the Year Award. It was also declared one of the ten most important children's novels of the past 70 years by judges of the CILIP Carnegie Medal for children's literature. The story is about Michael who moves to a new house with his family and has to come to terms with the new surroundings. Michael's baby sister is very ill and in danger of dying. In the garage at the back of their new house, he finds a decrepit creature with – as he later discovers – angels' wings growing out of his shoulder blades. Michael's mother goes to hospital with the baby that has to undergo heart surgery, and dreams she sees *Skellig* enter and hold the baby high up in the air. The child subsequently recovers. This encounter with superhuman otherness, spiritual elements in this case and Michael's and Mina's development in the course of the story is an example of magical realism, which, as the name implies, is concerned with the manifestation of the supernatural in everyday life (Latham, 2006). As Lois Parkinson Zamora and Wendy B. Faris explain, it is concerned with 'liminal territory (. . .) phenomenal and spiritual regions where transformation, metamorphosis, dissolution are common, where magic is a branch of naturalism, or pragmatism' (Zamora et al., 1995, p. 6).

Faris points out five characteristics of magical realism as a framework for comparison, which can be found in Almond's novel. These are:

- An irreducible element of magic;
- A grounding in the phenomenal world, that is, the realistic world;
- The production of unsettling doubts in the reader because of this mixture of the real and the fantastic;
- The near merging of two realms or worlds; and
- Disruptions of traditional ideas about time, space and identity. (Faris, 2004, pp. 7–27 passim)

They can be referred to in second language education to speculate about the nature of otherness, as displayed in the following passage from Almond's novel:

> I thought he was dead. He was sitting with his legs stretched out, and his head tipped back against the wall. He was covered in dust and webs like everything else and his face was thin and pale. Dead bluebottles were scattered on his hair and shoulders. I shone the torch on his white face and his black suit. 'What do you want?' he said. (Almond, 2009, p. 8)

Students can work on a number of creative writing tasks to reflect their perception of the stranger and his situation, they can analyse how the language contributes to Michael's feeling of confusion and speculate on the origins of the stranger in the garage. The dialogue between him and Michael can be continued and the students can collect all available information about the visitor in the garage. They can also work on the above-mentioned characteristics of magic realism in order to come to terms with literary features of the text, for example the depiction of the phenomenal world and elements of magic, the doubts produced in the reader because of the mixture of the real and the fantastic and the development of the children in the face of outward challenges and uncertainties.

Otherness turned magic: Rowling's *Harry Potter*

Encounters with otherness abound in the *Harry Potter* series. Curious creatures and fantastic beasts, wizards and muggles in varying degrees of good and evil constitute the magic of a reading adventure that heavily relies on plot structures based on the very existence of differences and otherness. As Dendle points out, Rowling devotes significant attention to animals and animal sentience and to the relationship between humans (or wizards) and the natural world (Dendle, 2009, p. 163). Here we find many conventional 'us and them' binaries, but they often appear in unusual and unexpected situations and sometimes transcend and blur allegedly stable oppositions. Encounters with otherness apply to different spheres, for example magic otherness (wizards, squibs and muggles), evil otherness (Voldemort, Slytherin), nonhuman otherness (house-elves and garden-gnomes), exotic otherness (Centaurs), even cultural otherness – through Hogwarts' Britain-based perspective (Durmstrang and Beauxbatons). As it is through Harry's eyes that the readers follow the young wizards into the magical world, they become very much aware of how the protagonists themselves have to come to terms with the unexpected created by the encounters with 'othernesses' on various levels. Again, otherness within the self is a strong motif, for example in *The Prisoner of Azkaban* that introduces the frightening creature of a 'boggart' taking on different shapes every time it faces people and confronts them with their greatest fears.

> So the boggart sitting in the darkness within has not yet assumed a form. He does not yet know what will frighten the person on the other side of the door. Nobody knows what a boggart looks like when he is alone, but when I let him out, he will immediately become whatever each of us most fears. (Rowling, 2000, p. 146)

The only remedy is ridiculing it, that is coming up with an idea of a funny situation for the boggart and thus fighting back both the danger and the fears. Learning to confront one's fears and accepting the daemons inside as part of an individual's personality is not a lesson to be taught at Hogwarts only. The common experience of Harry Potter's classmates facing their individual boggarts is an experience that may not only be shared by the readers of *Harry Potter* but that is also transferable into classroom situations in a 'muggle' EFL context. The students can work on this topic creatively, in pairs or in groups, and discuss a number of questions, preferably first referring to a character in a book about whose boggart the student does not know anything, but may be able to speculate from previous reading. In a second step, a transformation into the students' world is possible:

- What would Hermione's boggart look like?
- How could she successfully ridicule him?
- Together with a partner, think of what you can learn from this episode concerning your own fears? What may your boggart look like?

In a foreign language classroom, a collection of words referring to dangerous or frightening situations will prove useful so as to enable the students to explore the emotional intricacies and nuances of both fear and humour, and in literary encounters of tension and comic relief. Imagining one's boggart, possibly drawing or visualizing it – but also finding solutions to these threats can be both a stimulating and rewarding experience of coming to terms with the challenge of otherness within the self. The *Harry Potter* series offers many more highly suitable situations for second language education and its intercultural contexts. Interestingly, rather than condemning this story from the wizarding world as escapist and apolitical, Brycchan Carey rates *Harry Potter* 'among the most politically engaged novels to have been written for children in recent years' and suggests that 'Harry's personal struggle with the dark lord Voldemort [...] provides a site for discussion of a democratic society's response to elitism, totalitarianism, and racism' (Carey, 2003, p.105).

Perspectives for the EFL classroom

Raising an awareness of different levels of otherness is one of the big potentials of children's and young adult literature in second language education. Processes of imagining and imaging otherness can be investigated when it comes to visualizing these notions: how do pupils imagine otherness as presented in texts? How do they relate them to images of otherness displayed in films? The film versions – not only in the case of the *Harry Potter* series but also of *Skellig* (2009, dir. Annabel Jankel) – allow for critical discussions of these visual representations.

Creative tasks exploiting the reader's fascination can be the first steps towards engaging with the unknown – both in classical and contemporary children's literature. In the case of Alice this may result in questions like these:

- Alice managed to enter the looking-glass world. What could be different here? What will she discover in this other world?
- Look inside a mirror. Describe the looking-glass world you see. Imagine you could enter it, how different would it be from your old world?

The mirror also plays an important role in *Harry Potter and the Philosopher's Stone*. Here, it is the 'Mirror of Erised' that makes visible one's desires, individual innermost wishes and longings – in opposition to the boggarts of the third volume. The readiness to enter parallel worlds and come to terms with situations beyond one's grasp is a recurrent motif in children's literature. Similarly, a feeling of 'not-belonging' is a common feature, maybe the most remarkable common denominator of much children's and young adult literature. This is true for many picturebooks that feature outsiders like David McKee's *Elmer*, an elephant that suffers from his outward – colourful – otherness and worries about his being different. It is also true for Shaun Tan's graphic novel *The Arrival,* that leads the student into the outsider's feelings as an immigrant through visual representation only. Multicultural children's and young adult literature in a multitude of settings displaying otherness as a relational category rather than as a binary opposition is analysed by Brown and Stephens (1998). Their collection of essays entitled *Unity in Diversity. Using Multicultural Young Adult Literature in the Classroom* refers to the increasing heterogeneity in classrooms suggesting constructive ways of thinking about diversity.

Literary texts are relevant for second language education and intercultural understanding because they encourage us to put ourselves into the shoes of others and see the world through their eyes (Bredella, 2008, p. 25). In fact, they bring many different voices from various cultural backgrounds into the classroom. But they may also transport their readers to another world and engage and fascinate one's senses in that other world. In terms of discussing the notion of otherness, one may refer to Appiah who suggests that literary texts 'link us, powerfully to others, even strange others' (Appiah, 2005, p. 257). According to Cunningham fantasy may be able to play a part in this process 'because it strips away the veneer of the familiar and the ordinary, and gives the reader distance to view the world iconically' (Cunningham, 2010, pp. 125–6). Despite all discussions about the alleged escapist nature of much of young adult fantasy literature and the very fact that there may well be a tendency of juxtaposing good and evil, the imaginative world of fantasy often challenges the readers' preconceptions and prejudices, thus opening up unusual perspectives. Children's literature provides excellent opportunities for encountering otherness on different levels, for experiencing a sense of child-like curiosity for the unknown as well as coming to terms with feelings of uncertainty about not belonging. Teaching children's literature in its diverse shapes and forms, offers a fascinating platform for exploring questions of identity, values and worldviews, the basic ingredients for intercultural learning.

Bibliography

Almond, D. (1998), *Skellig*. London: Hodder Children's Books.

Carroll, L. (1865/1966), *Alice's Adventures in Wonderland and Through the Looking-Glass*. London: Dent et al.

Mc Kee, D. (1989), *Elmer*. London: Andersen.

Rowling, J. K. (1997), *Harry Potter and the Philosopher's Stone*. London: Bloomsbury.

— (1999), *Harry Potter and the Prisoner of Azkaban*. London: Bloomsbury.

Tan, S. (2011), *The Arrival*. New York: Levine.

References

Appiah, K. A. (2005), *The Ethics of Identity*. Princeton: Princeton University Press.

Bredella, L. (2000), 'Literary texts', in M. Byram (ed.), *Routledge Encyclopaedia of Language Teaching and Learning*. London: Routledge, pp. 375–82.

— (2008), 'What makes reading literary texts pleasurable and educationally significant?', *Fremdsprachen Lehren und Lernen*, 37, 12–26.

Brown, J. E. and Stephens, E. C. (1998), *United in Diversity: Using Multicultural Young Adult Literature in the Classroom*. Urbana, IL: National Council of Teachers of English.

Byram, M. (1997), *Teaching and Assessing Intercultural Communicative Competence*. Clevedon: Multilingual Matters.

Carey, B. (2003), 'Hermione and the house-elves: The literary and historical contexts of J.K. Rowling's antislavery campaign', in G. L. Anatol (ed.), *Reading Harry Potter: Critical Essays*. Westport, CT and London: Praeger, pp. 103–15.

Council of Europe (eds) (2001), *Modern Languages: Learning, Teaching, Assessment. A Common European Framework of Reference*. Cambridge: Cambridge University Press.

Cunningham, A. (2010), 'Engaging and enchanting the heart: Developing moral identity through young adult fantasy literature', in J. Alsup (ed.), *Young Adult Literature and Adolescent Identity across Cultures and Classrooms: Contacts for the Literary Lives of Teens*. New York: Routledge.

Dendle, P. (2009), 'Monsters, creatures, and pets at Hogwarts: Animal stewardship in the world of Harry Potter', in E. E. Heilman (ed.), *Critical Perspectives on Harry Potter* (2nd edn). New York: Routledge, pp. 163–76.

Dickerson, M. and O'Hara, D. (2006), *From Homer to Harry Potter: A Handbook on Myth and Fantasy*. Grands Rapids, MI: Brazos Press.

Faris, W. B. (2004), *Ordinary Enchantments: Magical Realism and the Remystification of Narrative*. Nashville, TN: Vanderbilt University Press.

Kramsch, C. (1993), *Context and Culture in Language Teaching*. Oxford: Oxford University Press.

Krashen, S. D. (2004), *The Power of Reading* (2nd edn). Portsmouth, NH: Heinemann.

Kristeva, J. (1991), *Strangers to Ourselves*. New York: Harvester Wheatsheaf.

Latham, D. (2006), 'Magical realism and the child reader: The case of David Almond's Skellig', *The Looking Glass: New Perspectives on Children's Literature*, Vol. 10, No. 1.

Rosenblatt, L. (2005), *Making Meaning with Texts*. Portsmouth, NH: Heinemann.

Russell, D. H. (1970), *The Dynamics of Reading*. Toronto: Ginn-Blaisdell.

Zamora, L. P. and Faris, W. B. (1995), 'Introduction: Daquiri Birds and Flaubertian Parrot(ie)s', in L. P. Zamora and W. P. Faris (eds), *Magical Realism: Theory, History, Community*. Durham, NC: Duke University Press, pp. 1–11.

Doing Identity, Doing Culture: Transcultural Learning through Young Adult Fiction

Susanne Reichl

Introduction

For years, intercultural learning has been a staple ingredient of European EFL curricula, and yet, there seems to be a cheerful variety of visions as to what exactly its aims are and how they might be reached. In this chapter, I will sketch an ideal learning process that is based on theories of culture, identity and understanding, and will then demonstrate how particularly books for young adults can help foster this kind of learning in the EFL classroom.

As a first step towards a better understanding of the notion of cultural learning, I would like to suggest the term 'transcultural learning', rather than 'intercultural learning', which is usually the standard term used in curricula. By proposing 'trans' rather than 'inter', I am following recent developments in cultural theory that conceive of cultures not as stable categories but as a network of relations and seek to transcend the essentializing binarism and territorial connotations that are sometimes inherent in investigations of intercultural learning (Doff et al., 2011, p. 1). However, this is a view that many recent articulations of the intercultural subscribe to as well, and rather than claim 'transcultural' as the new theoretical paradigm that makes all the difference and implies a whole new practice, I would go along with Werner Delanoy's argument that both concepts, the intercultural and the transcultural, have been used within frameworks that conceptualize culture as dynamic, changing and interconnected networks, rather than having stable borders or concrete (national) manifestations (Delanoy, 2008a, pp. 96–7). Because of the productive diversification that the terms have undergone, I will abstain from a prescriptive evaluation and the terminological nitpicking that is often implied in these discussions, in favour of a position that tentatively rather than authoritatively uses the term 'transcultural' in the sense that Frank Schulze-Engler has proposed (2006a and b, with Sabine Doff, 2011), as the basis for a sketch of an ideal learning situation that outlines the aims of the approach I suggest. With this article I hope to contribute to the debate on culture and literature in the EFL classroom in a way that indicates a possible bridging of the gap between cultural theories and dialogic practice in English language teaching.

The theory: Culture, identity, understanding and young adult literature

My theoretical background owes to contributions on cultural theory, identity theories, theories of understanding that mostly come from cognitive psychology and reading research, teaching methodology and the field of literature for young readers. Rather than constitute a coherent theoretical framework, I would suggest seeing the following as loose building blocks of an approach to transcultural learning that will be explored in more detail below.

Cultural theory has long accepted as a paradigm a conceptualization of culture as a network rather than as a container with boundaries and national demarcations, and this can be traced back to early theorists of culture, such as Clifford Geertz, who referred to culture as a 'web of significance', and to its analysis as an 'interpretative [analysis] in search of meaning' (Geertz, 1973, p. 5). Recent cultural theory sees culture increasingly in flux, intersecting, constantly changing, and also constituting a web rather than a monolithic whole, a notion that informs a body of work on transculturality, globalization and modernity, and the sociocultural practices and realities that make up modern life (Hannerz, 1996; Welsch, 1997, for a detailed overview see Schulze-Engler, 2002, 2006a, 2006b). The basic position of their arguments is that an adherence to territorial notions of culture essentializes individual differences, much in the same way that the category 'race' used to, rather than focusing on the individual subjectivities themselves and on the ways that collective identities shape themselves and negotiate their boundaries and their conflicts (Schulze-Engler, 2006a, pp. 45–6; Doff et al., 2011, pp. 1–2).

From a transcultural perspective, the notion of culture loses its territorial connotations and becomes absorbed in a network of identity positions, always in flux, always developing over time and place. The individual subject with its contingencies can then enter into clusters and collectives with other individuals along the same contingencies. This view of culture echoes what Stuart Hall (e.g. 1987), among others, has suggested about the notion of identity, that is that it is instable, in flux and performative. Similarly, transdifferential theory, a line of argumentation which has been developed over the past decade by a group of cultural theorists in Erlangen, has suggested that a more fruitful way of thinking about identity and difference is to investigate into the ways that people 'do' identity (Allolio-Näcke et al., 2003). Firmly based in poststructuralist discourse, transdifference studies rule out the idealistic notion of a stable, inner self, question boundaries between categories and focus on the moments of doubt that engender the day-to-day business of doing identity. Identity, in this view, is a phenomenon that consists of outside and inside moments, an oscillation between positioning oneself and being positioned by others and is characterized through scepticism, which results in a less secure, less self-assured and less monolithic understanding of identity and one that resists the binaries more successfully than often emerges in discussions of intercultural learning (Breinig et al., 2002, p. 23; Allolio-Näcke et al., 2003, pp. 153–4).

The ground is well prepared, then, it seems, from the perspective of cultural theory, to investigate learning about culture(s). However, I would strongly argue for a consideration of not just the theoretical side of culture itself, but also of the more fundamental question of how something like culture, or a text in which cultural identity is negotiated, can be understood in the first place. The German terms, *Fremdverstehen* and *interkulturelles Verstehen*, seem to be based on an a priori notion that understanding is a given, a product, whereas the English terms, intercultural learning or intercultural communication, have a more process-oriented ring to them. In the interdisciplinary range of theory available on understanding processes, from areas such as language learning, cognitive psychology, narratology or philosophy, there seems to be a general agreement that understanding is something fragmentary and tentative, is subject to construction (rather than reconstruction) by the individual, has a subjective as well as an intersubjective component, and can be constructed through and in dialogue (for a summary see Reichl, 2009, 24–6).

Research into language teaching has been concerned with the notion that something like total comprehension can never be fully achieved. Eva Burwitz-Melzer entitled her study on processes of intercultural learning at lower secondary level 'Allmähliche Annäherungen' (2003), which suggests a gradual process of understanding rather than a product at the end of a straightforward process. Claire Kramsch has said about communication in the EFL classroom in general that 'understanding and shared meaning, when it occurs, is a small miracle' (Kramsch, 1993, p. 2). Michael Steig in his book on literary understanding in classroom settings has defined understanding as a 'condition of satisfaction arrived at subjectively and (...) intersubjectively' (Steig, 1989, p. xiv), and has pointed out how subjective understanding can be extended and modified intersubjectively in the classroom through interaction and dialogue. And dialogue is a crucial theoretical ingredient that Werner Delanoy has recently contributed in his work on dialogic competence, one which includes key abilities such as a self-distancing from one's own position, a respectful confrontation with other viewpoints, and a positive appraisal of contradiction and irritation as opportunities for learning (Delanoy, 2008b). This coincides with a view of identity as made up of moments of doubt and scepticism. It also provides a frame for the observation that processes of understanding usually go unnoticed, since they are automatic and therefore not usually consciously experienced, while a failure to understand is something that people notice as unpleasant and disconcerting. All this suggests that understanding is to be conceived of as anything but complete if we want to learn. This is not simply a theoretical position but it is a precondition for active learning processes: if understanding was a straightforward process, a normative one and one with a clear single outcome, there would not be much room for individual or intersubjective learning and construction processes, which are the basis for a realization of the meaning potential as well as the basis for a discussion of the processes involved in understanding. Another useful ingredient that learning and understanding theories have contributed is the significance of meta-cognitive skills, or in other words 'thinking about one's own thoughts' (Hacker, 1998, p. 3), for the development of learning and understanding processes. Especially when it comes to the comprehension of sociocultural practices, which will inevitably include the use of cultural schemata on the part of the learner, the ability to reflect on one's own perception and comprehension is extremely valuable.

How and why should these learning processes be instigated with reference to a literary text? What are the special generic features of narratives, and young adult fiction especially, that lend themselves to these processes? Claire Kramsch has advocated the use of literary texts in the foreign language classroom because they have 'the ability to represent the particular voice of a writer among the many voices of his or her community, and thus to appeal to the particular in the reader' (Kramsch, 1993, p. 131). For the understanding of cultural practices and social realities, this seems especially relevant, because rather than tend to easy conclusions of the kind that would essentialize culture in the way that has been discussed above (e.g. 'she behaves like this because she is Arabian'), it is important to remember that there are always other voices, other stories as well.

It is potentially reductive to argue that literature for young readers has special generic features that lend themselves well to transcultural learning processes. There is such a broad range of texts that constitute a rather massive body of work, that any overgeneralizations are problematic. So on a very broad level, we could argue, young adult novels tend to have the potential for empathic understanding that is a result of the fictional world being in one way or another reconcilable with the learner's world. This is not only an important motivational factor that might determine the student's willingness to engage with a text, it also enables a very subjective kind of understanding, one that relates to the characters' motives and desires. Young adult fiction also tends to employ a relatively direct narrative perspective, that is a first-person narrative or a figural narrative situation that both provide insight into the protagonists' thoughts and ideas. Other features that are meant to facilitate the reading process, such as illustrations, short chapters or gripping narratives, enhance the sense of immediacy and the motivational power of the narrative, which seems to be a first step towards learning.

An ideal learning process?

How can these ingredients from the realms of cultural theory, cognitive psychology and language learning theories be integrated in a proposal for cultural learning that can be seen to apply to the reading of a young adult novel in the context of an EFL classroom?

Rather than argue at some length for such an integration, I would like to propose a sketch of an ideal learning process – in the full awareness that learning processes are hardly predictable in the way that my suggestions might indicate. I envision a constructive, more conscious learning process about cultural practices and identities, along the following lines:

1. The student constructs a subjective understanding of a particular identity encountered in a text. This is facilitated by a rather intimate narrative situation that allows the reader to engage intellectually and empathetically with the story.

2. The student realizes that there is a particular voice, a particular subjectivity in the story, as well as the fact that there are other stories, other voices and other subjectivities, too, and observes the negotiation processes involved in the group formation.

3. In the reading process, the student experiences moments of doubt, cognitive dissonances (often experienced simply as confusion), lack of understanding, and is thus made aware of his or her constructive understanding processes and the processes of cultural signification. The student also realizes that there are cultural schemata and other thinking patterns at work in understanding processes – to be detected, questioned, resisted and, in the process, learned more about. All this leads to the development of meta-cognitive skills, that is the power to reflect on and monitor learning and understanding processes.

4. The student extends or adjusts his or her understanding in dialogue with others (i.e. peers, the teacher, other texts), and thus moves from subjective understanding to intersubjective understanding.

What looks like a checklist of cultural learning needs extensive hedging to the effect that it should not be understood as a learning programme that can be expected to be activated by each and every text, each individual learner and in any situation. If we know one thing about understanding and learning processes, we know that they are subject to their social context, and even if reading often happens in isolation, the various possible EFL contexts can be expected to have some effect on the reading. In addition, the diverse cultural contexts that students can resort to in their understanding processes also produce a broad range of possible comprehension processes. Therefore I would like to suggest these points as potential moments of learning about culture and identity, rather than a programme that can be installed, and would like to illustrate these points with some examples from young adult fiction that seem to lend themselves well to cultural learning.

Select young adult fiction for transcultural learning

It is often suggested, especially in extensive reading contexts, that those novels that enable easy reading without many interruptions should be chosen for language learners to maintain their motivation. To teachers and teacher educators alike, this seems convincing as much as it is reductive. Many students are motivated by features that are a long way from being simple, and that appeal to them for entirely idiosyncratic reasons. Moreover, 'easy' is a hard concept to define. Quite apart from the truism that a text tends to be as easy as the task that is set (Purves, 1991, p. 167), I would argue that a certain degree of difficulty in the more conceptual areas of comprehension, especially when it concerns characters' motivations and identity positions, can result in a number of fruitful learning opportunities. Therefore, a young adult novel that refers to cultural identity positions which one would assume might cause problems to the teenage reader, should not be discarded as 'too difficult'. Rather, this perceived difficulty should be regarded as an opening for a dialogue about cultures and identities.

My first example comes from *Benny and Omar* (1998), a novel by Eoin Colfer, who is better known for his fantasy series featuring Artemis Fowl (which in itself might constitute a major motivational factor for some learners). In this novel, Benny Shaw, an Irish pre-teen, who has just migrated to Tunisia with his family, is the focalizer, who shares his understanding processes:

> Benny looked around at the people. They weren't Irish for a start. Now Benny was no eejit, he wasn't expecting the Tunisian nationals to be Irish. What he did expect were darkish people with Irishy personalities. That was not what he got. The Tunisians weren't interested in conforming to Benny's preconceptions. They stubbornly insisted on being themselves. You couldn't even categorize them. Successive waves of Muslim and European invaders, combined with darker genes from south of the Sahara, made appearances unpredictable. It was like every race in the world was focused here. One second you were looking at a black lad all dressed up like one of them rappers, the next some little red-haired pale-faced chap was trying to sell you flowers. (Colfer, 1998, p. 20)

The reader can accompany Benny's comprehension processes and is confronted with a sudden awareness of how our preconceptions might no longer hold in an unexpected situation. Here, we have a case of someone 'doing identity' not in the sense of performing it but of identifying other people around him and learning about the world and about cultural connections in the process. Benny's confusion at first and growing awareness of the complexities of his new environment is a good starting point for teachers to discuss the use of the term 'race' in this context, and invite comparisons to the students' own environments, as well as to observations they have made at airports and other places, including their classrooms, to encourage a meta-discussion of identities and cultures. In the passage above, even though Benny is engaged in a process of othering, there is no clear 'other' that would predetermine Benny's responses. On the contrary, there are familiarization processes ('them rappers') as well, and they can also be regarded as an attempt to make sense of globalization processes of a different kind than what students might be used to. This passage, as indeed much of the story that follows, invites a critical view of the way we categorize people and countries, and tend to think differently of identity in contexts that challenge our established preconceptions of cultures and identities. The dialogic learning that Delanoy advocates is present in the ways in which Benny gets to know Tunisia with the help of his Tunisian friend Omar – both engage in a mutual cultural learning process – and makes the book an excellent example of a teenage novel that encourages some of the thinking and learning processes sketched above.

An example in which the confusion is not in the novel but can be expected to arise in the reading process, and at its very beginning, too, is the opening paragraph of Morris Gleitzman's *Boy Overboard* (2002):

> I'm Manchester United and I've got the ball and everything is good. There's no smoke, or nerve-gas, or sand-storms. I can't even hear any explosions. Which is really good. Bomb wind can really put you off your football skills. (Gleitzman, 2002, p. 1)

Just these first three lines cause cognitive dissonance: how do Manchester United and explosions and bomb wind go together? For me, this text suggests an 'in-at-the-deep-end' approach, rather than any pre-reading activities that are often advocated as an integral part of any reading activity. In this case, I feel, there is a unique learning opportunity if students are simply presented with the beginning of the novel, and then asked what their explanation might be for the unusual combination of war references, a desert setting and Manchester United. A passage later on could be added for a more extensive discussion of readers' expectations:

> I turn and look fearfully at the figure behind us. It's not what I thought. It's not an angry man in black robes with a long beard and an even longer swishing cane. It's something even scarier. A kid in a very familiar dress and headcloth.
>
> 'Bibi,' I gasp.
>
> 'Eeek,' croaks Aziz, face slack with amazement. 'It's your sister.'
>
> For a moment there's silence except for the wind blowing in off the open desert and the distant sound of someone drilling bomb fragments out of their wall in the village. (Gleitzman, 2002, pp. 3–4)

The novel makes it impossible for the reader (and here I am thinking of a European teenage reader) to make any sense of the story yet. This strategy of delayed decoding is repeated several times, until the reader can build a clearer idea of the context of this story: the setting is Afghanistan, we learn that it is against Sharia law for a woman to walk about outside with an uncovered face, and that it is against the law for girls or women to play football. What we also get is an impression of a country in which war and references to war are omnipresent. The story is narrated by first-person narrator Jamal, whose metaphors tend to be taken from the realm of bombs, tanks, shelling and weapons, so the teenage reader is given one very particular voice and story. Rather than being given an exposition of the time and place of the story, the students are given direct access to the children's living conditions, and in such a way that they need to keep asking questions: this is not due to a lack of understanding on the basis of language, but on the basis of world knowledge, and it becomes an opportunity to learn something about the cultural practices and malpractices in question. The way that war features as a given reality in the story is something that students will quickly notice, and this noticing is the first step to learning. The learning process, then, is not a colourful intercultural one that involves food and clothes and so on, but one that introduces the young adult learner to the sociopolitical realities of one part of the modern world from the narrative perspective of a teenage boy. Here, too, identity becomes an important issue: it is interesting to see how Jamal identifies with Manchester United, a football club that most learners in Europe would be familiar with, even though the setting is completely different. This way of 'doing identity' seems to work as a protection or as an alternative to the world of war for Jamal, and again we have a dialogue between the very local social realities of Afghanistan on the one hand and the less contextualized globalization processes on the other. Students might grow to understand the story of Jamal and his sister better on an intellectual level because they have started out by not understanding, and they might understand the story better on an empathic level because they have a global cultural framework in place that allows them not to see the Afghani children as completely 'other', and they are being helped by a narrative situation that gives them access to the protagonist's perception.

A book that is perfectly teeming with cognitive dissonances for the first 80 pages or so and has its dialogic structure firmly embedded is Malorie Blackman's *Noughts and Crosses* (2001), the first volume of what was eventually to become a tetralogy. The dialogic structure in this case lies in the way in which the narrative situation reflects the binary social structure of the fictional world: the story is told alternatingly from Sephy's and Callum's perspective, the former a Cross, the latter a Nought, and sometimes the same situation is told from these two diverging voices and perspectives. This already implies the recognition of perspective and particularity that Kramsch emphasizes in her consideration of fiction for language learning. The particular story here is one that is at the same time familiar and strange: familiar, because we are faced with a world of racism, prejudice, institutional segregation, a history of slavery and a resulting situation in which the oppressed minority turns to violence to fight for their rights. Strange, because the segregation in this world is the opposite of what we know: the ruling majority are black, and the oppressed minority, who used to be kept as slaves, is white.

This situation results in many dialogues such as the following, in which the usual hegemonic roles are negotiated and stereotypical positions are reflected:

> 'Stick to your own kind. If you sit with the blankers again, everyone in the school will treat you like one of them.'
>
> 'You need to wake up and check which side you're on,' added Joanne.
>
> 'Why d'you want to be around them anyway?' Dionne piped up. 'They smell funny and they eat peculiar foods and everyone knows that none of them are keen to make friends with soap and water.' (Blackman, 2001, p. 83)

Most readers tend to read these episodes with the original black/white schema in place, that is as if the minority was black and the majority white, even though it is the other way round. This shows how firmly our world schemata are in place, and how a scripted conversation like the one above can activate them rather easily. But this, of course, provides ample opportunity for learning: as a reader, you become aware of the sociocultural patterns you apply when trying to make sense of a situation like that. In *Noughts and Crosses*, these schemata can be felt to jam and jar, or in other words, the reader experiences a cognitive dissonance, a mental conflict which is the result of contradictory beliefs or assumptions. On the whole, people build up quite a resistance to any input that would result in cognitive dissonance, which leads to phenomena that some of my students reported, which is that it took them 60 to 100 pages to keep track of who was black and who was white, even though there are hints and indications from the first chapter onwards.

Such a moment of doubt, or a cognitive dissonance, provides a promising learning opportunity; in this case the learning outcome is not focused on a culture or on a particular identity so much as on the more general processes of identification and signification. In fact, learning happens on a meta level, that is students learn about the way their own perception and cognition works, how quickly they fall into easy comprehension patterns, and awareness of these processes sharpens their meta-cognitive skills.

Conclusion

Understanding, as I have stipulated above, is always incomplete, fragmentary and subjective, and making any claims as to how learners deal with transcultural learning and the development of their meta-cognitive skills in practice would wrongly assume that we could be certain about what happens when they read these texts. Rather than make any such grand claims or attempt the impossible and investigate empirically into transcultural understanding, I will proceed along the lines of the tentative and the potential, and sooner throw up more questions that relate to the realities of the EFL classroom than try and close some that seem to evade closure anyway.

The first set of questions concern one of the focal points in this volume, extensive reading. If young adult students read these novels as part of an extensive reading programme, is there any way in which their learning processes can be controlled or gained insight into? How can we make sure that the transcultural learning potential is actually realized? Does the complexity of cultural learning and understanding processes not necessitate the return of the class reader, even in a setting and with an age group that would otherwise demand free voluntary reading?

Rather than discard extensive reading in favour of a class reader for all students in a class, I would suggest using passages like the one quoted above as appetizers or teasers to make students interested in some of the texts available for extensive reading, and to use them for training reading strategies as well. Young adult novels do not have to be read in their entirety, and passages like the opening chapter from *Boy Overboard* make very good short texts with which strategic reading can be practised and the processes involved in transcultural learning can be made visible for the learner. Whether or not the book is then read as a whole in an extensive reading project or as a class reader is less important, but it is more than likely that the students' curiosity will have been aroused.

Eventually, the question needs to be raised whether and how the teacher is expected to intervene in such learning processes in the first place, regardless of whether the books are class readers or part of a range of books that students chose from for free voluntary reading. I would argue that the teacher, in the role of facilitator more than one who imparts information, is well advised to intervene to an extent in order to make processes of learning explicit, but then step back again to allow the subjective and intersubjective learning processes to unfold. Again, as a facilitator, it is the teacher's responsibility to provide a setting in which meanings can be intersubjectively shared and intervene when the discussion becomes too detached from the texts in question.

Bibliography

Blackman, M. (2001), *Noughts and Crosses*. London: Corgi.
Colfer, E. (1998), *Benny and Omar*. London: Puffin.
Gleitzman, M. (2002), *Boy Overboard*. London: Puffin.

References

Allolio-Näcke, L. and Kalscheuer, B. (2003), 'Doing identity – Von Transdifferenz und dem alltäglichen Skeptizismus', in H. Fitzek and M. Ley (eds), *Alltag im Aufbruch: Ein psychologisches Profil der Gegenwartskultur*. Gießen: Psychosozial-Verlag, pp. 152–62.

Breinig, H. and Lösch, K. (2002), 'Introduction: Difference and transdifference', in H. Breinig, J. Gebhardt and K. Lösch (eds), *Multiculturalism in Contemporary Societies: Perspectives on Difference and Transdifference*. Erlangen: Universitätsbund, pp. 11–36.

Burwitz-Melzer, E. (2003), *Allmähliche Annäherungen: Fiktionale Texte im interkulturellen Fremdsprachenunterricht der Sekundarstufe 1*. Tübingen: Gunter Narr Verlag.

Delanoy, W. (2008a), 'Transkulturalität und Literatur im Englischunterricht', *FLuL*, 37, 95–108.

— (2008b), 'Dialogic communicative competence and language learning', in W. Delanoy and L. Volkmann (eds), *Future Perspectives for English Language Teaching*. Heidelberg: Winter, pp. 173–88.

Doff, S. and Schulze-Engler, F. (2011), 'Beyond "other cultures": An introduction', in S. Doff and F. Schulze-Engler (eds), *Beyond 'Other Cultures'. Transcultural Perspectives on Teaching the New Literatures in English*. Trier: WVT, pp. 1–14.

Geertz, C. (1973), *The Interpretation of Cultures: Selected Essays*. London: Fontana Press.

Hacker, D. J. (1998), 'Definitions and empirical foundations', in D. J. Hacker, J. Dunlosky and A. C. Graesser (eds), *Metacognition in Educational Theory and Practice*. Mahwah, NJ: Lawrence Erlbaum Associates, pp. 1–23.

Hall, S. (1987/96), 'New ethnicities', in H. A. Baker, M. Diawara and R. H. Lindeborg (eds), *Black British Cultural Studies: A Reader*. Chicago, IL: University of Chicago Press, pp. 163–72.

Hannerz, U. (1996), *Transnational Connections: Culture, People, Places*. London: Routledge.

Kramsch, C. (1993), *Context and Culture in Language Teaching*. Oxford: Oxford University Press.

Purves, A. C. (1991), 'Indeterminate texts, responsive readers, and the idea of difficulty in literature', in A. C. Purves (ed.), *The Idea of Difficulty in Literature*. Albany, NY: State University of New York Press, pp. 158–70.

Reichl, S. (2009), *Cognitive Principles, Critical Practice: Reading Literature at University*. Göttingen: Vienna University Press.

Schulze-Engler, F. (2002), 'Transnationale Kultur als Herausforderung für die Literaturwissenschaft', *ZAA*, 50/1, 65–79.

— (2006a), 'Von "Inter" zu "Trans": Gesellschaftliche, kulturelle und literarische Übergänge', in H. Antor (ed.), *Inter- und Transkulturelle Studien: Theoretische Grundlagen und interdisziplinäre Praxis*. Heidelberg: Winter, pp. 41–53.

— (2006b), 'What's the difference? Notes towards a dialogue between transdifference and transculturality', *Journal for the Study of British Cultures*, 13/2, 123–32.

Steig, M. (1989), *Stories of Reading: Subjectivity and Literary Understanding*. Baltimore: Johns Hopinks University Press.

Welsch, W. (1997), 'Transkulturalität: Zur veränderten Verfassung heutiger Kulturen', in I. Schneider and C. W. Thomsen (eds), *Hybridkultur: Medien, Netze, Künste*. Cologne: Wienand, pp. 67–88.

11

Developing Intercultural Competence by Studying Graphic Narratives

Carola Hecke

This chapter investigates how secondary school and university EFL students can develop intercultural communicative competence (ICC) with the help of teaching and studying graphic narratives. It describes the results of a project in which university students taught the graphic novels *Persepolis* (Satrapi, 2003) and *La Perdida* (Abel, 2006) to secondary school students. The results suggest that ICC can be developed in the course of teaching and studying graphic novels.

We currently assume that studying literature in EFL classes can lead to a higher ICC of students (Hallet, 2010, p. 5; Nünning, 2007; Nünning et al., 2006, pp. 27–38). Conditions for this are that the literary texts are written in English and that the authors are either from the target cultures or deal with the target cultures or with intercultural interaction. As graphic novels have been accepted as a literary medium (Chute, 2008) one may speculate that through their use, students would be able to develop and sustain ICC, too. A project at Georg-August University Göttingen researched whether this was really possible. In this project, two graphic novels were studied – the excellent English translation of Marjane Satrapi's graphic novel *Persepolis* (2003) and Jessica Abel's *La Perdida* (2006), originally written in English. Both texts fulfil the necessary conditions posed on literary texts in order for them to possibly lead to a higher ICC. *Persepolis* (Figure 11.1) is a graphic novel about cultural diversity in Iran and Austria and addresses a multitude of facets of intercultural understanding. It deals with growing up in a multicultural environment and depicts a series of personal experiences to which the German students taking part in this project, living in an increasingly multicultural society themselves, should be able to relate from different perspectives.

La Perdida, by a US author (see Figure 11.2), also deals with intercultural encounters and (mis-)understanding across cultural boundaries as it tells the story of a young American who moves to Mexico City to learn about her heritage. As both novels can be read in English and deal with intercultural interaction, plus one author is from an English-speaking culture and her novel deals with target cultures, the two texts meet the requirements for literary texts which foster intercultural learning and were therefore selected for the project to investigate whether studying graphic novels can help students develop ICC.

Figure 11.1 *Persepolis: The Story of a Childhood and The Story of a Return* by Marjane Satrapi and transl. Anjali Singh © (2003). Used by permission of Vintage, a division of the Random House Group Limited.

Figure 11.2 *La Perdida* by Jessica Abel © (2006). Used by permission of Pantheon Books, a division of the Random House Group Limited.

ICC and how it can be measured

According to the German educational standards (*Bildungsstandards*) of foreign language learning, ICC consists of three major components: (a) it is based on sociocultural knowledge, (b) it involves the willingness and ability to understand other people – for instance by a conscious change of perspective, and (c) it allows successful intercultural interaction (KMK, 2003, p. 9). ICC thus combines knowledge, attitudes and abilities. In order to develop ICC in students, teachers have to work on these three levels: they have to provide or help students gather information on other cultures, stimulate students' motivation to interact successfully with someone from a different culture and offer their students chances to practise intercultural interaction and understanding. Consequently, to prove whether ICC has developed, one has to run tests on these three levels and – since they are very complex – on every aspect related to them. This amounts to a very large number of matters to be researched. Due to this complexity of ICC, there is no testing tool for this competence as a whole. However, some rather successful attempts have been made in the field of psychology for the investigation of individual aspects of ICC, such as cultural knowledge and understanding (e.g. Gosch et al., 2006). At the beginning of the first project run in 2006, though, such testing tools were not yet available, and I had to find a way to measure the students' ICC. As in the discipline of psychology, I decided to focus on just one aspect, which was 'willingness and ability to understand other people'. This decision was motivated by the fact that intercultural understanding was the main goal of EFL classes. Therefore, research on this aspect is not only of interest for teaching with comics but for EFL teaching methodology in general. In addition, basic understanding of the graphic novel (which here means an understanding on the level of the language and the text together with the images) has to be seen as the starting point for an increase of ICC through graphic novels: students can only learn through texts if the texts make sense to them. Thus understanding of language and text is a precondition for the positive impact of any piece of literature on the development of ICC and therefore rather important. To test the students' ICC in the project, they filled in questionnaires on their understanding. In addition, student interaction in class as well as in the breaks before and after class was observed.

According to Ansgar Nünning, intercultural understanding concerns four different levels of interaction (Nünning, 2007, p. 126). The levels Nünning identifies are the level of the language, the text, the culture and the individual. One has to be able to understand the foreign words to know what the communication is about (language level). Words have to be related and the text that results from this process has to be interpreted (textual level). This interpretation has to be guided by cultural knowledge of the speaker's or author's/narrator's/characters' cultural background to allow an understanding, for instance of connotations (cultural level). Finally, to understand an individual one has to take on this person's individual perspective to see the reason for his or her actions – which does not imply that one has to agree with the decisions made by that person but to be able to understand why he or she has arrived at them (personal level). Understanding communication in a foreign language thus demands knowledge and skills in the fields of the foreign language, text interpretation, culture and socio-affective interaction. Accordingly, the project lessons provided students with exercises on all four levels: The students learned new vocabulary, they solved tasks which aided their textual understanding, they researched the cultures addressed in the novels and they were urged to take on the perspectives of different characters of their texts. Whenever the students complied successfully with these tasks (e.g. used words they had learnt recently in their own conversation) it was logged, too.

The Reading Project

The Reading Project involved high school students from grades 9 to 12, mostly 10th grade, and advanced university students. The high school students had voluntarily signed up for a one-semester on-campus English reading class in which they read *Persepolis* in the first and *La Perdida* in the second project run. Their classes were conducted by the university students who were enrolled in a seminar on teaching comics and graphic novels in EFL education. In the course of the semester the university students read *Persepolis* or *La Perdida* and prepared, presented and taught one 90-minute lesson, which was later discussed in the seminar. In their lessons, the university students helped the high school students read and understand the graphic novel by providing them with tasks that supported their understanding on all four levels. Interestingly, although the texts were authentic and not adapted for teaching language and text, understanding did not seem to pose any problem for the high school students at first (see 'potential difficulties'), as they confirmed themselves in the questionnaires. They said they used the pictures for support so that despite the lack of simplification or vocabulary annotations they could easily cope with the novels. This corresponds to research results from the field of reading psychology, which has shown that pictures aid textual understanding because they can contextualize the communicative situation or visualize the topic of the text, thus guiding the students' guesses on the meaning of a word or the content of the communication (Carney et al., 2002). So one can assume that the ease with which students understand graphic novels can be attributed to the positive impact of visual aids on reading. As pictures are a core element of comics they are probably always more accessible than novels without images, so that it can be claimed that graphic novels lend themselves extremely well for the purpose of fostering ICC since a very important precondition – language and textual understanding (Nünning's understanding on levels one and two) – is more likely to be met with graphic novels than with purely verbal texts. However, reading graphic novels still has to be trained because reading graphic novels differs from reading conventional text (see below).

To foster the understanding of the graphic novels on the cultural and personal levels, the ongoing teachers asked their students to do exercises such as researching the setting of a novel with the help of a map, gathering information on time and place from other texts, reflecting on stereotypes, developing character constellations, writing letters from the characters' perspectives, taking on a character's role and holding speeches, creating freeze frames and performing a talk show in which they took on the roles of characters. These exercises were adapted from resource books for the study of regular novels in literature classes and aimed at a change of perspective and an intensification of the students' reflection on the story.

Understanding graphic novels

The understanding of graphic novels does not mean reading and interpreting the text in the speech bubbles and captions alone but also reading them and interpreting them with the aid of the clues given by the pictures (Carter, 2008, pp. 48–50; Versaci, 2008, pp. 96–102). The pictures have to guide the interpretation, which means that readers have to switch back and forth between text and images. This is necessary because a word or sentence can have different meanings if it is said in different contexts. 'Hello' asked by a character tapping through a dark labyrinth pleads for help, whereas 'Hello' yelled aggressively by someone in an argument demands that his interlocutor should reconsider his opinion. Here, the decoding of the text and the pictures must obviously happen interrelatedly, and the understanding of each mode is supported and added to by the other input: text adds to pictures and pictures contextualize words. But which competences does this demand of the readers? Nancy Frey and Douglas Fisher have pointed out that reading the pictures requires visual literacy (Frey et al., 2008, pp. 1–4) which means that readers have to be familiar with the visual conventions used to depict the action of a comic. It also requires creativity for the interpretation of the story as the sequence of pictures of a comic or graphic novel does not show every step of the action minutely; the raising of a hand for instance does not need five pictures but one with motion lines for lifting the arm. Usually, the steps are only alluded to, as in our example by using motion lines below the elbow to indicate the raising of the arm. The readers have to interpret such clues based on their world knowledge and familiarity with the medium to constitute the meaning(s) intended by the author (McCloud, 1993, p. 68). Due to the relevance of the images and the importance of visual literacy for reading graphic novels these combinations of image and text should never be treated as verbal texts alone but as verbal *and* visual texts. In addition, since visual literacy is a major precondition for understanding graphic novels on the textual level it has to be trained because – as stated before – understanding on the textual level is the basis for any learning from texts (Frey et al., 2008, pp. 1–4). According to this claim, university and high school students did not only study graphic novels on the level of the story but also learned about graphic novels as a medium and the conventions of comics imagery.

More results

The high school students' performance during class, their responses in questionnaires and comments that were overheard during the lessons suggest that they could develop their ICC in the field of understanding through studying graphic novels. On the language level, they learned new words, understood them when they appeared in the speech bubbles and captions and used them in their communication. On the text level they were able to answer questions and showed that they were able to constitute a meaning for the graphic novel. According to the students, the pictures of the graphic novel helped them to get the meaning of a scene. Interestingly, it could be observed that the students really struggled harder with other text genres (e.g. interviews, short stories), which were read for additional information in class too, as they asked more questions and needed help with unfamiliar words. On the third, the cultural level, the students improved too, as they picked up information about the cultures addressed in the novels. For example, they were able to correct their own wrong, previously stated assumptions from a brainstorming session at the beginning of a lesson, for instance the belief that there were no cars in Iran. Also, in their discussions, the students referred to research done in class on the setting and cultures involved. In the *Persepolis* project run, students became aware of their own stereotyped opinions, as one student wrote: 'The lesson on stereotypes made me realize that people are different even though they are from the same country.' He or she seemed to have become aware of the inadequacy of lumping together one member of a culture with everybody else. Another student even seemed to have overcome his or her own prejudices, as he or she stated: 'Now I have more background knowledge and can understand people better.' These comments are persuasive that in the future real-life cultural understanding between them and members of the cultures researched in class will be more successful. However, whether the attitudes and patterns of reaction will truly be transferred to situations outside the classroom cannot be proven with the results of the project, as it did not follow the participants' extracurricular activities and neither surveyed nor compared the students' attitudes before and after the project run. Yet, the students' performance in class was a positive indication of respect and acceptance, since the students were willing and able to imagine themselves in the protagonists' place and complied willingly and successfully with tasks such as writing letters in the foreign language from the perspective of a character or performing in the talk show. These tasks revealed that the students would at least be able to switch to another perspective to understand members of other cultures on a personal level. All this led to the cautious assumption that working with graphic novels helps students develop or sustain ICC and can prepare them for successful real-life intercultural interaction in the target language.

Potential difficulties

However, graphic novels are no silver bullet to the increase of ICC. First, even graphic novels can be difficult to understand on the story level. The project showed that if the text addresses unfamiliar topics (e.g. communism in the case of *La Perdida*) and the pictures do not explain the concept (e.g. when the characters only discuss the topics) it is very difficult for the students to understand the text at all. One high school student wrote on the question whether reading English graphic novels was easier than reading other texts that it depends ('*kommt drauf an*') and he explained: 'there is no difference between English words in regular text and comics' and of course, he is right. Unfamiliar words that are not explained through images will not be understood more easily just because they appear in a speech balloon. For that reason, some high school students checked 'as easy as' regarding the questions whether it was easier, as easy as, or more difficult to understand the words in the speech balloons, the plot, and the cultures presented in the comics than in regular texts. In the lessons, one student had to struggle very hard to understand the plot and cultures of *La Perdida* at all. He argued that the text was 'to (sic) long and a part is difficult'. Due to this difficulty, personal understanding was 'more difficult' for *La Perdida* than for the graded readers the students had already read at school – according to the questionnaires. This was probably because of the long heated conversations on abstract topics between the characters. Nevertheless, the students of the *La Perdida* project run were able to perform well in those tasks that aimed at taking on the roles of the characters from the novel. However, due to the results from the questionnaires I would not recommend reading *La Perdida* with high school students before 11th grade because the successful compliance with tasks for personal and cultural understanding cannot be guaranteed if the text is not understood. Selecting a graphic novel to be read in class, one has to keep in mind the students' pre-existent knowledge because graphic novels are no easy material per se, as the students' responses indicated.

Secondly, besides ensuring that students can understand the text and fostering intercultural learning through adequate methods, teachers have to prevent the development of problematic ideas that would disturb intercultural communication rather than support it. The *La Perdida* project run showed that prejudices and stereotypes – if addressed in the novel and not sufficiently discussed in class – can even be affirmed by graphic novels, as by any text. For instance, when the students were asked what they had learned about Mexico they answered that Mexico City and Mexico in general were very dangerous places ('*Mexico ist gefährlich*') with a high crime rate. Yet this notion, which is partly true for Mexico City, should not be generalized undifferentiatedly for a whole country as it might be offensive for its inhabitants.

Performance of university students

Now let us take a look at the university students' results. The university students who had studied and taught a graphic novel yielded positive results regarding their own development of ICC, too. They learned new vocabulary and collocations, became aware of the characteristics of graphic novels which should aid their reading and broaden their cultural knowledge. One student teacher in the *Persepolis* course wrote in the questionnaire: 'It [*Persepolis*] provided me with a whole new perspective on a land I virtually knew nothing about' (student teacher A). *Persepolis* obviously changed the image of Iran for the student teachers as they gathered new information on the country. At the end of the course the university students said that they knew more about Iran and Mexico and their cultures than before. This knowledge helped them understand the characters, as they affirmed. Hopefully it will help them interact successfully with real persons from Iran or Mexico in real life, as one student teacher from the *Persepolis* class suggested: 'My attitude towards Iranians has changed in so far as that I have got an idea about their way of life and an idea about the Iranian history' (student teacher B). Another ongoing teacher wrote:

> I was also full of stereotypes and also uncertainty about Iranian life and now think to have acquired a much better understanding of Iranian life; and most of all am aware of the fact that there are many similarities despite the differences with regards to the political situation. (Student teacher C)

Another student teacher claimed that his or her 'stereotypes vanished' – and in parentheses added 'by learning about their culture'. In how far existing stereotypes really vanished or were rather replaced by new ones can be questioned, of course. Ideally new perspectives lead students to a more differentiated view of a country, its cultures and its people and to a successful interaction with someone from the country in the target language English. In any case, the university students seemed to have developed an awareness of the existence and potentially negative impact of stereotypes.

One very interesting finding was that university students voluntarily researched cultures addressed in their graphic novel and wanted to learn about them and ICC when it came to preparing their lessons. Their responsibility to teach others on the topic had obviously motivated them to learn about the subject matter of their lessons. It seems that in their case, it was this learning through teaching approach and not so much the medium that led to the increase of ICC. The university students stated in the questionnaire: 'my own lesson helped me to get an inside view about Marjane and about the Iranian culture' and 'it has helped [me to develop my own ICC] that I had the responsibility to make them [the students] more open to ICC' (student teacher D). Another university student explained: 'Because you always have to reflect about what you want to teach. So you reflect about intercultural interaction and therefore learn about it' (student teacher E). These findings suggest that teaching graphic narratives aiming at the students' development of ICC helps ongoing teachers to become aware of the characteristics of ICC and ideally to develop ICC themselves. The learning through teaching approach seems to matter strongly because it forces the student teachers to reflect on the characteristics of ICC which eventually leads to a more profound knowledge and awareness regarding the matter.

Conclusion

The research questions of this chapter were whether EFL students could develop or sustain ICC with the help of graphic narratives or through teaching graphic novels. The findings of the reading project suggest that both is not only possible but very likely if certain preconditions are met: the text is written in English, deals with intercultural matters, is written by someone from the target cultures or deals with the target cultures, the topic is age-appropriate and the methods fit their purposes. Graphic novels are suitable because their pictures facilitate understanding, yet do not explain everything. But thanks to visual aids, graphic novels can even deal with complex intercultural topics, which they treat in similar depth to other texts (Tabachnick, 2009, p. 2). Therefore, this type of comic should unreservedly be integrated into EFL lessons. Recently gathered positive results with 9th graders at a German school confirms this claim. Especially boys seem to enjoy working with this medium, as in a 9th grade English class in which the students individually could choose a novel from eleven books – half of them graphic novels – every boy chose a graphic novel. For the development of ICC the results on the learning through teaching approach to graphic novels suggest that student teachers benefit strongly from their involvement in teaching graphic novels. All these positive results of the Reading Project are rather strong arguments in favour of the use of graphic novels as one type of multimodal text in EFL classes. Hopefully the results will encourage teachers to integrate graphic novels in their English lessons more often.

Bibliography

Abel, J. (2006), *La Perdida*. New York: Pantheon.

Satrapi, M. (2003), *Persepolis: The Story of a Childhood and The Story of a Return*. Transl. Anjali Singh. London: Vintage.

References

Carney, R. N. and Levin, J. R. (2002), 'Pictorial illustrations still improve students' learning from text', *Educational Psychology Review*, 14(1), 5–26.

Carter, J. B. (2008), 'Comics, the canon, and the classroom', in N. Frey and D. Fisher (eds), *Teaching Visual Literacy Using Comic Books, Graphic Novels, Anime, Cartoons, and More to Develop Comprehension and Thinking Skills*. Thousand Oaks, CA: Corwin, pp. 47–60.

Chute, H. (2008), 'Comics as literature? Reading graphic narrative', *PMLA*, 123(2), 452–65.

Frey, N. and Fisher, D. (2008), 'Introduction', in N. Frey and D. Fisher (eds), *Teaching Visual Literacy Using Comic Books, Graphic Novels, Anime, Cartoons, and More to Develop Comprehension and Thinking Skills*. Thousand Oaks, CA: Corwin, pp. 1–4.

Gosch, C. and Hany, E. (2006), *Interkulturelles Verständnis aus entwicklungspsychologischer Perspektive: Was Kinder und Jugendliche von Kultur wissen und verstehen*. Erfurt: Universität Erfurt.

Hallet, W. (2010), 'Romane lesen lernen', *Der fremdsprachliche Unterricht Englisch*, 44(107), 2–8.

KMK (2003), *Bildungsstandards für die erste Fremdsprache (Englisch/Französisch) für den Mittleren Schulabschluss*. <db2.nibis.de/1db/cuvo/datei/bs_ms_kmk_erste_fremdsprache.pdf> 31 July 2010.

McCloud, S. (1993), *Understanding Comics: The Invisible Art*. New York: Kitchen Sink-Harper Perennial.

Nünning, A. (2007), 'Fremdverstehen und Bildung durch neue Weltansichten: Perspektivenvielfalt, Perspektivenwechsel und Perspektivenübernahme durch Literatur', in W. Hallet and A. Nünning (eds), *Neue Ansätze und Konzepte der Literatur- und Kulturdidaktik*. Trier: WVT, pp. 123–42.

Nünning, A. and Surkamp, C. (2006), *Englische Literatur unterrichten: Grundlagen und Methoden*. Seelze-Velber: Klett-Kallmeyer.

Tabachnick, S. (2009), 'Introduction', in S. Tabachnick (ed.), *Teaching the Graphic Novel*. New York: MLA, pp. 1–15.

Versaci, R. (2008), 'Literary literacy and the role of the comic book. Or, you teach a class on what?', in N. Frey and D. Fisher (eds), *Teaching Visual Literacy Using Comic Books, Graphic Novels, Anime, Cartoons, and More to Develop Comprehension and Thinking Skills*. Thousand Oaks, CA: Corwin, pp. 91–111.

12

'We are Britain!' Culture and Ethnicity in Benjamin Zephaniah's Novels

Sigrid Rieuwerts

It is argued in this chapter that the novels of this British-Caribbean author make ideal reading in the EFL classroom – they represent authentic reading material and enhance the pleasures of listening, reading and writing at school. Since Zephaniah is widely regarded as the face of a new, multicultural Britain, my particular focus is on the development of intercultural competence through the teaching of his novels.

Benjamin Zephaniah is high up on the official lists in Britain of 'authors every teenager should read' (*The Independent*, 2007). He is seen as representing the face of a new, multicultural Britain and as such his work is regarded as an extension of the traditional canon. The Britishness he promotes is inclusive, multicultural and multi-ethnic. Zephaniah identifies himself as a British-Caribbean author. Born in Handsworth, a multi-ethnic neighbourhood of Birmingham, to parents of the first generation of 'Empire Windrush', he grew up in the 'Other' Britain, a multi-ethnic, non-white Britain (see Zephaniah, 2011; also Parker, 2007 and Wilkins, 1999). Only when his family moved to a poor white working-class area did he understand what it meant to be black and Jamaican. He felt discriminated against and the scars of a brick thrown at him in a racist attack are still visible today. Small wonder therefore that 'Otherness' and the problems of race relations are recurrent themes in his work. Time and again he argues for an extension of the concept of Britishness – so for example in his introduction to his children's poetry anthology called *We are Britain!*:

> The British are not a single tribe, or a single religion, and we don't come from a single place. But we are building a home where we are all able to be who we want to be, yet still be British. That is what we do: we take, we adapt, and we move forward. We are the British. We are Britain! (Zephaniah, 2002, unpaginated)

In *We are Britain!*, 13 young children with diverse backgrounds introduce themselves in rhymes and pictures and thus give a face and a story to the British. Their contributions are designed to answer the question: 'Who are the British?'

Ask us, and you will find that we dance to music from America, Africa and Asia; we eat food from Ireland, Italy and Jamaica; we speak more than three-hundred languages and we know over four-hundred different ways to cook a potato. We look Celtic, Arab and Bengali; we wear kilts, saris and football shorts; and if you get very close to us and look right into our eyes, you can almost see the history of the whole world. (Zephaniah, 2002, introduction)

Ethnicity is not only a matter of differences and cultural commonalities but it is also a matter of categorization and at times discrimination. It is this divide between 'us' and 'them' and the potential for racism that Zephaniah attacks in his poetry and prose. Although I will focus exclusively on his novels, it is worth pointing out that his mission to extend the concept of Britishness is prevalent in all his work.

To look beyond the face

Face is his first novel, written for a young readership and published in 1999. It was hailed as a ground-breaking novel about prejudice, forcing you 'to look beyond the face / To see the person true' (Zephaniah, 1999b, p. 208). Zephaniah was already a well-established poet when he conceived the idea of writing a novel about prejudice and racism without the colour of the skin playing any role in it. In order to make the topic more accessible to a wider readership, he opted for the story of a burn victim. 'I wondered what prejudices a person with a disfigured face would come across. Was discrimination by face the same as discrimination by race? Was he ever bullied? What does real beauty mean? Who were his friends and lovers? These were the issues I wanted to explore in *Face*' (Zephaniah, 1999a).

The story is set in East Ham and Newington, London's multicultural East End. It is the area, as the narrator explains, where 'in the sixteenth century French Protestant refugees called Huguenots settled (. . .), then Germans, Chinese, Vietnamese, Jews and Poles (. . .) and the latest arrivals were Caribbeans, Africans, Asians and Bosnians' (Zephaniah, 1999b, p. 15). The main character Martin, however, is white and seems to be largely unaware of the people from many different cultures that live in his neighbourhood. The 'Gang of Three' as Martin and his two friends, Matthew and Mark, call themselves, had 'a reputation for mischief making and playing tricks, (. . .) for chasing girls' (Zephaniah, 1999b, p. 9) and for pushing people around. Gangs, drugs and violence were part of their lifestyle and even racist remarks were not out of the ordinary if they could get away with it. Yet 'Martin knew that there was no way he would get away with a racist remark here. The group they had been talking to had ethnic origins that ranged from the Philippines, to Africa and Bosnia and he was not going to upset any of them' (Zephaniah, 1999b, p. 27).

One day this is all going to change. Martin makes one wrong decision, gets caught up in a joy-riding accident and the facial injuries he sustains change his life forever. While he starts on his long journey of rehabilitation, his lover and his friends leave him. He also has difficulties in dealing with the reactions to his new appearance, let alone with accepting his disfigurement. Before the crash Martin was a good-looking, fashion-conscious, happy-go-lucky young student; a chancer living for the moment. After that fateful night, he is confused and in emotional and physical pain. The world he knew has fallen apart for him. Martin finds himself 'othered' and is forced to confront a sense of estrangement and discrimination. On his long journey towards self-acceptance he becomes sensitized to the prejudices of others and he, a white boy, starts to connect afresh with those around him, black and white.

Martin's changing fate and attitude lend themselves to practising changing perspectives and role play in the English foreign language classroom. While *Face* is listed on the national curriculum for Year 9 in England, teaching this novel in Year 10 is more appropriate in the EFL classroom in Germany, given the difficulties some students might have with the occasional colloquialisms from East London. These are minor problems, however, for generally speaking, students will find it easy to relate to the narrative. Some teachers tend to have doubts concerning the educational value of the book. However, their concerns are often motivated by political rather than educational considerations as the following remark in a teacher's forum on 'teachit. co.uk' reveals. Asked why *Face* is not worth teaching, one teacher replied:

> Because it's fashionable, middle class twaddle, that's why. If boors like Zephaniah hate their adopted country so much, then why are they here? Answer: because they like being in a civilized, industrialized nation, where the arts and humanities matter (. . .). Stuff like his – and all that appalling 'other cultures' stuff in the anthologies – is, at root, a sham. (St. Paul, 5 May 2008)

To teach ' "other cultures" stuff' may not be to everybody's liking, but it is part of the curriculum in the United Kingdom, Germany and other countries. It is precisely this 'otherness' that students need to learn about, and Zephaniah is giving the issue a voice in his teenage novels. He does not shy away from the big issues of today.

An inclusive Britain?

'"Welcome to England, Mr Kelo," said the immigration officer as he handed back the passports to Alem's father. Alem stared up at the tall officer; the officer looked down at Alem. "Have a good holiday now" ' (Zephaniah, 2001, p. 11). This is the beginning of *Refugee Boy* – a powerful, angry book about Alem, a 14-year-old African boy, who finds himself stranded in England. His father had not come to England to have a good holiday as the customs officer and Alem himself expected, instead Mr Kelo wanted his son to seek refuge in England from the war between Ethiopia and Eritrea. Alem's life is at risk in Africa for with an Ethiopian father and an Eritrean mother, he was not welcome in either place. In fact, as the family lay sleeping one night, soldiers had kicked down the door of the house, entered waving their rifles erratically and asking them to leave. When Alem finds himself alone in a foreign country he is shocked and bewildered, asking himself whether this was meant to be some kind of rite-of-passage thing and he wonders about his parents: 'Was bringing him to England really the best thing to do? Did they really love him or was this a plan to get rid of him? Would they

care so much about his upbringing, his health, his education and then dump him?'
(Zephaniah, 2001, p. 33). He soon realizes that he is not welcome in England either,
even when he learns that his mother has been murdered. When his asylum is refused,
his friends organize a series of protests and an appeal. Only after his father is murdered
too, after he had managed to come back to 'safety' in England, is he allowed to stay in
Britain due to 'exceptional circumstances' (Zephaniah, 2001, p. 288).

The novel is set in England in the 1990s and although the name of the conflict
might have changed, its main theme – seeking refuge in a European country – is
as topical as ever. With his teenage novel, Zephaniah is addressing the cognitive,
emotional and ethical dimensions of asylum seeking and this makes *Refugee Boy* an
ideal novel to read in the EFL classroom. It shows the interconnectedness of the world
and the global challenges we are facing today. As Jill Murphy (2001) writes in a review
of the novel:

> *Refugee Boy* is a fantastic story on a personal level, telling of individual courage,
> of the capacity of the young to overcome and, despite the frighteningly sad things
> which happen, it is a story of hope, and of looking forward and of the value and
> potential of friendship and community. It's beautifully, vividly written and a very
> personal perspective on one of today's big issues.

It is this very personal perspective on one of today's big issues that appeals to teenagers,
and teaching ideas should include these personal and wider issues. Especially the
teaching of wider, political issues will benefit from project work on refugees and
asylum – these can best be explored in pre- and post-reading sessions.

Given the many opportunities to respond to the text, writing skills lend themselves
as focus for while-reading activities. For Year 9 or 10, the following exercises are
designed to practise style and diction in response to the issues of the novel:

– Describe Alem's journey 'Out of Africa . . . Into England' in a creative way.
– Write Alem's first letter to his parents after he finds himself abandoned in England.
– Write Alem's letter to his friends in Africa after he learns that his mother was
  killed and that he cannot go back (just yet).
– Read the report by Heaven Crawley ('Chance or choice? Understanding why
  asylum seekers come to the UK') and summarize its findings.
– Write a letter of appeal to the Home Secretary on behalf of Alem and his father,
  asking that they are given asylum in England.
– Design a campaign poster and make sure that it contains a catchy phrase.
– Write a newspaper article about Alem and his family.
– Write a character study of Alem.

These activities take up the themes of the book, but a more focused approach on 'Life
in Britain' (e.g. in the form of Alem's diary account) helps to engage the students in
transcultural and intercultural discourses. The community that Alem becomes part
of in East London is a multi-ethnic and multicultural society that understands his
problems with acculturation and his legal predicament. In particular, when Alem

reflects on his life in Africa and compares it to his experience in England, students are not only engaged by adopting this 'very personal perspective', but they will also have to reflect on Alem's problems with ethnic boundaries and the legal interpretation of them. What divides 'us' from 'them' is in this case partly our perception of race and ethnicity and as such part of our identification, classification and interpretation of self and other, but also partly a decision in court, made in the name of the British people. In *Refugee Boy*, it is clearly marked as a wrong decision that 'the state believes that the appellant faces no personal threat if he were returned to his country' (Zephaniah, 2001, p. 149). These are the wider, political issues the novel addresses.

Also worth exploring in the EFL classroom are issues of intercultural competence especially since intercultural communicative competence is a key element of English language teaching and can well be achieved through the teaching of literature (see Nünning, 2007). Adopting Byram's model (1997), Alem's engagement with the other culture and his ability to deal with cultural differences can be described as a development of intercultural competence. Initially he lacks the knowledge and the skill of interpreting and relating – examples are his initial response to the English weather and his misinterpretation that every cloud signifies rain (Zephaniah, 2001, p. 15) as well as his inability to relate to different British dialects (Zephaniah, 2001, pp. 18–20). In addition, skills of interaction are also at play in his discovery of the sounds of London: 'Can you hear the nothing, Father? There are no animal noises – no birds, no donkeys, no hyenas, nothing.' As he finished speaking, a car roared through the streets. ' "I don't think they have so many wild animals here, only wild drivers in loud cars," his father replied' (Zephaniah, 2001, p. 26).

Similarly, he cannot understand that a room full of books does not translate into an 'amount of knowledge' (Zephaniah, 2001, p. 94) or 'why some kids would play truant when they had the privilege of going to school. School was preparation for the future, as far as Alem was concerned, and he had no intention of going into the future unprepared' (Zephaniah, 2001, p. 124). Here the development of critical cultural awareness is recognizable. Alem is fascinated with the opportunities in Britain and cannot come to terms with its reality nor indeed can he identify with his British classmates' laziness, self-preoccupation and their unwillingness to prepare for adult life. He has developed a critical cultural awareness and remains true to himself. When almost at the end of this novel a policeman suggests a more British-sounding name to him, he insists on his African birth name.

'It's Alem.'

'Al-em – I'm sorry, can I call you Alan or Al maybe?'

'No,' Alem replied firmly, 'my name is not Alan, it's Alem'. (Zephaniah, 2001, p. 284)

He is no longer the shy refugee boy who does not understand what is happening to him. ' "Everything is politics" he explains to his father. "We are here because of politics, the judge is there because of politics, and we are being sent home because of politics"' (Zephaniah, 2001, p. 239). He feels strongly about his right to live and be protected –

he is fighting a Britain that does not live up to its own standards. He is arguing for an inclusive Britain.

In London's multicultural East End

Ethnicity and race are also prominent features in *Gangsta Rap*. Zephaniah's third novel, published in 2004, follows the real life story of the rap artist Tupac Shakur, drawing at the same time also upon his own story as a drop-out, involved in gang warfare who later made it through music and music-making.

The plot evolves around Ray, a teenage boy who is frequently in trouble at school and at home with his younger sister and parents. When he is eventually expelled from school after he has broken every rule in the book, he joins his two previously expelled friends Prem and Tyrone and roams the streets of London. They find it difficult to fit in and attract a lot of trouble. 'So what your parents gonna say? Did they threaten to send you back to the Caribbean like mine were going to send me to India? Prem asked' (Zephaniah, 2004, p. 20). He himself comes from 'a working-class, trying hard to be middle-class, Indian family' (Zephaniah, 2004, p. 21) and his parents feel 'very let down by their only son leaning towards black culture and by his indifference to education' (Zephaniah, 2004, pp. 21–2). Also Ray's father is disappointed by his son and calls him 'a failure' (Zephaniah, 2004, p. 31). Yet while he refuses to talk to his son about it, Tyrone's parents try everything from talking to threatening to beatings to church-going, they even consider sending him to relatives in Trinidad, but they cannot control him. Thus, they only have each other and since Ray, Tyrone and Prem all share a passion for hip-hop music, they spend most of their time in a local music shop. The owner is 'a Jamaican-born reformed bad boy who weighed nineteen stone before breakfast' (Zephaniah, 2004, p. 15) and is known to all as Marga Man. To the three drop-outs, he is a sort of father-figure who is in tune with their way of life and listens, but would also give them a piece of his mind, especially when he finds their attitude or behaviour unacceptable.

> Marga Man turned the volume of the music down low and folded his arms. 'What you mean, all three of yu now not going school?' His voice was deep, his accent heavy Jamaican, the type of voice that had never made any attempt to sound more English. 'Listen, all I know is dat if you three roam de streets is trouble, yeah man, big trouble, and de tax payer will not foot de bill'. (Zephaniah, 2004, p. 17)

With the help of Marga Man and a Social Inclusion Project, the three boys eventually turn their lives around and do what they always dreamed off: produce their own hip-hop music and become a successful band. School, what school? 'My name is X-Ray-X, / (. . .) / The teacher kicked me out of the classroom / Now I'm rapping in the Rex' (Zephaniah, 2004, p. 137):

> We are the Positive Negatives
> We live the Hip-Hop philosophy

So if you wanna live
You gotta know not to fuck with we,
We come out of the East
Where we are not ethnic minorities
So just leave us in peace
We are the immoral majority. (Zephaniah, 2004, p. 138)

British hip-hop is the music of resistance, the angry music on the streets of East London, mainly performed by young men with an ethnic Caribbean background. But as Ray explains at a press conference, hip-hop is not about violence. 'Hip-hop is a philosophy, hip-hop is about the way we live, it's about the way we see life. We are outsiders and we survive by creating new families for ourselves' (Zephaniah, 2004, p. 226).

Once they find their own voice, produce their first CD and are generally at peace with themselves and society, they are drawn into violence and gang warfare with another London hip-hop band. But the ending of the novel is almost too patronizing. All is well in the end and the guns are silent again and they all 'dance to true hip-hop' (Zephaniah, 2004, p. 335). The underlying question of the novel is whether children from ethnic minorities are failing school or whether schools are failing these children. Zephaniah opts for the latter.

Nothing is what it seems

Benjamin Zephaniah's latest novel, *Teacher's Dead*, was published in 2007. As with his previous novels, it is primarily aimed at teenagers. The way in which Zephaniah for example describes 'The Crime Scene' in chapter two may serve to illustrate this point. It is written from the perspective and the life-setting of a teenage boy and thus very engaging.

My name is Jackson Jones. I stood and watched a teacher die. For the first time in my life I felt real shock. I didn't panic. I just froze. I wanted to walk away but I couldn't. I was the quickest at the one hundred metres in my year, I had only been beaten once in the long jump, and my reflexes were sharp, but all that stuff was useless. My whole body actually went numb. They say the brain is like a computer – well, my computer crashed. (Zephaniah, 2007, p. 7)

Jackson is a deep-thinking and intelligent 15-year-old who is trying to come to terms with seeing his teacher murdered by two boys (Lionel and Ramzi) of his own age. What he saw was not going to go away. When others stop asking questions and settle on the explanation that both boys came from broken homes – the media headline read: 'Fatherless Killers' (Zephaniah, 2007, p. 12) – Jackson begins to think and embark on the quest for the story behind the headlines. He himself is growing up without ever having seen his father: 'I didn't even know who he was, but that didn't make me evil. I'd been alive for fifteen years and I'd never felt the need to kill someone because I didn't have a dad' (Zephaniah, 2007, p. 13). When Jackson starts his own investigation after the case is officially closed, he is confronted not only with a wall of silence but also with prejudice and some big issues (like cruelty to animals and bullying) that led to the stabbing in the first place. In the end, nothing is as straightforward as it first appeared and Zephaniah's dedication 'for the truth, and the seekers of truth' is also an open invitation not to accept everything you have been told but to remain critical.

From a teacher's point of view this book makes ideal reading in the EFL classroom. First, the mission the main protagonist sets himself provides the students with a task in a natural context for language use. The information that slowly comes to light in the course of the novel can be organized as an information-gap activity. Teams are given specific lines of inquiry (passages in the book) that need to be worked on and the information must then be exchanged with other teams in order to complete the task. Secondly, bullying is one of the major themes in *Teacher's Dead* and this is ideal for project work. Students are given the challenge to come up with a series of possible solutions for eradicating bullying. Thirdly, remaining critical, especially in connection with the media coverage of one and the same event, is another point worth pursuing (see Rieuwerts, 2009), either as project work or as a close reading of the instances in the book where 'nothing is what is seems'.

With *Teacher's Dead* as with his previous novels, Zephaniah rides straight 'through everybody's taboo and everybody's prejudices' (Murphy, 2007). All his novels are powerful and hard-hitting real-life novels that are informed by his own experience of racism and injustice in London's notorious East End. It is a poor and diverse area that many people forget about when they talk about Britain. Time and again he complains about racial discrimination in Britain and gets involved in the debate on multiculturalism. 'Anybody who knows anything about Britain knows that you are five times more likely to be stopped and searched by the police if you are African-Caribbean' (Zephaniah, 2005, p. 12) he complains in 'What am I going on about?', the introduction to his book of poetry called *Too Black, Too Strong*. With rare understanding, Zephaniah addresses questions of culture and ethnicity. Today, with the recent riots in Britain, Zephaniah's novels about life of teenagers in London are more topical than ever. Not only his poetry but also his novels comment on his own community in true Jamaican dub tradition. He deliberately uses real street names in his novels so that his community, the local East Enders, living in London E7, are able to recognize it as their world. In his novels he depicts their lives, their griefs and their joys – indeed he argues, this is also Britain. 'We are Britain' – a multicultural and ethnically diverse Britain.

While Zephaniah's children's book *We are Britain!* celebrates a multicultural Britain, his novels portray the darker side of 'otherness'. When he argues in *Too Black, Too Strong* for an inclusive concept of Britishness, he sees himself as a cultural ambassador at home and abroad: '[Britain] is probably one of the only places that can take an angry, illiterate, uneducated, ex-hustler, rebellious Rastafarian and give him the opportunity to represent the country' (Zephaniah, 2005, p. 12). His outspoken views on discrimination and injustice offer incisive commentaries on Britain today; and since Zephaniah's teenage novels also embody youth culture, it makes them accessible in an educational context. His passionate plea for a multi-ethnic and multicultural Britain has made a valuable contribution to a multicultural and anti-racist education.

Bibliography

Zephaniah, B. (1999a), 'Face – Inspiration: Where did the idea of the book come from?'
    Accessible at www.benjaminzephaniah.com/content/205.php
— (1999b), *Face*. London: Bloomsbury.
— (2001), *Refugee Boy*. London: Bloomsbury.
— (2002), *We are Britain!* London: Frances Lincoln.
— (2004), *Gangsta Rap*. London: Bloomsbury.
— (2005), 'What am I going on about?', in B. Zephaniah (ed.), *Too Black, Too Strong*. Tarset:
    Bloodaxe Books, pp. 9–14.
— (2007), *Teacher's Dead*. London: Bloosmbury.
— (2011), *Benjamin Zephaniah: My Story*. Illustrated by Victor Ambrus. London:
    HarperCollins. Accessible at www.benjaminzephaniah.com

References

Anon (2007), 'The authors every teenager should read', *The Independent* (12 July).
Byram, M. (1997), *Teaching and Assessing Intercultural Communicative Competence*.
    Clevedon: Multilingual Matters.
Crawley, H. (2010), 'Chance or choice? Understanding why asylum seekers come to the
    UK'. Accessible at www.refugeecouncil.org.uk/policy/position/2010/18jan2010
Murphy, J. (2001), 'Review: Refugee boy'. Accessible at www.thebookbag.co.uk/reviews/
    index. php?title=Refugee_Boy_by_Benjamin_Zephaniah
— (2007), 'Review: Teacher's dead'. Accessible at www.thebookbag.co.uk/reviews/index.
    php/ Teacher's_Dead_by_Benjamin_Zephaniah
Nünning, A. (2007), 'Fremdverstehen und Bildung durch neue Weltansichten:
    Perspektivenvielfalt, Perspektivenwechsel und Perspektivenübernahme durch Literatur',
    in W. Hallet and A. Nünning (eds), *Neue Ansätze und Konzepte der Literatur- und
    Kulturdidaktik*. Trier: WVT Wissenschaftlicher Verlag Trier, pp. 123–42.
Parker, V. (2007), *Writers Uncovered: Benjamin Zephaniah*. Oxford: Heinemann.
Rieuwerts, S. (2009), ' "How do you like your Truth? . . . How do you like your Youth?"
    Teaching Benjamin Zephaniah's Teacher's Dead', in B. Reitz (ed.), *Essays in Honour
    of Peter Erlebach and Thomas M. Stein*. Trier: WVT Wissenschaftlicher Verlag Trier,
    pp. 125–38.
Wilkins, V. (1999), *Benjamin Zephaniah: A Profile*. Black Profiles. London: Northwood.
    Accessible at www.teachit.co.uk.

13

Taiwanese Adolescents Reading American Young Adult Literature: A Reader Response Study

Li-Feng Lee

Introduction

Including literary texts in the English as a second language (ESL) or English as a foreign language (EFL) classroom is not a new concept (British Council, 2008). Some scholars particularly advocate the use of children's and young adult literature with ESL or EFL students at different levels (Custodio et al., 1998; Ghosn, 2002). This is not only because such literature can be more accessible to young and adolescent English students in terms of age appropriateness and language complexity, but also because there are at least three benefits that reading literature can bring about: (1) literature offers a rich source of linguistic input and facilitates the integration of skills; (2) literature engages students, gives them the pleasure of reading and thus motivates them for language learning; and (3) literature helps to develop students' understanding and awareness of cultural differences and to broaden their perspectives of other cultures as well as their own (British Council, 2008; Custodio et al., 1998; Ghosn, 2002).

Some scholars have documented their efforts at using children's or young adult literature with English learners (e.g. Ho, 2000; Watts, 1999), and some have reported effects of reading such literature on students' language development and reading motivation (e.g. Cho et al., 1994; Ho, 2000). However, few studies have investigated the nature of EFL students' literary experience, let alone how such experience can contribute to their development of intercultural understanding and awareness.

To fill this lack of knowledge, this study was conducted to explore and describe Taiwanese EFL adolescents' literary responses and cross-cultural awareness when they read American young adult literature (YAL) in an after-school book club for a six-week period. Specifically, the study attempted to answer the following two questions: (1) How did Taiwanese adolescents make meaning from the selected American short stories for young adults? (2) What were the characteristics of the adolescents' cross-cultural awareness?

Theoretical framework

The theoretical framework that informed this study was based on three areas: reader response theories, second language acquisition (SLA) theories and multicultural literature.

Reader response theories

For reader response theorists, meaning is not found in the text but is constructed by the reader in transaction with the text by drawing on his or her linguistic-experiential reservoirs. Transactional reader response theorists focus on the transaction between the reader and the text and characterize this dynamic meaning-making process in different terms. For Rosenblatt (1994, p. 30), reading literature is an event, a 'lived-through experience'. For Benton (1992, p. 18), reading a story is the realization of a 'secondary world'. Similarly, Langer (1995, p. 9) defined reading as an 'envisionment building' process. It is such a 'lived-through experience' or virtual experience of the 'secondary world' that engages readers and gives them the pleasure of reading.

Recently, literary response scholars have examined response through sociocultural perspectives, and response to literature is regarded as a cultural practice (Galda et al., 2001; Lewis, 2001). Simply put, readers respond to literature according to certain 'subject positions' which they acquire through socialization by cultural institutions, and which they act out in various cultural practices. When readers respond, they take positions appropriate to their gender, class, race and other social roles, and thus define and construct their subjectivities, revealing their membership to certain cultural groups.

Second language acquisition theories

Krashen's (1982, 1985, 2003) SLA theories, especially his acquisition/learning hypothesis, input/comprehension hypothesis and affective-filter hypothesis, are often cited to support the use of authentic literature with English learners. For Krashen (1985), language acquisition is a subconscious process, and we acquire language only when we understand messages, that is, when we obtain 'comprehensible input'. In addition to language factors, characteristics of comprehensible input include contextual clues, topics students have prior knowledge about or topics that are interesting and meaningful to students. Moreover, the affective filter determines how comprehensible input is going to be processed. Students with a higher affective filter tend to seek less input.

Krashen (1985) accordingly emphasized the importance of authentic texts and meaningful tasks because the focus is on meaning rather than on form. He also suggested that using extended texts can provide more contextual clues for comprehensible input. Finally, he highlighted the importance of a low-anxiety environment because it lowers students' affective filter and increases the input they receive.

In light of Krashen's theories, using YAL with EFL adolescents should be appropriate because (1) these are authentic texts, (2) they are extended texts with interesting and meaningful topics, and (3) the response-centred approach to reading YAL (i.e. reading for pleasure) can help to create a low-anxiety environment.

Multicultural literature

The assumptions concerning response to literature from other countries or about people of other cultures are grounded within a broad frame of multicultural literature. The intercultural reason for using literary texts with EFL students is also a goal that educators try to achieve through multicultural literature (Dressel, 2003; Landt, 2006). In fact, when EFL students read the target language literature, they are indeed reading across cultures.

Research on response to multicultural literature also helped to shape my theoretical framework. Studies have shown that cultural differences do not interfere with readers' engagement in reading literature of other cultures (Altieri, 1995; Ho, 1990). Studies have also demonstrated that intercultural understanding could be achieved through reading multicultural literature (Dressel, 2005; Enriquez, 2001; Lehr et al., 2000) or foreign literature (Stover et al., 1990). In particular, Enriquez (2001) discovered that the process of ESL adolescents' understanding of different cultures tends to undergo a progression of making sense and reflecting.

Method

This study adopted a qualitative research design because qualitative research methods are generally deemed appropriate for uncovering complexities of meaning or the nature of experience (Glesne, 2010).

Research context and participants

The study was conducted in a public junior-senior high school in a metropolitan area in southern Taiwan. Most students were from middle- and lower-middle classes. The school curriculum was strictly oriented towards preparing students for college education. Since there was no way for the study to fit into the established curriculum, the main part of the study was conducted in an after-school book club in a schoolroom.

Purposeful sampling was used in this study, and the selection criteria were students' English reading ability (intermediate or upper levels) and their willingness to express their responses honestly in writing and orally. Six girls volunteered to join the study, and all of them were from the 11th grade Honors Language Class, which ensured that their English reading ability met the criteria of this study. On the pre-study questionnaire, all participants identified themselves as diligent students and avid readers. Most of them studied English only with the aim of passing the College Entrance Exam, and their English reading experience was limited to textbooks and language learning magazines. Overall, their understanding of American culture seemed quite shallow and limited to holidays.

Literature selection

Six realistic American short stories for young adults were used in this study. The selection criteria were readability, age appropriateness and literary quality (Vardell et al., 2006). All the stories were selected from the titles on the ALA (American Library Association) Best Books for Young Adults Lists and, based on my teaching experience, would match the 11th graders' language level and interests. The story topics included child–parent relationship, boy–girl relationship, friendship, peer pressure, work experience and teenage pregnancy.

Data collection and procedures

Every week participants read one story at home and kept a response journal, following the guidelines for journal writing that Benton (1992, p. 35) developed for use with adolescents. Then students brought their response journals to our weekly meeting to talk about their responses to the story they had read that week. Our discussion lasted about 50 minutes each time. I adopted Chambers' (1996) 'Tell me' approach as the framework for discussion, and I led the discussion by asking response-centred, open-ended questions. Individual interviews with each participant were conducted at the beginning, in the middle and at the end of the study in order to clarify their written and oral responses. All the literature discussions and individual interviews were audio-taped, transcribed and analysed.

Data analysis

Data were analysed to answer the research questions. Data sources included response journals, group discussions and semi-structured individual interviews. Part of my coding scheme was adapted from Benton et al. (1985) in terms of literary responses and from Enriquez (2001) in terms of cultural awareness. The same data were analysed twice, first for literary response types and patterns, and secondly, cultural awareness. The unit of analysis was a message unit, a focused thought, which varied in length, ranging from one to several sentences to one paragraph. The constant comparative method was employed throughout the process of data analysis in order to define and refine the coded concepts or categories.

Results

Three major categories emerged from data analysis of students' literary responses: interacting, interpreting and evaluating. Table 13.1 displays the frequency and percentages of response categories. The majority of students' responses were coded as 'interpreting', with 50.9% of their responses in response journals and 68.8% in group discussions. Each major category encompassed several subcategories, which referred to the mental activities that each major response category involved. Table 13.2 provides the description of coded response categories.

Table 13.1 Frequency and percentages of categories of literary responses in response journals and group discussions

Response categories	Response journals	Group discussions	Totals
Interacting	42 (32.3)	33 (19.8)	75 (25.2)
Interpreting	66 (50.8)	115 (68.9)	181 (60.9)
Evaluating	22 (16.9)	19 (11.4)	41 (13.8)
Totals	130 (43.8)	167 (56.2)	297 (100.0)

Table 13.2 Categories of literary responses in relation to response activities

Response categories	Response activities
Interacting	Picturing
	Associating
	Predicting and speculating
	Becoming emotionally involved
Interpreting	Describing, explaining and judging the character
	Determining thematic meanings and making generalizations
Evaluating	Evaluating the story on the basis of its subject matter
	Evaluating the story as a literary work of art

Interacting

When the students interacted with the text, they tried to build up the storyworld by drawing on their prior language knowledge, personal life experience and intertextual connections to other literary and cultural texts. They were engaged in various response activities: picturing, associating, predicting and speculating, and becoming emotionally involved. For example, Jane (all student names are pseudonyms) associated the story 'Dead End' (Anaya, 1993) with her personal life experience. In the story, the protagonist Maria was under a lot of peer pressure. Jane wrote in her response journal:

> The story reminded me of what happened in my junior high school life. At that time, those playful boys and girls in my class always regarded the diligent students as an eyesore. Seeing the diligent students studying, they would say something that made you feel bad, something like, 'Study, study, and study. All you know to do every day is study, and nothing else'. It really made me feel bad. (Jane, Journal 3)

Interpreting

This category of responses involved students' interpretation of the storyworld as they assessed characters' behaviour and defined thematic meanings. Sometimes they described and explained characters' behaviour in terms of characters' motives and feelings, based on textual clues, and such responses were coded as 'descriptive'. At other times, students stated whether they liked or disliked the characters, approved or disapproved of their behaviour, by drawing on their own cultural values as judgmental criteria. Such responses were coded as 'judgmental'. In students' response journals, of all interpretive responses concerning characters, 15% were descriptive and 85% were judgmental. Moreover, among their judgmental responses, their likes and approvals were found to be outnumbered by their dislikes and disapprovals in the proportion of one to three.

In the following example, Kelly's questions about the character's motive demonstrated her strong disapproval of the heroine's choice to lead a corrupt life because it was illegal and immoral.

> Why did the heroine want to be like the other girls who smoked dope? Smoking dope is obviously a wrong thing. I felt that Maria seemed to suffer a lot, and that she was struggling as to whether she wanted to go with the crowd, leading a corrupt life just like others. But what was there to consider after all? It is strange! (Kelly, Journal 3)

When students made thematic statements about a story or applied the thematic messages to life in general, their responses tended to be moralistic or didactic. For example, Jane wrote in her journal that she learned two lessons from the story entitled 'Lessons' (Sachs, 1997). The first was 'Do not hate others', and the second was 'Life's meaning lies in how you live, not how long you live' (Journal 5). Jane also felt inclined to draw a moral lesson from 'My Sweet Sixteenth' (Wilkinson, 1993), writing 'I think the moral lesson of this story should be: being too liberal in attitude toward sex will bring about terrible consequences' (Journal 6).

Students' didactic orientation in determining story themes as moral platitudes was somewhat challenged and laid bare by 'My Sweet Sixteenth'. Some students felt that the author seemed to invite them to see the teenage pregnancy problem from a perspective that was deviant from their sociocultural frame. For example, when discussing about their responses to 'My Sweet Sixteenth', Vivian explained why she was having difficulty determining its thematic meanings:

> Chinese stories always present this topic in a scary way so that you would not dare to try something morally wrong. But in this story, Monique's life was not changed drastically by the incident. The result is quite different from those in Chinese stories. (Group Discussion 6)

Vivian's response illustrated that students' assumption about the designated thematic message was actually conditioned by their past experience of reading Chinese stories on similar topics.

Evaluating

In this category of response, students evaluated their literary experience, stating whether and how they liked or disliked the story. Students expressed favourable responses when the subject matter was dealt with in a way that reflected their concerns or needs. For example, Lindsey evaluated the story 'Dead End' positively in her journal because the main character's inner conflict reflected her own problem:

> Oh – how I love this story. It touched me deeply, especially when the main character was thinking about whether she wanted to be like other girls. I once wanted to be like them, wearing beautiful clothes and going shopping. (. . .) Finally, the main character did not choose to follow the other girls, and this is the part that I like most about the story. On the whole, this is a very positive story. I love it very much. (Lindsey, Journal 3)

Students also measured stories against some literary criteria, and they preferred stories with humour, action and a happy ending. For example, Vivian stated in her journal what she disliked about 'My Sweet Sixteenth', that the 'narrative was somewhat tedious and uninteresting, especially for the first few pages. It did not become "exciting" until the last few pages when it came to the description of Monique's birthday' (Journal 6).

Cultural awareness

Students' cultural awareness was categorized as background information, stereotyped conceptions, comparing and contrasting and reflective understanding.

Background information Sometimes students asked questions concerning the sociocultural background of the story to help them better understand the story. For example, they asked whether it is common for American children to call parents by their first names or whether Americans apply as much value to diplomas as people in Taiwan do. Such questions were not the major issues in the stories, but, for these students who were not familiar with American culture, they couldn't help wondering.

Stereotyped conceptions Students' responses also revealed their stereotyped conceptions about the American sociocultural context. Most of the participants commented that the culture represented in the text confirmed their previous impressions that American people are more liberal and open-minded than Taiwanese, and that American teenagers are more mature and independent. Students' stereotyped conceptions were often found in their responses to the topics of teenage drug problem and sexual relationship in 'Dead End' and 'My Sweet Sixteenth' and work experience in 'Lessons'.

Comparing and contrasting Most instances of students' cultural awareness were revealed when they made comparisons and contrasts between their own culture and American culture in order to make sense of characters and their actions. They found that American adolescents face similar developmental problems just like themselves, such as peer pressure, parent–child relationship and boy–girl relationship. For example, 'Dead End' reflected a dilemma that these students were often faced with. Like the protagonist Maria, they found it difficult to decide whether 'to insist on one's own ideals' or 'to go with the crowd' (Anne, Interview 3).

The students also found cross-cultural differences in the ways people react to the same problems. For example, the students found that American parents, as represented in 'I've Got Gloria' (Kerr, 1997) and 'She' (Guy, 1984), were less authoritarian figures and gave children more respect and freedom. The following discussion shows a contrast they made:

Lindsey:	Scott's father admitted his attitude toward Scott was bad, right? I was thinking, if they were Chinese people, nobody would admit his own mistake. Chinese people are just like that.
Multiple voices:	Yeah, that's right.
Vivian:	Chinese parents would never admit their mistakes.
Lindsey:	Because Chinese are more authoritative. In foreign countries (America), kids are treated as equals and people are more willing to talk to kids.
Researcher:	You mean more democratic?
Lindsey:	That's right.
Anne:	It feels more like friends. They are more willing to listen to kids about what they really think. (Group Discussion 1)

Reflective understanding The final category of cultural awareness is composed of students' reflections upon the differences between their own culture and the one portrayed in the text. The students gained a new understanding and learned to adopt a broader view of culture as Lindsey stated in an interview:

I knew that one cultural difference between Western and Asian cultures is that we are more conservative and they are more liberal. There's nothing wrong with either side. But now that I have read these stories, I understand better the way they think and live, and in what ways they are more liberal. (Lindsey, Interview 3)

Students also learned to modify their initial impressions of American culture that they acquired from watching American movies. After reading the selected realistic short stories, the students learned that there are realities that differ from the always-positive, feel-good and pleasant reality that they had often seen in American movies. For example, Vivian pointed out some unpleasant reality about American education in an interview: 'It's not the "ideal American education" that we used to imagine. For example, Maria is very smart and capable, but she can't afford to go to a better school. I think their education system doesn't give poor people equal opportunities' (Interview, 3).

Responses like this indicated students' reflection upon their earlier perceptions of the ideal image of America. The experience of reading American YAL exposed students to different aspects of the society and invited them to reach a more balanced, broadened view of reality.

Discussions

The findings of this study support and extend existing reader response theories and research. In line with transactional reader response theories (Benton, 1992; Rosenblatt, 1994; Langer, 1995), this study found that the participants actively constructed meanings from the text by drawing on their past experience and knowledge. They were able to have a virtual experience through the text, interpret the characters and meanings of the fictional world and make an evaluation of their literary experience. In this way, the students' literary responses revealed their involvement and enjoyment in reading American YAL.

In addition, more than half of the participants' literary responses were interpretive, and the primary response mode was didactic. This finding echoes the studies by Cai (1992) and Ho (1990), both of whom found that Asian students tended to provide didactic or moralistic interpretations of characters and themes. This is probably because Asian cultures emphasize moral education and Asian students are taught to read for morals in literary works. In other words, the interpretive responses in this study greatly reflected readers' cultural values and the influence of schooling.

The findings of this study also unveil how the students increased their intercultural understanding as a result of reading literature. In agreement with Enriquez (2001), this study found that the students adopted a strategy of cognitive progression from wondering to reflection as they tried to understand a different culture. In this study, the students' cross-cultural awareness was especially apparent when they were interpreting characters' actions in terms of parent–child relationships and sexual relationships. To make sense of the characters' motivation and behaviour, the students applied their own cultural values to the characters. By testing out their own values against those of the characters, they were induced to reflect upon cultural differences. In this way, they increased their intercultural understanding and broadened their view of cultures.

Bibliography

Anaya, R. (1993), 'Dead end', in D. R. Gallo (ed.), *Join in: Multiethnic Short Stories by Outstanding Writers for Young Adults*. New York: Delacorte Press, pp. 101–26.

Guy, R. (1984), 'She', in D. R. Gallo (ed.), *Sixteen: Short Stories by Outstanding Writers for Young Adults*. New York: Delacorte Press, pp. 147–53.

Kerr, M. E. (1997), 'I've got Gloria', in D. R. Gallo (ed.), *No Easy Answers: Short Stories about Teenagers Making Tough Choices*. New York: Delacorte Press, pp. 67–78.

Sachs, M. (1997), 'Lessons', in A. Mazer (ed.), *Working Days: Short Stories about Teenagers at Work*. New York: Persea Books, pp. 72–82.

Wilkinson, B. (1993), 'My sweet sixteenth', in D. R. Gallo (ed.), *Join in: Multiethnic Short Stories by Outstanding Writers for Young Adults*. New York: Delacorte Press, pp. 128–41.

References

Altieri, J. L. (1995), 'Multicultural literature and multiethnic readers: Examining aesthetic involvement and preferences for text', *Reading Psychology: An International Quarterly*, 16, 43–70.

Benton, M. (1992), *Secondary Worlds: Literature Teaching and the Visual Arts*. Philadelphia: Open University Press.

Benton, M. and Fox, G. (1985), *Teaching Literature: Nine to Fourteen*. Oxford: Oxford University Press.

British Council (2008), *Teaching English Using Literature*. Accessed 14.04.12 at www.teachingenglish.org.uk/transform/teachers/specialist-areas/ using-literature-introduction

Cai, M. (1992), *Toward a Multi-Dimensional Model for the Study of Reader Response to Multicultural Literature*. PhD thesis, Ohio State University.

Chambers, A. (1996), *Tell Me: Children, Reading, and Talk*. Portland, ME: Stenhouse.

Cho, K.-S. and Krashen, S. D. (1994), 'Acquisition of vocabulary from the Sweet Valley Kids series: Adult ESL acquisition', *Journal of Reading*, 37(8), 662–7.

Custodio, B. and Sutton, M. J. (1998), 'Literature-based ESL for secondary school students', *TESOL Journal*, 7(5), 19–23.

Dressel, J. H. (2003), *Teaching and Learning about Multicultural Literature: Students Reading Outside their Culture in a Middle School Classroom*. Newark: International Reading Association.

— (2005), 'Personal response and social responsibility: Responses of middle school students to multicultural literature', *The Reading Teacher*, 58(8), 750–64.

Enriquez, G. (2001), 'Making meaning of cultural depictions: Using Lois Lowry's The Giver to reconsider what is "multicultural" about literature', *Journal of Children's Literature*, 27(1), 13–22.

Galda, L. and Beach, R. (2001), 'Response to literature as a cultural activity', *Reading Research Quarterly*, 36(1), 64–73.

Ghosn, I. (2002), 'Four good reasons to use literature in primary school ELT', *ELT Journal*, 56(2), 172–9.

Glesne, C. (2010), *Becoming Qualitative Researchers: An Introduction* (4th edn). Upper Saddle River, NJ: Prentice Hall.

Ho, L. (1990), 'Singapore readers' response to U.S. young adult fiction: Cross-cultural differences', *Journal of Reading*, 33(4), 252–8.

— (2000), 'Children's literature in adult education', *Children's Literature in Education*, 31(4), 259–71.

Krashen, S. (1982), *Principles and Practices of Second Language Acquisition*. Oxford: Pergamon.

— (1985), *The Input Hypothesis: Issues and Implications*. New York: Longman.

— (2003), *Explorations in Language Acquisition and Use: The Taipei Lectures*. Portsmouth, NH: Heinemann.

Landt, S. M. (2006), 'Multicultural literature and young adolescents: A kaleidoscope of opportunity', *Journal of Adolescent & Adult Literacy*, 49(8), 690–7.

Langer, J. A. (1995), *Envisioning Literature: Literary Understanding and Literature Instruction*. New York: Teachers College Press.

Lehr, S. and Thompson, D. L. (2000), 'The dynamic nature of response: Children reading and responding to Maniac Magee and The Friendship', *The Reading Teacher*, 53(6), 480–93.

Lewis, C. (2001), *Literary Practices as Social Acts: Power, Status, and Cultural Norms in the Classroom*. Mahwah, NJ: Lawrence Erlbaum.

Rosenblatt, L. M. (1994), *The Reader, the Text, the Poem: The Transactional Theory of the Literary Work*. Carbondale and Edwardsville: Southern Illinois University Press.

Stover, L. T. and Karr, R. (1990), 'Glasnost in the classroom: Likhanov's Shadows across the Sun', *English Journal*, 79(8), 47–53.

Vardell, S. M., Hadaway, N. L. and Young, T. A. (2006), 'Matching books and readers: Selecting literature for English learners', *The Reading Teacher*, 59(8), 734–41.

Watts, E. L. (1999), 'Using young adult literature with adolescent learners of English', *The ALAN Review*, 26, 25–30.

14

Developing Intercultural Competence through First Nations' Children's Literature

Grit Alter

Through reading children's and young adult fiction, students can engage in exciting adventures and explore other cultures and nations. Additionally, and some may argue more importantly, the appeal and potential of literature for children and young adults can be summarized by 'pleasure', as is done in Margaret Mackey's (2011) and Perry Nodelman and Mavis Reimer's (2003) publications. With the context of second language education, the literature serves as a source for the development of intercultural communicative competence (ICC) (Oliver, 1994; Brown et al., 1998; Willis, 1998; Nünning et al., 2008; Bredella, 2010). This is especially the case when the protagonists represent cultural entities that are different to the reader's. Literature, thus, provides insights into constructed secondary worlds, which 'may help readers develop empathy with and solidarity for the characters portrayed (. . .) (and the portrayal thus) also has a strong ethical dimension' (Delanoy, 2005, p. 57). The development of ICC and the quality of empathy strongly depend on the media to which children are exposed to, because based on a medium the reader receives a certain image of the represented culture and transfers this image into a construction of a perceived reality. One example in which fictional representation of otherness has led to a superficial and false image of otherness is the perceived and constructed knowledge of First Nations and Native Americans.

This chapter uncovers the problematic representation of First Nation and Native American cultures by analysing a selection of contemporary children's books with regard to their representation of the 'other' culture. That the representation of 'Indians'[1] or 'Savages', as they are called in the selected titles of children's fiction, is highly stereotypical and essentialized will be revealed by a comparison with titles written by First Nation and Native American authors. These will be suggested as alternatives that avoid the undifferentiated amalgamation of various indigenous cultures, as they allow readers to develop a more balanced picture of indigenous peoples of North America.

Distorted representation of 'otherness'

Three titles in which young readers find a rather superficial and demeaning representation of 'otherness' are to be presented and collectively discussed, a choice of which is based on availability and popularity. More attention is to be paid to books that are considered to be useful in a language-teaching context, and which involve raising awareness of other cultures. Among other places, in Rosa's and Barks' comic book *Uncle Scrooge Adventures*, Scrooge and his nephews travel to *The Land of the Pygmy Indians* and are part of the *War of the Wenidgo* (2007). Already on the cover of this double issue, two of the most common stereotypes are revealed when the Native Americans wear feathers in their hair and, with an aggressive facial expression, threaten to throw the visitors, Uncle Scrooge and his nephews into a river of crocodiles to kill them. The four main protagonists visit the village of the Natives during a back-to-nature trip that allows them to escape the busy city for a few days. It seems natural and fits the essentialized image of North American indigenous people that the village is untouched by modernity and civilization and that they live within a culture that has not developed for hundreds of years. When civilization threatens to destroy the natural way of life of the indigenous population, it is Scrooge and his nephews who have to support the Natives in their fight against Western influences and signs of progress. As the indigenous population is not able to help itself, the support and expertise of the civilized visitors is essential to their survival.

Ernest Seton's *Two Little Savages: The Adventures of the Two Boys who Lived as American Indians* tells the story of two boys, Yan and Sam, who after trouble with their families, find refuge in the woods where they independently enjoy the outdoors. Having to fend for themselves, they learn how to build a teepee, make a fire without matches, use the stars for orientation and read animal tracks. Additionally the two boys craft a drum and make their own arrows, which they use to kill animals. As the title of the adventure story suggests they do everything just as 'American Indians' would do it, and as Boy Scouts Yan and Sam find themselves on a great adventure imitating the 'American Indian's' lifestyle.

Daniel Farside's books series for young readers *The Adventures of One Feather* invites children to read about a boy, One Feather, and his 'tribe'. The reader learns about the need to make wise decisions in the face of peer pressure (*One Feather Takes a Leap of Friendship*, 2008a), experiences the challenges of an exciting mountain race (*The Race up Rattlesnake Mountain*, 2008b), and encounters the escape of dangerous bears (*Earning the Golden Feather*, 2008c). All three stories are set within the 'Kittywampa tribe' who live in the 'Valley of the Endless Breath' (Farside, 2008a, p. 1). The covers of all three volumes show that indigenous people never walk normally, but usually flee, race or hurry up trees, they are always in some kind of danger and have to escape. Additionally, they always wear feathers in their hair and are dressed in leather suits, which could already be interpreted as *progress* when considering that on the cover of *The Land of the Pygmy Indians* the 'Indians' are half naked, which supports the image of the 'Indian' as nature-loving and primitive.

What all these example texts have in common is the presentation of a highly stereotyped, essentialist and distorted image of North American indigenous people.

This is especially due to their representation as 'somewhat' in the past, the stories 'take place in an unidentified "sometime" and "somewhere" ' (Susemihl, 2008, p. 127). The covers, which usually show mountains, a river or a lake, and woods do not allow for any differentiation of the manifold aspects in which indigenous cultures are different. The general illustration of feathers and leather clothes allows for a generalized perception of *the* 'Indian' as a member of a culture without recognizing the different peoples' characteristics. This blending of different simplified cultural aspects of indigenous identities has been labelled as a 'pan-Indian mash' (Lutz, 2002, p. 53), which prevents the establishment of a balanced view on cultural otherness.

When Yan and Sam pretend to be 'American Indians' their imitation of cultural elements that are said to be elements of the 'American Indian' lifestyle suggests that 'being Native' is 'something' that can be done by everyone, everywhere. The activities that are said to be typically 'Indian' confirm those stereotypes that Genevieve Susemihl discovered in her recent empirical study on the students' knowledge of North American indigenous peoples (Susemihl, 2008, pp. 122–3). At the same time, this pretence of *going Native* recalls the practice of using 'Indian' costumes for carnivals, leaving in children the impression that 'being Indian' is comparable to other occupations which are likely to be represented at dressing-up festivals. Imitating indigenous people at carnivals or pretending to be 'Indian' in the wilderness shows a lack of respect towards people who actually exist in the present. An understanding of this aspect as problematic is regarded as one of the aims of developing intercultural competence.

Through a representation that is false, arbitrary and superficial, these books (re-) create and transmute the indigenous person as a mythical figure, which transcends any real-world reflection and rather reveals a construction of a perceived reality of First Nation cultures (Edwards, 2008). Studies conducted in German schools and universities (Lutz, 1985 and 2002; Krebes, 2002; Susemihl, 2008) have shown that a strong interdependency between the media presentation of cultures and the opinion people share about them exists. Luhmann (1996, p. 120) explains that media representations affect public discourses in that fiction is taken for granted and perceived as a contribution to society's factual background knowledge. With books like those mentioned above, children are deprived of the chance to gain knowledge of indigenous people of North America but are rather left to re-implement a myth. This reflects what Clark already stated in 1981:

> Children's attitudes toward [Native Americans] are determined chiefly not by contact with [Native people], but by contact with the prevailing attitudes towards [Native Americans]. It is not the [Native people], but the idea of the [Native person] that influences children. (Clark in Moore et al., 1981, p. 8)

When children's literature is employed in language teaching, the dimension of cultural representation is of essential significance. With books such as the above, children reading at home or students reading in classroom environments hardly have a chance to learn something about First Nation and Native American culture, as the distorted images deprive them of opportunities to move beyond an essentialist and superficial knowledge, but rather ingrain existing misconceptions.

Intercultural learning with original literature on First Nations

One means to 'defeather the Indian' (LaRogue, 1975) is to offer reading material that avoids a stereotypical representation of indigenous cultures but rather uses specific geographical, historical, social and cultural contextualization in order to develop in students an awareness of other cultures.

In the following I will suggest children's literature titles by First Nations and Native American authors, which can be regarded as useful examples for developing intercultural competence, one of the key topoi in second language education. In an educational context, learning about different cultures, learning to appreciate and respect otherness and to challenge one's own viewpoint have been important objectives ever since foreign language teaching transcended the mere learning of a language to include cultural studies, which has nowadays developed into ICC. The development of ICC depends, among other factors, on the media to which children are exposed. In the light of the children's books analysed, the ethical dimension of the insights into secondary worlds (Delanoy, 2005, p. 57) and the quality of empathy achieved is highly challengeable. In order to achieve the aim of intercultural learning as inscribed in the Common European Framework (2001, pp. 101–3), the stereotypical images of indigenous people need to be replaced. The narrative approach followed in the aforementioned titles cannot contribute to gaining differentiated knowledge about First Nations, not to mention developing intercultural awareness. For this to be realized, more appropriate material, which offers deeper insights into First Nation cultures and differentiated background knowledge, is essential.

Chief Jake Swamp's *Giving Thanks – A Native American Good Morning Message* states at the beginning, that the text in its original version belongs to the Thanksgiving Address of the Haudenosaunee. The book reveals an 'ancient message of peace and appreciation of Mother Earth and all her inhabitants' (Swamp, 1995, unpaginated). The Haudenosaunee are a people who are also known as the Iroquois or Six Nations, comprised of the Mohawk, Oneida, Cayuga, Onondaga, Seneca and Tuscarora. The words of respect and thankfulness addressed to the different elements of the earth, such as sun, earth, thunder, stars, are still spoken at ceremonies. The students gain a very honest and approachable access to First Nation philosophy and perception of the interdependency of different life forms. This is mainly achieved by the easily understood and lyrical sentences author Chief and Elder Swamp, himself a member of the Akwesasne Mohawk, uses to convey the essence of the ritual.

Tomson Highway, author of the Cree story *Fox on the Ice/Maageesees Maskwameek Kaapit* has created his book bilingually, indicating that First Nation languages are still being spoken. The story is set in Northern Manitoba and the people are dressed in warm winter coats, driving a dogsled and fishing in the ice. Moreover their representation resists any contextualization with teepees, horses and headdresses as seen above, but rather raises the students' awareness for the manifold characteristics of First Nation and Native American peoples. The story centres around Joe and Cody who are fishing on a frozen lake, when all of a sudden their sled dogs sniff a fox across the lake and chase it, pulling the sled with them on which Joe and his mother were dozing. Cody and his father do not have any other choice but run after the dog sled and try to save

Cody's mother and brother. This short, easy to read adventure on the ice helps students realize that indigenous people are not backward or simpleminded at all, but are rather able to find a strong balance between modern progress using jiggers for fishing while at the same time appreciating their cultural heritage.

In Jeanette Armstrong's *Neekna and Chemai* the back cover introduces the author as Okanagan. This book is about two girls growing up in the Okanagan Valley and is set before the arrival of the Europeans. When the two best friends set out on a walk with their grandmother, the students may almost feel as if they are part of the small group as well and directly receive the grandmother's teachings about nature and the natural life pattern of the Okanagan people. Together with Neekna and Chemai, they learn about the different plants and fruit which, if picked moderately and with due respect, provide a living for the people. As their lifestyle and culture is determined by their surrounding environment and the seasonal patterns, this story, moreover, illustrates that First Nation people cannot be as homogenous as presented in the stories discussed in the beginning of this chapter.

Anne Renaud's *Missuk's Snow Geese* invites young readers to meet Missuk, a little girl who dreams of becoming a great wood carver, just like her father. When her father leaves for a hunt, she stays at home with her mother and improves on her sewing and woodcarving skills. Disappointed by her insufficient results, she rather goes outside to explore the tundra, which is about to wake up from the long winter. Lying in the snow, she watches the returning snow geese, imitating their wing movements and honks. The figures and prints she leaves in the snow survive an upcoming snowstorm, which however causes Missuk to worry about the well-being of her father. When her father returns, she learns that indeed it was her snow geese that guided her father safely home. This is not only a wonderful story about the trust in one's abilities, but additionally offers a readable insight into a First Nation culture in Northern Quebec. Especially the sketch-like illustrations in light pastel colours present an engaging picture of the snow-covered tundra.

Morning on the Lake by Jan Bourdeau Waboose is an Anishinawbe Ojibway story of a 'Mishomis' (grandfather) and his 'Noshen' (grandchild) who in their birchbark canoe embark on a journey across the lake in the morning, the rocky cliffs at noon and the woods at night to witness the tranquil wilderness and different animals in their natural habitat throughout the day. This quiet story teaches students the beauty of nature and that it is worthwhile stopping for a moment in time to discover small wonders. At the same time, Morning on the Lake also teaches of the respect for one's family heritage and the environment, both of which are essential to the Anishinawbe Ojibway understanding of self.

The latter books introduced in this chapter counteract the romanticized conviction that Indian children are named according to their character traits and their resemblance in nature. In the example texts discussed earlier, the 'Indians' either do not have a name at all, or, as in Fraside's story, are called 'One Feather' or 'Big Bear' (Farside, 2008a, b and c). Both of these approaches de-humanize indigenous people. Armstrong, Swamp, Renaud, Waboose and Highway do not make use of any such terminology but authentically name their protagonists Neekna and Chemai or Joe and Cody.

Original First Nation children's books additionally refrain from presenting First Nation people in the past but, directly or indirectly, refer to their present existence and usage of 'modern' features in their daily routines. Swamp tells the reader exactly where the Mohawk Nation lives and refers to the present in which the address is still being shared. This is supported when the book includes the address in the Nation's traditional language kaniakehaka (Mohawk); the culture is present and practised, not a 'thing' of the past. Moreover, the pictures of the authors in the back of the book show members of First Nations who are far from wearing leather and headdresses, as was prominent in the illustrations analysed above. Tomson Highway's inclusion of fishing methods as they are applied today support this aspect.

It should be noted that in the illustrations of Swamp's *Giving Thanks – A Native American Good Morning Message* (illustrated Erwin Printup), Renaud's *Missuk's Snow Geese* (illustrated Geneviève Côté), Armstrong's *Neekna and Chemai* (illustrated Barbara Marchand) and Highway's *Fox on the Ice/Maageesees Maskwameek Kaapit* (illustrated Brian Deines) not one single feather can be seen, thus these books especially support LaRouge's call to 'defeather' the Indian. Compared to that all three books by Farside, as well as Rosa and Barks' title, display feathers on the cover and on almost every page – be it as a decoration in headbands, decoration for bags and clothes or bow, arrow and spear. Especially the decoration of hunting tools is senseless, as feathers would prevent the hunter from aiming precisely and arrow and spear from flying with the required speed.

Raising awareness of 'otherness'

In summary, the First Nation titles achieve high potential for the development of intercultural competence because of the clear contextualization of the stories they tell and the characters they introduce. Students learn that *the* 'Indian' does not exist, but that the indigenous population of North America is as diverse as any other population of any other nation. The books offer important insights into the diversity of indigenous people and through their narratives offer a balanced perspective on 'other' cultures. By specifically contextualizing indigenous identities presented in the books, First Nation authors avoid generalizations and, thus, also limit the options for a stereotypical perception. Books on First Nations such as those suggested above need to be included in English language teaching to counteract the images transported in the books criticized at the beginning of this chapter. Literature represents 'otherness', and through fictional texts students are offered insights to worlds they may not be familiar with (Volkmann, 2010, p. 250). As experiencing otherness through fiction lays the foundations for the development of intercultural competence, children need to be provided with literature that allows them to engage in balanced intercultural encounters.

It is the aim of intercultural learning to develop in students an understanding of otherness that reflects respect, and develops the ability to show empathy (Nünning et al., 2008, p. 17). With any kind of literature that represents otherness students need to be enabled to broaden their knowledge of cultures they may not be a part of. The achievement of this objective with the children's books mentioned at the beginning of the chapter is highly problematic as the reader perceives an image of North American indigenous people that is inaccurate, condescending and derogative. In order for intercultural learning to be beneficial for a student's perception of self and otherness, a balanced representation of other cultures is essential. This chapter uses a comparison of different children's books on First Nations and Native Americans to illustrate this importance. In the course of the discussion, titles have been suggested which pay tribute to the diversity of indigenous peoples in North America by defining a specific cultural background of the protagonists and by creating a more nuanced image which counteracts the stereotypical and fanciful image young readers may still be growing up with. Students thus have the chance to become aware of the fact that 'I' is not for Indian, but rather for identity.

Note

1 Usage of 'Indian' when referring to the context of representation in books published by non-members of indigenous peoples. The author is aware of the derogative connotation and uses First Nation and Native American to refer to the indigenous people in North America in the remaining discussion.

Bibliography

Armstrong, J. (1991), *Neekna and Chemai*. Penticton: Theytus Books.
Farside, D. (2008a), *One Feather Takes a Leap of Friendship*. Reno: 3 Point Land Publishing.
— (2008b), *The Race up Rattlesnake Mountain*. Reno: 3 Point Land Publishing.
— (2008c), *Earning the Golden Feather*. Reno: 3 Point Land Publishing.
Highway, T. (2011), *Fox on the Ice/Maageesees Maskwameek Kaapit*. Markham: Fifth House.
Renaud, A. (2008), *Missuk's Snow Geese*. Vancouver: Simply Read Books.
Rosa, D. and Barks, C. (2007), *Uncle Scrooge Adventures Land of the Pygmy Indians / War of the Wenidgo*. Timonium: Gemstone Publishing.
Seton, E. (2010), *Two Little Savages: The Adventures of the Two Boys who Lived as American Indians*. Edinburg, VA: Axios Press.
Swamp, Chief J. (1995), *Giving Thanks – A Native American Good Morning Message*. New York: Lee and Low Books.
Waboose, J. B. (1997), *Morning on the Lake*. Toronto: Kids Can Press.

References

Bredella, L. (2010), *Das Verstehen des Anderen. Kulturwissenschaftliche und literaturdidaktische Studien*. Tübingen: Narr.
Brown, J. E. and Stephens, E. C. (eds) (1998), *United in Diversity – Using Multicultural Young Adult Literature in the Classroom*. Urbana: National Council for Teachers of English.

Council of Europe (eds) (2001), *A Common European Framework of Reference: Learning, Teaching, Assessment*. Straßbourg.

Delanoy, W. (2005), 'A dialogic model for literature teaching', *ABAC Journal*, 25.1, 53–66.

Edwards, B. F. R. (2008), ' "He scarcely resembles the real man": Images of the Indian in popular culture'. Available at: //scaa.sk.ca/ourlegacy/exhibit_popularculture#fn3.

Krebes, S. (2002), 'Zum Bild des nordamerikanischen Indianers im Deutschland des 21. Jahrhunderts: Versuch einer empirischen Analyse vorherrschender Stereotypen und Untersuchungen ihres realhistorischen Ursprungs', State examination thesis. Rostock: University of Rostock.

LaRogue, E. (1975), *Defeathering the Indian*. Agincourt: The Book Society of Canada Ltd.

Luhmann, N. (1996), *Die Realität der Massenmedien*. Opladen: Westedeutscher Verlag.

Lutz, H. (1985), '*Indianer' und 'Native Americans': Zur sozial- und literaturhistorischen Vermittlung eines Stereotyps*. Hildesheim: Olms Verlag.

— (2002), 'Images of Indians in German children's books', in H. Lutz (ed.), *Approaches: Essays in Native North American Studies and Literatures*. Augsburg: Wißner Verlag, pp. 13–47.

Mackey, M. (2011), *Narrative Pleasures in Young Adult Novels, Films, and Video Games*. New York: Palgrave Macmillan.

Moore, R. B. and Hirschfelder, A. (1981), 'Feathers, Tomahawks and Tipis: A study of stereotyped "Indian" imagery in children's books', in Council of Interracial Books for Children (ed.), *Unlearning 'Indian' Stereotypes: A Teaching Unit for Elementary Teachers and Children's Librarians*. New York: Council for Interracial Books for Children, pp. 5–23.

Nodelman, P. and Reimer, M. (2003), *The Pleasures of Children's Literature*. Boston: Allyn and Bacon.

Nünning, A. and Surkamp, C. (2008), *Englische Literatur unterrichten 1 – Grundlagen und Methoden*. Seelze: Klett/Kallmeyer.

Oliver, I. E. (1994), *Crossing the Mainstream: Multicultural Perspectives in Teaching Literature*. Urbana: National Council for Teachers of English.

Susemihl, G. (2008), 'The imaginary Indian in German children's non-fiction literature', in K. Knopf (ed.), *Aboriginal Canada Revisited*. Ottawa: University of Ottawa Press, pp. 122–57.

Volkmann, L. (2010), *Fachdidaktik Englisch: Kultur und Sprache*. Tübingen: Narr.

Willis, A. I. (ed.) (1998), *Teaching Multicultural Literature in Grades 9–12: Moving Beyond the Canon*. Norwood: Christopher-Gordon Publishers.

Part Four

Empowerment and Creativity
through Story

15

Creative Writing for Second Language Students

Alan Maley

Why is it that most institutional systems of education develop such narrow and unadventurous teaching procedures? How is it that joyful learning somehow gets overwhelmed by institutional rituals: the worship of the syllabus, the obsession with 'covering' the textbook, the manic preoccupation with the exam, the compulsion to conform? It seems that only in rare cases, through the determination of individual teachers, is joyful learning achieved. In most other cases, the language is reduced to drumming in material as if it were a set of mathematical formulae in preparation for the exam, after which it can safely be discarded. Small wonder that many students simply switch off and develop a lifelong aversion to the language in question. What they learn is neither enjoyable nor perceived as useful in the 'real' world outside the classroom.

This applies to much English language teaching too: all too often, it lacks a creative spark. John McRae goes so far as to say,

> In future years, the absence of imaginative content in language teaching will be considered to have marked a primitive stage of the discipline: the use of purely referential materials limits the learner's imaginative involvement with the target language, and leads to a one-dimensional learning achievement. Representational materials make an appeal to the learner's imagination ... (McRae, 1991, p. vii)

In this chapter I shall be arguing for the need to develop more creative approaches to writing as a way of enriching the learning experiences of both teachers and students.

What is creative writing?

Creative writing is often contrasted with expository writing. I have summarized the principal differences between them in Table 15.1.

When writing an expository text we are essentially instrumentally motivated. We have a quantum of facts, ideas and opinions to put across. Expository writing rests

Table 15.1 Expository writing versus creative writing

Expository writing	Creative writing
Instrumental	Aesthetic
Facts	Imagination
External control	Internal discipline
Conventions	Stretching rules
Logical	Intuitive
Analytical	Associative
Impersonal	Personal
Thinking mode	Feeling mode (plus thinking!)
Appeal to the intellect	Appeal to the senses
Avoidance of ambiguity	Creation of multiple meanings

on a framework of externally imposed rules and conventions. These range from grammatical and lexical accuracy and appropriacy to specific genre constraints. The aim of expository writing is to be logical, consistent and impersonal and to convey the content as unambiguously as possible to the reader.

Creative writing, by contrast, is aesthetically motivated. It deals less in facts than in the imaginative representation of emotions, events, characters and experience. Contrary to what many believe, creative writing is not about license. It is a highly disciplined activity. But the discipline is self-imposed: 'the fascination of what's difficult' (Yeats). In this it stands in contrast to expository writing, which imposes constraints from without. It often proceeds by stretching the rules of the language to breaking point, testing how far it can go before the language breaks down under the strain of innovation. Creative writing is a personal activity, involving feeling. This is not to say that thought is absent – far from it. The ingenuity of a plot, or the intricate structure of a poem are not the products of an unthinking mind: they require a unique combination of thought and feeling. An important quality of creative writing however is the way it can evoke sensations. And, unlike expository writing, it can be read on many different levels and is open to multiple interpretations.

The case for creative writing

It is reasonable to ask however, how we can justify the inclusion of creative writing, in addition to aesthetic reading, in our language teaching practices. A recent small-scale survey (unpublished data) I conducted among some 50 leading ELT professionals, especially teachers of writing, yielded the following reasons:

1. Creative writing aids language development at all levels: grammar, vocabulary, phonology and discourse. As learners manipulate the language in interesting and demanding ways, attempting to express uniquely personal meanings (as they do in creative writing), they necessarily engage with the language at a deeper level of processing than with expository texts (Craik and Lockhart, 1972). The gains in

grammatical accuracy, appropriacy and originality of lexical choice, and sensitivity to rhythm, rhyme, stress and intonation are significant.

2. Creative writing also fosters 'playfulness'. In recent years there has been a resurgence of interest in the role of play in language acquisition (Crystal, 1998; Cook, 2000). In some ways the 'communicative movement' has done a disservice to language teaching by its insistence on the exclusively communicative role played by language. The proponents of play point out, rightly, that in L1 acquisition, much of the language used by children is almost exclusively concerned with play: rhythmical chants and rhymes, word games, jokes and the like. Furthermore, such playfulness survives into adulthood, so that many social encounters are characterized by language play (puns, jokes, 'funny voices', juggling with words, and so on) rather than by the direct communication of messages. In creative writing, learners are encouraged to do precisely this: to play creatively with the language in a guilt-free environment. As Crystal states, 'Reading and writing do not have to be a prison house. Release is possible. And maybe language play can provide the key' (Crystal, 1998, p. 217).

3. This playful element encourages learners to take risks with the language, to explore it without fear of reproof. By manipulating the language in this way, they also begin to discover things not only about the language but about themselves. They effectively begin to develop a 'second language personality'.

4. Much of the teaching we do draws and focuses on the left side of the brain, where our logical faculties are said to reside. Creative writing puts the emphasis on the right side of the brain, with a focus on feelings, physical sensations, intuition and the like. This is a healthy restoration of balance between the logical and the intuitive faculties. It also allows scope for learners whose hemisphere preference or dominance may not be left-brain, and who, in the usual course of teaching, are therefore at a disadvantage.

5. The dramatic increase in self-confidence and self-esteem which creative writing tends to develop among students leads to a corresponding increase in motivation. Dornyei (2001), among others, has pointed to evidence that suggests that among the key conditions for promoting motivation are:

   5. Create a pleasant and supportive atmosphere in the classroom.
   6. Promote the development of group cohesiveness. (...)
   13. Increase the students' expectancy of success in particular tasks and in learning in general. (...)
   17. Make learning more stimulating and enjoyable by breaking the monotony of classroom events.
   18. Make learning stimulating and enjoyable for the learner by increasing the attractiveness of tasks.
   19. Make learning stimulating and enjoyable for the learners by enlisting them as active task participants.
   20. Present and administer tasks in a motivating way. (...)
   23. Provide students with regular experiences of success.
   24. Build your learners' confidence by providing regular encouragement.

28. Increase student motivation by promoting cooperation among the learners.
29. Increase student motivation by actively promoting learner autonomy. (...)
33. Increase learner satisfaction.
34. Offer rewards in a motivational manner. (Dornyei, 2001, pp. 138–44, numbered as in the original)

All these conditions are met in a well-run creative writing class. This increase in motivation is certainly supported by my own experience in teaching creative writing. Learners suddenly realize that they can write something in the foreign language which no one else has ever written before. And they experience not only a pride in their own products but a joy in the process.

6. Creative writing also feeds into more creative reading. It is as if, by getting inside the process of creating the text, students come to intuitively understand how such texts work, and this makes them easier to read. Likewise, the development of aesthetic reading skills provides students with a better understanding of textual construction, and this feeds into their writing. There is only one thing better than reading a lot for developing writing – and that is writing a lot too!
7. Finally, the respondents to the questionnaire survey were almost unanimous in agreeing that creative writing helps to improve expository writing too. In fact, by helping learners to develop an individual voice, it makes their factual writing more genuinely expressive.

All of the above factors were mentioned by the respondents to the questionnaire. Respondents noted that students who become engaged in creative writing tasks demonstrate a robust sense of self-esteem and are consequently better motivated (Dornyei, 2001). They also become more aware both of the language and of themselves as learners. The virtuous cycle of success breeding more success is evident with such students. As they become more self-confident, so they are prepared to invest more of themselves in these creative writing tasks. Above all, students derive not just 'fun' but a deeper sense of enjoyment from their writing.

Some practical ideas

There are a number of general points that will help make implementing creative writing activities more likely to succeed:

- Try to establish a relaxed, non-judgmental atmosphere, where your students feel confident enough to let go and not to worry that their every move is being scrutinized for errors.
- Ensure that the students' work is 'published' in some way. This could be by simply keeping a large notice-board for displaying the students' work. Other ways would include giving students a project for publishing work in a simple ring binder, or as part of a class magazine. Almost certainly, there will be students able and willing to set up a class website where work can be published. Performances, where students

read or perform their work for other classes or even the whole school, are another way of making public what they have done.

- Encourage students to discuss their work together in a frank but friendly manner. We get good ideas by bouncing them off other people. Help them establish an atmosphere where criticism is possible without causing offence.
- Explain regularly how important accurate observation is, and encourage 'noticing' things. They also need to be encouraged to be curious and to follow up with 'research' – looking for more information, whether in books, on the internet or by asking people.
- Make it clear that what they do in the classroom is only the tip of the iceberg. To get real benefit from these activities, they need to do a lot of work outside class hours. Most of what we learn, we do not learn in class. You can capitalize on that fact.
- Do the activities regularly in order to get the best effects. Maybe once a week is a sensible frequency. If you leave too long between sessions, you have to keep going back to square one. That is a waste of time and energy.

The following are a sample of some possible activities:

Hello/Goodbye poems

Tell the class that they are going to write a poem. It will have only two lines, and each line will have just two words. The first line will start with *Hello*, the second with *Goodbye*. Give students one or two examples:

> Hello sunshine,
> Goodbye rain.
> Hello smoking,
> Goodbye health.
> Hello paper,
> Goodbye trees.

Then, ask if they can think of any new ones. Note them on the board. Ask students to work in pairs (or alone if they prefer), and try to come up with at least two new poems. Allow 10 minutes for this task.

Ask for their examples and put them on the board. Ask students to give feedback on each other's examples. Collect all the poems. Display them on the class noticeboard or upload them onto the class/school website. The activity is very simple yet it does require students to call on their vocabulary store and to think about words that have a mutual or reciprocal relationship of meanings (smoking/ health etc.) If you prefer, this can be used as a short warm-up for other activities. It is a very good starter activity for younger students.

Stem poems

Explain to students that they will be writing some lines that will fit together into a poem. Then, write up the stem you intend to use. For example: *I wish I could . . .*

Elaborate further by eliciting samples of completed sentences, as in these examples:

I wish I could have an ice cream.
I wish I could speak French.
I wish I could visit Australia.

Then, ask each student to write three sentences following the same pattern.

After about 10 minutes, ask students to work in groups of 4 and to share their sentences. They should choose six sentences that they think are most suitable and then decide what order to put them in to form a six-line poem. There is no need for the poems to rhyme but if they do, fine. Lastly, tell them to add one final line, which is: *But I can't.*

Ask groups to read their poems aloud to the class. Can they suggest any ways to improve the poems? Collect all the poems. Display them on the class noticeboard or upload them onto the class/school website. You can decide on other stems to use in subsequent classes. For example:

Loneliness is ...
I used to ... but now ...
I love the way ...
Nobody knows ...
Who knows...?
I don't know why ...

It would be a good idea to choose stems that give practice in language points you are working on with the class at that time.

Acrostics

An acrostic poem is based on a word written vertically. The letters then each form the first letter of a word, and all the words are related to the meaning of the original word. For example:

Docile
Obedient
Growling

Explain what an acrostic is and write up one or two examples on the board. Then, ask them to write an acrostic based on their own name or the name of someone they know well. The words they choose should somehow describe the person. For example, *Vuthy*:

V Very
U Unlikely
T To
H Help
Y You

Collect all the poems. Display them on the class noticeboard or upload them onto the class/school website. Ask students to write at least one more acrostic before the next class. This time, they can choose any word they like (it doesn't have to be someone's name). For example:

Lying
Everywhere =
Autumn
Falling.

Acrostics involve a kind of mental gymnastics that engages students in reactivating their vocabulary in an unusual way. Acrostics do not usually produce great poetry but they certainly exercise the linguistic imagination.

Acknowledgement: Some of the ideas were developed by Tan Bee Tin.

If you were ...

First you make copies of this outline:

If I were a fruit, I would be ...
If I were a vegetable, I would be ...
If I were a tree, I would be ...
If I were a flower, I would be ...
If I were a fish, I would be ...
If I were a bird, I would be ...
If I were a book, I would be ...
If I were a song, I would be ...
If I were the weather, I would be ...
If I were a season, I would be ...

Then distribute the sheets that you have prepared. Ask students to work individually for about 10 minutes, completing the outline of the poem with words they prefer. For example: *If I were a fruit, I would be a grape.*

Let students share what they have written in groups of four. Then conduct a class discussion and go through the poems line-by-line, asking for examples of what they have written.

Ask students to think of someone they like and to write the person's name as the title of their poem. They then write a 12-line poem addressed to that person using the following format:

Line 1: describe the person as a kind of food
Line 2: describe the person as weather
Line 3: describe the person as a tree
Line 4: describe the person as a time of day
Line 5: describe the person as some kind of transport
Line 6: describe the person as an article of clothing
Line 7: describe the person as part of a house
Line 8: describe the person as a flower
Line 9: describe the person as a kind of music/a sound
Line 10: describe the person as something to do with colour
Line 11: describe the person as an animal

The last line should be the same for everyone: *You are my friend.*
So, their poem would look something like this:

For Sharifa
You are mango ice-cream
You are a cool breeze on a hot day
You are a shady coconut palm
You are dawn
You are a sailing boat crossing the bay
You are my comfortable sandals
You are the sunny verandah
You are jasmine
You are a soft gamelan
You are light blue
You are a playful kitten
You are my friend.

Metaphor poems

Make copies of this list of words and phrases for use during the class:

Love	an egg
Hate	a toothbrush
Disappointment	a vacuum cleaner
Marriage	a spoon
Friendship	a knife
Hope	a mirror
Life	a window
Work	a cup
Time	a banana

Check that students know what a metaphor is – a form of direct connection between two things. Give examples of metaphors in everyday life:

A blade of grass
A sharp frost
Spending time
Save time
Opening up a can of worms
She's a snake in the grass
He clammed up
He shelled out
A wall of silence

In fact, everyday language is so full of metaphorical expressions that we hardly notice them. They have become an accepted way of speaking. Explain that poets make great use of metaphor to make their words more vivid and easier to visualize.

Hand out the sheets. Tell students to write three metaphors by combining one item on the left with another on the right (students will have to join the words using 'is'). They should not spend time thinking about the combinations. For example:

Life is a window.
Friendship is a knife.
Love is a vacuum cleaner.
Marriage is a banana
Hate is a mirror.

Now, ask them to choose just one of their new metaphors. They should now write two more lines after the metaphor to explain what it means. For example:

Marriage is a banana:
when you've eaten the fruit,
only the skin is left.
Hate is a mirror:
it reflects back
on the one who hates.

Tell students not to use 'because' as it is unnecessary, and to keep the lines short. Ask students to share their metaphor poems with the class. Students should then make an illustrated display of their work.

Acknowledgement: This idea is adapted from Jane Spiro (2004)

The Asia teacher-writers project

In this final section, I shall describe the activities of a dynamically engaged group of teachers who have put these ideas into practice and become creative writers who produce materials for use by their students.

Background and history

This is a small-scale, grassroots / bottom-up initiative. Participation is entirely voluntary and the project is independent of institutions. It is predicated on the principle that 'small is beautiful' (Schumacher, 1974). There is no ambition to effect sweeping, large-scale changes, such as the many failed government schemes which litter the educational landscape. It has a local focus with no global ambitions. It works through persuasion at the personal level, and through the commitment of a small number of individual teachers. Small phenomena can nonetheless have large effects, as Chaos Theory teaches us (Gleick, 1988).

Significantly, it intersects with some important currents of contemporary professional concern. The role of the NNS (Non-Native Speaker) continues to preoccupy scholars of the spread of English, as does the development of English as an International Language, no longer the sole property of the metropolitan countries (Rubdy and Saraceni, 2006). This project is intimately linked with such concerns. It promotes the notion of NNS teachers able to find their own confident place and their own idiom in this rapidly changing global movement.

The project also reasserts the importance of the place of affect (Arnold, 1999), of visualization (Tomlinson, 1998, 2001), noticing (Schmidt, 1990), personalization, Multiple Intelligences (Gardner, 1985), motivation (Dornyei, 2001), authenticity, extensive reading (Day and Bamford, 1998; Krashen, 2004), the teaching of creative writing in a second language, and creativity in general (Boden, 1998; Carter, 2004).

The project started in 2003 with a small workshop in Bangkok. Teachers from a number of Asian countries gathered to discuss the desirability of writing creative materials in English for students in their countries. A collection of papers was the outcome (Tan, 2004), together with some stories which were also eventually published by Pearson Malaysia (Maley and Mukundan, 2005 a, b, c).

This first event was followed by workshops for roughly the same (but slowly expanding) group in Melaka, Malaysia (2004), Fuzhou, China (2005), Hanoi, Vietnam (2006), Salatiga, Indonesia (2007) Kathmandu/Kirtipur, Nepal (2008), Ho Chi Minh City, Vietnam (2009), Jakarta, Indonesia (2010), Dhulikhel, Nepal (2010) and Jember, Indonesia (2011). Each workshop produced poems and stories, which were published by Pearson Malaysia (Maley, 2007 a, b; Maley and Mukundan, 2005 a, b, c; 2011 a, b), as well as another volume of papers (Mukundan, 2006). As already noted above, the group is noteworthy for being independent of any institutional support, and is entirely voluntary. Each year, a volunteer takes on the responsibility for finding local sponsorship and organizing the workshop in a different venue in Asia.

Rationale and objectives

The group operates in the belief that NNS teachers are not only capable of but are also uniquely well-placed to write literary materials for use by their own and other students in the Asia region. By virtue of the fact that they share their students' backgrounds and contexts, they have an intuitive understanding of what will be culturally and topically relevant and attractive for them. What they all too often lack is the confidence in their own ability to write interesting material. The group operates to dispel this misconception.

The following rationale underpins the activities of the group:

- A belief in the value of creative writing in English both for teachers and for students.
- A belief in the ability of teachers in the region to produce their own English teaching materials.
- A belief that these materials will provide useful input for promoting reading (and other activities) in English.
- A belief in the value for professional and personal development of forming a closely knit, Asia-wide, mutually supportive learning community of teacher/writers.

The objectives are:

- To produce poetry and stories appropriate in level and content for use by Asian students of English at secondary level.
- To publish and promote these as widely as possible, thus creating a wider awareness of the value of creative writing.
- To develop materials and activities for the teaching of creative writing.
- To run creative writing conferences and workshops for the wider teaching community wherever possible.
- In this way, to boost the self-esteem and confidence of teachers of English in Asia.

In other words, the project aims at three main audiences:

~ a small group of writers who produce the materials, and in so doing develop professionally and personally.
~ English teachers in the region at large who will use the materials and hopefully go on to develop their own in due course.
~ secondary-school students of English in the region who will use the materials, and will themselves produce texts which can be fed back as input to other students.

Apart from peer editing and discussion, the workshops also include input sessions when new ideas for activities are shared. There are now many published sources for such ideas (Koch, 1990; Matthews, 1994; Frank and Rinvolucri, 2007; Spiro, 2004, 2007; Maley and Mukundan, 2011 a, b).

The importance of the project described here resides in the high degree of commitment by young, energetic professionals to its aims. Ultimately, change in our teaching practices will not come from top-down ministerial decrees but from the commitment of individuals with a belief in the value of their actions. 'A journey of 1000 li begins with the first step' (Chinese proverb).

References

Arnold, J. (1999), *Affect in Language Learning*. Cambridge: Cambridge University Press.

Boden, M. (1998), *The Creative Mind*. London: Abacus.

Carter, R. (2004), *Language and Creativity: The Art of Common Talk*. London: Routledge.

Cook, G. (2000), *Language Play: Language Learning*. Oxford: Oxford University Press.

Craik, F. I. M. and Lockhart, R. S. (1972), 'Levels of processing: A framework for memory research', *Journal for Verbal Learning and Verbal Behaviour*, II, 617–84.

Crystal, D. (1998), *Language Play*. London: Penguin.

Day, R. and Bamford, J. (1998), *Extensive Reading in the Second Language Classroom*. Cambridge: Cambridge University Press.

Dornyei, Z. (2001), *Motivational Strategies in the Language Classroom*. Cambridge: Cambridge University Press.

Frank, C. and Rinvolucri, M. (2007), *Creative Writing*. Innsbruck: Helbling Languages.

Gardner, H. (1985), *Frames of Mind*. London: Paladin Books.

Gleick, J. (1988), *Chaos*. London: Sphere Books.

Koch, K. (1990), *Rose, Where Did You Get That Red?* New York: Vintage Books.

Krashen, S. (2004), *The Power of Reading* (2nd edn). Portsmouth, NH: Heinemann.

Maley, A. (ed.) (2007a), *Asian Short Stories for Young Readers. Vol. 4*. Petaling Jaya: Pearson/Longman Malaysia.

— (ed.) (2007b), *Asian Poems for Young Readers. Vol.5*. Petaling Jaya: Pearson/Longman Malaysia.

Maley, A. and Mukundan, J. (eds) (2005a), *Asian Stories for Young Readers. Vol. 1*. Petaling Jaya: Pearson/Longman Malaysia.

— (eds) (2005b), *Asian Stories for Young Learners. Vol. 2*. Petaling Jaya: Pearson Malaysia.

— (eds) (2005c), *Asian Poems for Young Readers. Vol. 3*. Petaling Jaya: Pearson/Longman.

— (2011a), *Writing Poems: A Resource Book for Teachers of English*. Petaling Jaya: Pearson Malaysia.

— (2011b), *Writing Stories: A Resource Book for Teachers of English*. Petaling Jaya: Pearson Malaysia.

McRae, J. (1991), *Literature with a Small 'l'*. Oxford: Macmillan.

Matthews, P. (1994), *Sing Me the Creation*. Stroud: Hawthorn Press.

Mukundan, J. (ed.) (2006), *Creative Writing in EFL/ESL Classrooms II*. Petaling Jaya: Pearson Longman Malaysia.

Rubdy, R. and Saraceni, M. (eds) (2006), *English in the World: Global Rules, Global Roles*. London/New York: Continuum.

Schmidt, R. (1990), 'The role of consciousness in second language learning', *Applied Linguistics*. Vol. 11, No. 2, pp. 129–58. Oxford: Oxford University Press.

Schumacher, E. F. (1974), *Small is Beautiful*. London: Abacus/Sphere Books.

Spiro, J. (2004), *Creative Poetry Writing*. Oxford: Oxford University Press.

— (2007), *Creative Story-building*. Oxford: Oxford University Press.

Tan, B. T. (ed.) (2004), *Creative Writing in EFL/ESL Classrooms I*. Serdang: UPM Press.

Tomlinson, B. (1998), 'Seeing what they mean: Helping L2 learners to visualise', in B. Tomlinson (ed.), *Materials Development in Language Teaching*. Cambridge: Cambridge University Press, pp. 265–78.

— (2001), 'The inner voice: A critical factor in language learning', *Journal of the Imagination in L2 Learning*, VI, 123–54.

Wright, A. and Hill, D. (2008), *Writing Stories*. Innsbruck: Helbling Languages.

16

Young Adult Literature in Mixed-Ability Classes

Maria Eisenmann

In a competence-oriented foreign language classroom, students today have to deal with literature very early. A diverging and heterogeneous student population reads and interprets texts on more or less the same level even though their receptive skills can be very different. This contribution will try to answer questions on how teachers can promote the relationship between motivation and individual differentiation in dealing with children's literature and young adult fiction in heterogeneous learner groups. After expanding on opportunities for internal differentiation and individualization, the focus will be on student-centred methodologies such as extensive reading, keeping a reading log and implementing literature circles.

Heterogeneity in the classroom

The contemporary approach to differentiation has been shaped by recent research on multiple intelligences (Gardner, 1983, 1999; Haß, 2008) as well as the growing research on learning, e.g. DESI, 2001–6[1]). If students learn at a slower or faster pace it can be traced back to their being different learner types. There are concrete, analytical, communicative or authority-oriented learners (Nunan, 1999). Some can learn better by reading, others by listening, some like to write things down and some prefer to talk about a particular issue in the classroom (Looß, 2001; Nunan, 1999; Vester, 2007; Weidenmann, 2002). Today's teachers have to take leave of the expectation of illusive homogeneous learner groups and see heterogeneity as something very normal, as an opportunity for learning and as enrichment through variety.

Learning a language entails a complex network that is dependent not only on different forms of intelligence and different learner types but also on motivation, previous knowledge, personality, socialization, home life or simply on the student's form on that day (Bönsch, 2009; Boller et al., 2007; Eller et al., 2008; Kunze, 2008; Trautmann et al., 2007; Von der Groeben, 2008). Learning is a very individual and also subjective process and the contexts of learning not only depend on political and ideological agendas, cultural environment and school ethos, but also on emotional, physical and social differences of the learners.

Consequently, English literature lessons today can no longer be adjusted to an average anonymous learner, and following an obligatory curriculum (Bönsch, 1995, p. 14).

This realization poses many questions: if all students are different, do they all need to be treated differently? How can teachers deal with children's literature in mixed-intelligence, mixed-ability classes?

Differentiated instruction in the literature classroom

A literature classroom that caters for learner differentiation offers a variety of learning options designed to tap into different readiness levels, interests and learning profiles. Opportunities for internal differentiation and individualization can most commonly be found in contexts such as quantity, quality, goals, content, participatory structures, methods and media (Bönsch, 2009; Paradies et al., 2001; Schwerdtfeger, 2001). It is important to note that a class is not differentiated when assignments are the same for all learners and the adjustments consist of varying the level of difficulty of questions for certain students, grading some students differently or letting students who finish early play games for so-called enrichment. It is not appropriate to have more advanced learners do extra reading, extra book reports or after completing their regular work be given extension assignments. Asking students to do more of what they already know is hollow, asking them to do 'the regular work, plus' inevitably seems punitive to them (Tomlinson, 2001; for a list of key principles of a differentiated classroom see Tomlinson, 1999, p. 48).

As Morgan and Neil note '[d]ifferentiation is the provision of different levels of activities for students of varying abilities and interest levels' (2001, p. 49). Consequently, basic characteristics of a differentiated class are flexible tasks. Sometimes tasks are readiness-based, sometimes interest-based, sometimes constructed to match learning style, and sometimes a combination of readiness, interest and learning style. Another feature is the incorporation of many different types of participatory structures. Sometimes students work alone, sometimes in pairs, sometimes in groups.

Teachers do not assume that all students need a given task or segment of study, but continuously assess student readiness and interest, providing support when students need additional instruction and guidance, and extending student exploration when indications are that a student is ready to move ahead. This creates new roles for both students and teachers. Students are active explorers in reading and dealing with texts, teachers guide the exploration (Peschel, 2004; Prengel, 2004). Because varied activities often occur simultaneously in a differentiated classroom, the teacher works more as a guide or facilitator of learning than as a dispenser of information. As in a large family, students must learn to be responsible for their own work (Tomlinson, 1999, 2001).

Differentiation in the context of dealing with children's literature and young adult fiction does not simply mean to reduce or enlarge reading content but to individualize tasks and requirements of the learners. Means of differentiation within the methodology of foreign language teaching do not only provide a more intense concentration on the learner as individual, they also focus on intercultural communicative competence as one of the most important targets in teaching literature (Trautmann, 2010).

Cooperative methods are particularly suitable for the foreign language classroom as they have a high potential for student activation and enhance many communicative speaking opportunities. Cooperative learning techniques promote student learning and academic achievement as they increase student retention. It also helps them to develop skills in oral communication, social skills and it may even contribute to an increase in self-esteem.

Promoting literary proficiency in mixed-ability classes

Methodological possibilities with extensive reading

Reading a text, we activate our background knowledge, we have different reading strategies and semantic mapping systems in order to leave out some passages or lines; we are constantly predicting, decoding and reading between or even beyond the lines. Consequently, different people understand different things although they have read the same text. In a foreign language it is even more difficult to grasp the meaning of the text, because the lack of vocabulary leads to even more mistakes while applying all of these techniques. The lack of appropriate reading techniques, strategies and practice are the reasons for insufficient reading skills and the existence of reluctant readers (Henseler et al., 2007, p. 6). Students within the same classroom have different interest and abilities, they read at different paces and their reading skills vary a lot. Some are able to read an authentic children's book while others still struggle with short texts or course book texts. Consequently, while promoting literacy and reading skills it is not very reasonable to read the same book with the whole class at the same pace at the same time. How can reading be trained in the mixed-ability language classroom in order to gain a positive approach to dealing with literature? How can heterogeneous student groups be motivated to reading literature in the foreign language?

Many benefits emerge from **extensive reading**, and there are hardly any drawbacks for a differentiating classroom. It is a very individualized form of reading, usually for pleasure, as you can read a lot and as fast as you are able to (Bramford et al., 2004; Finkbeiner, 2005; Haß, 2006; Henseler et al., 2007). This can be put into practice by compiling reading lists, setting up a class library, making up a fixed time for silent reading, actually every form of sustained silent reading, which is based on the premise that as a skill, reading improves with practice (Henseler et al., 2007, p. 6).

A related approach to training reading skills is called **DEAR (= Drop Everything and Read)**. DEAR is classroom time set aside for teachers and students to Drop Everything and Read (www.dropeverythingandread.com/NationalDEARday.html). The goal of DEAR is to encourage independent silent reading for extended periods of time on a daily or weekly basis. Students choose the book they wish to read based on interest and ability. Guidelines for DEAR focus on protecting it as a sacred classroom time to encourage independent reading. This is not to be used as a filler activity or a graded task. Students should bring books if they want to and if they are available to them. Of course, they can also select books from the classroom library before DEAR time begins. Recommendations for a time frame usually suggest beginning with 5 minutes for younger students and 15 minutes for older students, increasing the time allowance as the academic year progresses. In this time the teacher functions as a role model and also reads.

To facilitate the process of identification and intercultural awareness, literary texts should be selected which tell about the lives of (young) people from other cultures, including the whole field of children's and young adult literature. Intercultural conflicts and causes for misunderstanding are dramatically presented in postcolonial literature and minority texts, that study race and ethnicity in literature such as Latino or African-American, Asian-American, Jewish-American or Native-American literature. In multicultural novels, experiences of alienation are often reflected, for example the alienation of strangers in a strange land, for example Latinos in Francisco Jiménez' *Breaking Through* (2002), life of Indian-English youths in Great Britain in Bali Rai's *(Un)arranged Marriage* (2001), problems of immigration in Will Hobbs' *Crossing the Wire* (2007), the experiences of African Americans in Angela Johnson's *The First Part Last* (2004) or the experiences of Native Americans in Sherman Alexie's *The Absolutely True Diary of a Part-time Indian* (2007).

In all these novels, imagination and empathy will help intercultural learning as these books show all the similarities young people have – usually problems specific to adolescents and their crossing the threshold between childhood and adulthood, especially regarding drug or alcohol abuse, violence, suicide, social norms and human sexuality, first love and friendship. Usually told from the teen perspective, the stories focus on multifaceted formation of hybrid identities set in a transcultural and globalized world. Thus these books offer great potential and an especially good opportunity for teenage readers to identify and empathize with the young protagonist.

All of the above activities entail that it is the students' choice of what they want to read. But what methods and possibilities do we have if we read a book together with all the students in class? Differentiation can either take place by pace of work or by providing the students with different forms of tasks and activities. Consequently, this means before and while reading the same text, or after having read the same text, students can work on different tasks in different participatory structures according to their readiness, interests, abilities and learning profiles. More open questions and a variety of tasks have to be supplied. But weaker students also need more support while working on their tasks, which means a different methodology, with the breaking down of tasks into smaller steps. Tasks should always be structured from easy to difficult. This way the students have a warm up and with succeeding in the easier tasks they are more motivated to undertake the more difficult ones. You can give the students a choice of tasks, which they can work on in groups, in pairs or alone according to their interest and abilities (Gardner, 1983, 1999; Haß, 2008).

Differentiation by keeping a reading log on Sherman Alexie's *The Absolutely True Diary of a Part-time Indian*

One major goal in the differentiated language classroom is to educate the learners to take over responsibility for their own learning, and thus become a self-directed and autonomous learner. One way to allow students to broaden their horizons in individual reading is by keeping a **reading diary** or a **reading log** as tools for monitoring one's reading progress (Bray, 2002; Henseler et al., 2007, p. 5).

A reading log is a written dialogue with a fictional text and basically functions as a record of anything a student wants to document while reading this text. It is used to monitor and evaluate how students are comprehending what they are reading and to be able to talk about it while reading or after reading it. Students set themselves a number of chapters to read and then, after this reading session, write in their reading log their reaction to what they have read. Usually reading logs are divided into the chapters of the book, as this is how the author intended the novel to be read. The following is an example of how to keep a reading log on Sherman Alexie's *The Absolutely True Diary of a Part-time Indian*, a novel about Junior, a budding cartoonist, who leaves the Spokane Indian Reservation in order to visit an all-white school in Reardan, Washington. The book deals with issues such as racism, poverty, alcohol abuse, friendship and love. My suggestion is to divide the reading log into the following four sections:

Important facts

Give character descriptions – Do the characters change or remain the same?
Note down ideas about plot, structure, setting, characters, point of view and style.
What do Junior's drawings tell us that his words in the diary don't?
What is the relationship between his pictures and his words?

Personal impressions

Does the text leave you with questions you would like to ask? What are they?
Would you like to direct any of your questions to the author or a particular character?
Would you have left the reservation? Why/Why not?
What does it mean for Junior to be a 'part-time Indian'? Do you sometimes feel your-
    self as belonging to something 'part-time'?
What is the last picture/cartoon Junior draws about? Why is it important?
Have you learned anything you did not know before?
Would you like to be one of the characters? Why (not)?

Language focus

Why does Rowdy call Junior a 'nomad'? What does the term mean literally and in a
    figurative sense? Is it a positive or a negative word?
Take notes of expressions/sentences you find difficult to understand.
Write down your favourite lines of the text. Explain what you like about them.

Creative tasks

Imagine you are Rowdy – Write a letter to Junior about your experiences, thoughts
    and feelings.

If you were the author, would you have changed the name of a character, or altered
    the location of a scene?
Interview Junior about the story or about anything your imagination comes up with,
    asking questions and giving answers for him.
If there is a dialogue or scene you do not like, go ahead and rewrite it.
Design a new cover for the book.

A reading log is a very individualized form of dealing with literature in the EFL
classroom because all students can read the text at their own pace and write down
their individual findings. Consequently, it embodies the students' personal responses
to a text, helps them to gain insight about theme and plot, enhances students' ability
to respond personally and critically, supports them to explore, clarify and reflect on
their own thoughts, experiences and learning. It also helps them find out about their
feelings towards the characters, it trains their ability to interpret, select and combine
information using a variety of strategies, resources and technologies and students
remember what they have read better.

Literature circles

Another method to encourage student choice and a love of reading is to organize a
literature circle in the classroom, an equivalent to an adult book club (Daniels, 2002;
Daniels et al., 2004; Eisenmann, 2012, p. 306). The students could choose books such
as Narinder Dhami's *Bend it like Beckham* (2002), Vikas Swarup's *Slumdog Millionaire*
(2005), Aravind Adiga's *The White Tiger* (2008), Jhumpa Lahiri's *Unaccustomed Earth*
(2008), Khaled Hosseini's *The Kite Runner* (2003) or *A Thousand Splendid Suns*
(2007).
    Literature circles, that involve small groups of learners exploring a piece of literature,
allow students to practise and develop the skills and strategies of good readers (DaLie,
2001). They 'gather together to discuss a piece of literature in depth. The discussion is
guided by students' responses to what they have read' (SchlickNoe et al., 1999, p. ix).
There are many ways to implement the strategies of a literature circle dependent on
class levels and subject areas. In most cases, the application of literature circles evolves
over time as students and teachers become more experienced readers.
    This strategy engages students in higher-level thinking and reflection by
encouraging collaboration. One of the main goals of literature circles is an enthusiastic,
natural and informal conversation that encourages a life-long love of reading. These
literary discussions are guided by student insights, observations and questions. For
implementing literature circles in the classroom the following steps are necessary
(Eisenmann, 2012, p. 306):

1. Members of the literature circles (= discussion groups) are selected. Usually
    the teacher forms these first groups of four or five students, making them as
    heterogeneous as possible by balancing personalities, gender and ability levels.
2. Generally, each literature circle will read the same book. Other groups in the
    same classroom may be reading different books and the groups may jigsaw or

participate in a class-wide culminating activity. In some cases, group members may be reading different texts by a particular author, different texts on the same theme or different texts from the same genre.

3. Group discussions are at the core of a literature circle. In order to have good discussions going on in the classroom, the teacher provides the students with some discussion guidelines that can serve as reminders (for an explanation of group discussions see www.litcircles.org/Discussion/discussion.html).

Each member of the circle is now assigned a specific role. The teacher determines what roles should be used depending on the age and ability of the students as well as the reading selections. These roles keep the discussions fresh and encourage students to focus on different cognitive perspectives related to their reading and draw on different intelligences. At first, the roles may be primarily directed at the readings. For example, for a given chapter one student writes discussion questions, another visualizes the setting through art, while still another student identifies new vocabulary or interesting passages. As these roles become a natural part of the circle, you may shift the roles to be more activity specific. Table 16.1 suggests possible roles (Grieser-Kindel et al., 2009; Eisenmann, 2012, p. 307; for further roles see http://olc.spsd.sk.ca/de/pd/instr/strats/literaturecircles/index.html):

Table 16.1 Roles for discussion groups

Discussion director	plans the meeting, keeps it going and develops questions for the group to discuss
Passage picker	chooses a selection that the group rereads and discusses because it is interesting, informative, the climax, well written etc.
Vocabulary reporter	chooses words that are either important or difficult or used in an unfamiliar way
Connector	Finds a connection between the story and another book, event in their personal life or the outside world
Illustrator	visualizes or draws a picture related to the reading
Summarizer	prepares and presents a brief summary of the assigned reading
Interest investigator	looks up background information related to the book

Conclusion

A first and basic step is that heterogeneity is not seen as an obstacle in teaching literature but as a very normal condition and a structural feature for the literature classroom, because homogeneous groups of students have never existed, not even in the very selective and subdivided German school system. Consequently, the challenge is not only to accept heterogeneity but also to find a positive approach and a productive response to this phenomenon. The focus should not be on how to remove or reduce weaknesses but on how to enhance students' strengths. Each reading of a (literary) text happens on an individual basis and this is why we need learner involvement, learner centredness and learner autonomy. Teachers have to be encouraged to identify with their role as a guide or facilitator of learning. Not only does such learner centredness give students more ownership of their learning, but it also facilitates the important goal of adolescence: growing independence in thought, planning and evaluation.

Websites

www.dropeverythingandread.com/NationalDEARday.html (January 2011)
www.learnnc.org/reference/Drop+Everything+And+Read (January 2011)
www.litcircles.org/Discussion/discussion.html (January 2011)
http://olc.spsd.sk.ca/de/pd/instr/strats/literaturecircles/index.html (January 2011)

Note

1   DESI (German English Student Assessment International) is a longitudinal study (N=11.000 in Germany) that investigated a range of language competences both in German (L1 and L2 for part of the population) and English (first foreign language) primarily in the German school system (ninth grade) (Beck et al., 2007).

Bibliography

Adiga, A. (2008), *The White Tiger*. London: Atlantic Books.
Alexie, S. (2007), *The Absolutely True Diary of a Part-time Indian*. Stuttgart: Klett.
Dhami, N. (2002), *Bend it like Beckham*. London: Hodder & Stoughton.
Hobbs, W. (2007), *Crossing the Wire*. New York: HarperCollins.
Hosseini, K. (2003), *The Kite Runner*. New York: Riverhead Books.
— (2007), *A Thousand Splendid Suns*. New York: Riverhead Books.
Jiménez, F. (2002), *Breaking Through*. New York: Sandpiper.
Johnson, A. (2004), *The First Part Last*. New York: Simon & Schuster.
Lahiri, J. (2008), *Unaccustomed Earth*. London, New York and Berlin: Bloomsbury.
Rai B. (2001) *(Un)arranged Marriage*. London: Transworld.
Swarup, V. (2005), *Slumdog Millionaire*. London: Scribner.

References

Beck, B. and Klieme, E. (2007), *Sprachliche Kompetenzen. Konzepte und Messung; DESI-Studie (Deutsch Englisch Schülerleistungen International)*.Weinheim: Beltz (Beltz-Pädagogik).
Bönsch, M. (1995), *Differenzierung in Schule und Unterricht. Ansprüche – Formen – Strategien*. München: Ehrenwirth.
— (2009), *Intelligente Unterrichtsstrukturen. Eine Einführung in die Differenzierung*. Baltmannsweiler: Schneider Hohengehren.

Boller, S., Rosowski, E. and Stroot, T. (eds) (2007), *Heterogenität in Schule und Unterricht*. Weinheim: Beltz.

Bramford, J. and Day, R. R. (2004), *Extensive Reading Activities for Teaching Language*. Cambridge: Cambridge University Press.

Bray, E. (2002), 'Using task journals with independent readers', *Forum*, 40(3), 6–11.

DaLie, S. O. (2001), 'Students becoming real readers: Literature circles in high school English classes', in B. O. Ericson, (ed.), *Teaching Reading in High School English Classes*. Urbana: NCTE, 84–100.

Daniels, H. (2002), *Literature Circles: Voice and Choice in Book Clubs and Reading Groups*. Maine: Stenhouse Publishers.

Daniels, H. and Steineke, N. (2004), *Mini-Lessons for Literature Circles*. Portsmouth: Heinemann.

DESI-Konsortium (eds) (2008), *Unterricht und Kompetenzerwerb in Deutsch und Englisch. Ergebnisse der DESI-Studie*. Weinheim: Beltz.

Eisenmann, M. (2012), 'Introduction: Heterogeneity and differentiation', in M. Eisenmann and T. Summer (eds), *Basic Issues in EFL Teaching and Learning*. Heidelberg: Winter, 297–310.

Eller, U. and Grimm, W. (2008): *Individuelle Lernpläne für Kinder. Grundlagen, Ideen und Verfahren für die Grundschule. Grundlagen, Ideen und Verfahren für die Grundschule*. Weinheim: Beltz.

Finkbeiner, C. (2005), *Interessen und Strategien beim Fremdsprachlichen Lesen: Wie Schülerinnen und Schüler Englische Texte Lesen und Verstehen*. Tübingen: Narr.

Gardner, H. (1983), *Frames of Mind: The Theory of Multiple Intelligences*. New York: Basic Books.

— (1999), *Intelligence Reframed: Multiple Intelligences for the 21st Century*. New York: Basic Books.

Grieser-Kindel, C., Henseler, R. and Möller, S. (2009), *Method Guide. Methoden für einen Kooperativen und Individualisierenden Englischunterricht in den Klassen 5–12*. Paderborn: Schöningh.

Haß, F. (ed.) (2006), *Fachdidaktik Englisch*. Stuttgart: Klett.

— (2008), 'Auf unterschiedliche Weise schlau werden', *Der Fremdsprachliche Unterricht Englisch*, 94, 30–5.

Henseler R. and Surkamp, C. (2007), 'Leselust statt Lesefrust. Lesemotivation in der Fremdsprache Englisch fördern', *Der Fremdsprachliche Unterricht Englisch,* 89, 2–10.

Kunze, I. (ed.) (2008), *Individuelle Förderung in der Sekundarstufe I und II*. Baltmannsweiler: Schneider Hohengehren.

Looß, M. (2001), 'Lerntypen? – Ein pädagogisches Konstrukt auf dem Prüfstein', *Die Deutsche Schule*, 93(2), 186–98.

Morgan, C. and Neil, P. (2001), *Teaching Modern Foreign Languages. A Handbook for Teachers*. London: Kogan Page.

Nunan, D. (1999), *Second Language Teaching and Learning*. Boston: Heinle & Heinle.

Paradies, L. and Linser, H. (2001), *Differenzieren im Unterricht*. Berlin: Cornelsen.

Peschel, F. (2004), 'Ganznormale Kinder! Differenzierung von oben oder Individualisierung von unten', *Friedrich Jahresheft*, 23, 21–3.

Prengel, A. (2004), 'Spannungsfelder, nicht Wahrheiten. Heterogenität in pädagogisch-didaktischer Perspektive', *Friedrich Jahresheft*, 23, 44–6.

SchlickNoe, K. L. and Johnson, N. J. (1999), *Gettting Started with Literature Circles*. Norwood, MA: Christopher-Gordon Publishers.

Schwerdtfeger, I. C. (2001), *Gruppenarbeit und innere Differenzierung*. Berlin: Langenscheidt.

Tomlinson, C. A. (1999), *The Differentiated Classroom. Responding to the Needs of All Learners*. Alexandria, VA: Association for Supervision and Curriculum Development.

— (2001), *How to Differentiate Instruction in Mixed-ability Classrooms* (2nd edn). Upper Saddle River, NJ: Pearson/Merrill Prentice Hall.

Trautmann, M. (2010), 'Heterogenität – (k)ein Thema der Fremdsprachendidaktik', in A. Köker, S. Romahn and A. Textor (eds), *Herausforderung Heterogenität*. Bad Heilbrunn: Klinkhardt, pp. 52–64.

Trautmann, M. and Wischer, B. (2007), 'Individuell fördern im Unterricht – Was wissen wir über Innere Differenzierung?', *Pädagogik*, 9, 44–8.

Vester, F. (2007), *Denken, Lernen, Vergessen. Was geht in unserem Kopf vor, wie lernt das Gehirn, und wann lässt es uns im Stich?* München: Deutscher Taschenbuch Verlag.

Von der Groeben, A. (2008), *Verschiedenheit Nutzen. Besser Lernen in Heterogenen Gruppen*. Berlin: Cornelsen Scriptor.

Weidenmann, B. (2002), 'Multicodierung und Multimodalität im Lernprozess', in L. J. Issing and P. Klimsa (eds), *Information und Lernen mit Multimedia. Lehrbuch für Studium und Praxis* (3rd revised edn).Weinheim: Beltz, pp. 45–64.

17

Enhancing Self-Esteem and Positive Attitudes through Children's Literature

Paola Traverso

The work presented in this chapter is based on the premises that positive social attitudes and self-esteem are important factors in effective learning, as research in the field of humanism in language teaching has shown. School can play an important role in affecting students' emotional development and in the English classroom the use of children's literature can be of great help in fostering positive feelings. Examples are given of how to address the themes of diversity and tolerance, self-acceptance and empathy exploiting graded readers and picturebooks for primary school pupils. In particular, the following texts are considered in detail: *The Owl's Song* (Paola Traverso, illus. Alida Massari, 2010; *Michael* (Tony Bradman, illus. Tony Ross, 2009); *My Travelin' Eye* (Jenny Sue Kostecki-Shaw, 2008).

Introduction

Research in the field of humanistic psychology has shown that children with low self-esteem are more likely to speak negatively about themselves and are often fearful of expressing opinions and trying out new things. They show a low tolerance of frustration and give up very easily. Reasoner (1992) states that children with low self-esteem exhibit a high degree of anxiety, are fearful of taking risks and are not able to relate positively to their mates. In contrast, children who feel good about themselves, who feel secure and respected, are more willing to welcome new challenges, to tolerate frustration and persist in the face of difficulty.

Coopersmith (1967) refers to self-esteem as the self-perceptions that an individual has of being capable, significant and worthy. He emphasizes that these self-perceptions develop mainly during childhood and depend on the experiences that children have in their environment and on the relationships they have with their parents and other significant figures around them: teachers, friends, peers. Also Rogers (1969) points out that we learn about ourselves through others and how they respond to us. In order to develop a good and healthy self-esteem we need positive recognition. We need to be valued and loved, we need to be listened to and to be accepted for what we are.

Teachers can play an important role in affecting students' self-image and personal growth, especially when children are very young and they are still proceeding along their psychological and social development. In the English classroom positive attitudes can be fostered by creating a friendly and supportive atmosphere, a safe and non-threatening environment where differences are valued and individual needs are taken into consideration. In addition, to encourage pupils to develop positive feelings and a better understanding of themselves and of others, the use of children's literature can be of great help.

The educational value of stories is widely recognized. Good stories evoke emotions, release tensions and offer models of how to overcome conflicts and problems. Bettelheim (1989) states that fairy tales develop around archetypal contents and carry messages that can speak to the conscious and unconscious minds of children and adults alike. They tell about universal themes and inner problems of human beings and show ways to cope with difficulties. Petter (2007) emphasizes that stories enlarge children's vision of the world and their knowledge of how relationships and feelings work. Through storytelling it is possible to support a balanced development of rationality, imagination and emotions.

The role of stories and storytelling has been appreciated also in the field of foreign language teaching. According to Ellis et al. (2002), stories offer a motivating learning experience and provide a rich context for a variety of activities: linguistic, cognitive, social and cultural. In order to fully exploit the potential of stories, selecting appropriate materials is important. Attention needs to be paid to which books contain narrative features that help the young learners of English memorize the story: rhymes, alliteration, onomatopoeia and repetitive language. High-quality illustrations and pictures that synchronize with the text can both stimulate imagination and support understanding. With regard to the content, it is useful to select stories which present themes that are related to children's interests and experiences and that offer opportunities for emotional development.

A multi-sensory approach to storytelling

Considering the principles described above, a multi-sensory approach to storytelling is presented in this section. The purpose is to take different learning styles into account (visual, auditory and kinaesthetic) and to propose a variety of activities in order to favour students' participation and involvement and facilitate comprehension. As research in the field of Neuro-Linguistic Programming has shown (Revell et al., 1997), a multi-sensory approach to language teaching can satisfy the needs of different learners and create a friendly learning environment. The graded reader *The Owl's Song* is an animal story that deals with the feeling of being different and with the experience of rejection and isolation. Examples are offered of how to introduce and exploit the story in the English classroom, how to stimulate the use of the foreign language and encourage reflection on personal attitudes and social issues. The activities described have been used, by the writer, in teacher training courses organized in Italy for primary school teachers.

If you ...

This activity is based on Total Physical Response (TPR) techniques. These techniques have been chosen because they emphasize the connections between language and action. According to Asher (1982), performing a series of actions in the target language is a way to make input comprehensible and to reduce stress. Attention is paid to the meaning of the message to be performed through actions and the focus is not on language performance.

The following activity can be used as an icebreaker. It has two purposes: getting to know each other in terms of likes, dislikes and abilities; and becoming familiar with some words of the story. The teacher shows some pictures of natural elements (moon, sun, wind), which have been placed on the classroom walls. The students are asked to point to the sun, the moon, the wind. Then they are asked to stand up, listen to some instructions and perform some actions. Before starting, the teacher demonstrates by showing the actions to be performed and saying the commands:

> *If you like the moon, arms up!*
> *If you like the sun, arms out!*
> *If you like the wind, arms down!*
> *If you can sing, turn around!*
> *If you can't sing, touch the ground and up!*
> *If you like animals, stamp your feet!*
> *If you like animal stories, clap your hands!*

The actions proposed are not chosen at random. They are part of a dance that is included in the *Owl's Song* story.

A magical journey

This relaxation and visualization activity has been included in order to create the right atmosphere for storytelling, to approach the story little by little and to allow the children to experience what it is like to be calm and to be in an environment where everything is quiet. The teacher tells the class that she knows a beautiful wood, where everything is quiet: the trees are quiet, the animals are quiet, the grass is quiet. The class is going on a magical journey to this wood. The students are asked to sit down in a comfortable position with their feet apart and their hands on their legs. They are asked to close their eyes and to breathe in and out, slowly and naturally. If they feel uncomfortable, they can keep their eyes open and look at a fixed point in front of them. The teacher guides the journey:

> *You are in a wood, in a beautiful wood. The trees are quiet, the grass is quiet, the animals are quiet and you are quiet. Your head is quiet, your shoulders are quiet, your*

arms are quiet, your hands are quiet. Your tummy is quiet, your back is quiet. Your legs are quiet, your feet are quiet. Your head is quiet, your eyes are quiet, your ears are quiet, your nose is quiet, your mouth is quiet. You are in a wood, a beautiful wood. The trees are quiet, the grass is quiet, the animals are quiet and you are quiet …

Now it's time to return to your classroom. Slowly open your eyes. Slowly stretch your arms.

The image of the wood and some expressions used during the visualization and relaxation exercise have been once again chosen because they are related to the text of *The Owl's Song*.

Story time

The teacher reads the story that begins describing a wood at night where everything is quiet: 'The wood is quiet. The trees are quiet, the grass is quiet, the animals are quiet. Everything is quiet and dark, very dark …' (Traverso, 2010, p. 2).

As the story goes on, the children discover that each morning some little birds fly through the wood and sing to wake the animals up. One day a big brown owl comes. He wants to join the little birds and sing with them, but they don't want him because he is big, ugly and he can't sing. The owl is very sad, he flies away and hides inside an old black tree. When finally the night comes and everything is quiet again, the owl sings his song. The moon likes the song very much and the fairies of the wood start dancing.

Since the book is a graded reader, the language is not difficult to understand. In addition, there are repetitive patterns, rhyming words and plenty of animal sounds, all of which make it easy for the children to join in. They can also perform the fairies' dance and sing along. The dance has simple sequences and includes many movements that have been already experienced during the ice-breaking activity.

From the story to children's experience

The story offers an opportunity to reflect on the theme of rejection and isolation, an experience that might be common among children. In the story the owl, when he is rejected, feels very sad and needs to go away and find a place to hide. In a situation like that, not all the children would react in this way because each of them has a different personality and a specific way of dealing with problems. In the classroom, some simple activities can be proposed to explore the students' feelings and to make them aware that even though we might experience similar situations, our reactions might be different.

What do you feel when …

The teacher gives each child a handout (see Figure 17.1) and tells them to write what they feel when they are not welcomed or accepted into a group. On the handout the pictures have been drawn using Wright's techniques (1996b).

Read, look and write

What do you feel when some children say to you:

'You can't come with us!'

'You can't play with us!'

'You're not like us!'

I feel ....

Happy

Sad

Angry

Worried

Surprised

Scared

Figure 17.1 Working on feelings.

These things make me feel …

The situations that can cause negative and positive feelings might be various and it is important to take into account the variety of personal experiences. When children are young and have a limited command of the language, using drawings is a good solution to allow them to express themselves. In this activity the students are invited to think and then draw things that make them sad, angry, worried, happy, etc. (see Figure 17.2).

For a follow-up, it is possible to organize some circle time to let the children speak freely about those situations where they have not felt accepted by others. During this activity the mother tongue can be used and the teacher can 'recast' and tell in English what the children say.

Figure 17.2 A student's work (San Giovanni Battista School, Genoa).

Stories as models to overcome problems

Animal stories, as the one examined in the previous section, are very good for young learners, because they can easily identify with the characters. As Piaget notes (1962) the fantasy story world, populated by objects that are alive and animals that have human characteristics, matches very well children's thought that is characterized by a high degree of animism. Later on, older learners may be more interested in stories where the protagonists are boys and girls. Reading or listening to stories that tell other children's adventures is involving and creates an emotional impact (Petter, 2007).

In the picturebooks *Michael* and *My Travelin' Eye* the protagonists are, respectively, a boy and a girl. They both have to deal with the fact of being different, in one way or another, from their peers.

Michael

This story is about a boy who is considered a bad pupil because he is different and he does not conform. At school Michael does not like doing the ordinary things the other children do during the lessons and he is always interested in something else. He loves spaceships and he has a big dream: to build a rocket. All his actions, that seem quite odd and disruptive, are directed to reaching that goal. During math lessons he does strange calculations; in the science lab he does his own experiments; during the break he keeps reading books on rockets and outer space. His teachers think he is hopeless and that working with him is worthless. Michael does not seem to care, because he knows what he is doing. And he is right because at the end he succeeds and his dream comes true. The book is written in a simple and repetitive language and the illustrations integrate very well with the text. The story offers opportunities to discuss aspects related to self-confidence and competence. Michael is an outsider and he is not supported at all by his teachers, who always negatively comment on him. Nevertheless, he never gets discouraged. He has great expectations and a strong will and he works very hard in order to reach his goal. In this sense Michael is a positive model and the story shows that creativity is not enough unless it is supported by hard work, study and practice, determination and a great sense of confidence.

To further exploit these points in class, the following activities can be used.

I can do

Each student is given a handout with the outline of a big star (see Figure 17.3). They are asked to write and draw inside the star something they can do very well. It could be anything and it could be related to study skills, art and craft, music, sports, games and hobbies. When the students have completed the task, they are invited to think of how they became good at doing a certain thing. They share their experiences in small groups and then with the whole class. This last task can be done using the mother

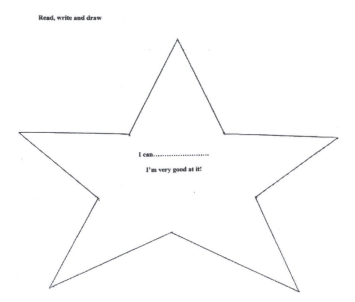

Read, write and draw

I can.............................

I'm very good at it!

Figure 17.3 Describing personal abilities.

tongue. The teacher can then summarize the results and write some key words in English. The goal of this activity is to make students aware of the strategies they have used in order to reach competence in a specific field. In addition, the sharing of experiences can offer an opportunity to discover and learn from each other about other successful strategies.

I can't do yet

Each child is given a handout with the outline of a big foot (see Figure 17.4). They are asked to write and draw inside the foot something they can't do very well yet. They are then invited to think about which actions they could undertake in order to improve their abilities. In this activity, the outline of the foot could be used as a visual metaphor to carry the message that in order to become good at something we need to walk a long way, we need to proceed step by step before reaching our goal. A class discussion could be organized to talk about transferring strategies from one field to another and about how to use new strategies in order to find out what can work best for us.

My Travelin' Eye

This story is about Jenny Sue, a girl affected by strabismus. When speaking of her vision problem, people say that she has a 'wandering eye'. She prefers calling her eye 'my travelin' eye' because she thinks her eye has the nature of an artist and adventurer. It reminds her to look around, to smell the flowers and kiss the butterflies, to look at the sky and read the clouds. Unfortunately, not all things are pleasant. At school the

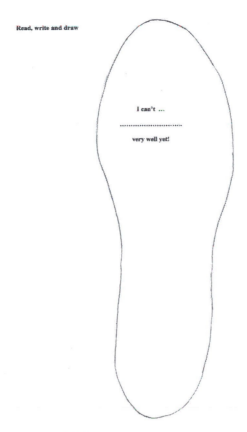

Read, write and draw

I can't …

....

very well yet!

Figure 17.4 Evaluating personal abilities.

other children tease her and say she has 'iguana eyes' that look in two directions at the same time. One day she is sent to an ophthalmologist, who makes her wear glasses and a patch over her eye. In class things are even worse and the kids call her names because of her patch. She is incredibly sad and does not want to go to school any more. Her mum comes up with wonderful suggestions: decorating the glasses and creating 'fashion-patches' with bright colours and lively designs. The result is so good that quite soon all the pupils want to wear a 'fashion-patch'.

Although the language used to tell the story is not easy for young learners of English, the narrative is often accompanied by artistic balloons that contain common children's expressions and sayings that are simple and effective. In addition, the author-illustrator uses mixed media and collage techniques that make the pages quite attractive and original. The book sends a positive message and offers a good example of how to overcome problems in a creative way. It can be used in class to discuss things that make us feel different, things that make us feel bad and feel good. The following activities can be proposed to investigate children's feelings and emotions in difficult situations, to improve communication in the classroom and favour empathy.

Pretend you are ...

The class is divided into two groups. The girls pretend to be Jenny Sue, the protagonist of the story. The boys pretend to be Johnny Blue, a new character that represents the male version of Jenny Sue. The purpose is to act out some parts of the story, miming situations where the protagonist is very sad or happy. The girls act first, and the boys observe. Then the boys act and the girls observe. Each time, the children follow the teacher's instructions:

> *You are Jenny Sue/Johnny Blue and you are at school. Kids make fun of you and say you have 'iguana eyes': 'Hallo Iguana Eyes!', 'What are you doing Iguana Eyes?', 'Bye bye Iguana Eyes!'*

> *You are sad, very sad. Your eyes are sad, your head is sad, your arms are sad, your hands are sad, your legs are sad, your body is sad, very sad.*

> *You are Jenny Sue/Johnny Blue and today you are wearing a beautiful 'fashion-patch'. Kids like it: 'Wow!', 'Cool!', 'Can I wear one of your patches, Jenny Sue/Johnny Blue?' You are happy, very happy. Your eyes are happy, your head is happy, your arms are happy, your hands are happy, your legs are happy, your body is happy, very happy.*

At the end, the teacher asks the students what happened in their bodies when they were sad and when they were happy and what they observed in their classmates. Even though each child might have interpreted the roles in different ways, it is usually possible to find some similarities. For example, in sad situations assuming shrinking positions, feeling smaller and looking down is quite common. On the contrary, in happy situations it is more likely students assume expanding positions, looking up, feeling bigger and wanting to move.

For a follow-up, the children examine in detail how the main character of the story in question, Jenny Sue, is pictured when she feels sad because she is teased, and how she is pictured when she feels happy because she receives compliments and positive comments by her classmates. The students can also examine, in various magazines, pictures of people portrayed while they are expressing vivid emotions. For this task, other picturebooks that the children already know can also be used. In addition, an interesting book for exploring emotions and facial expressions, is *Faces* by Pieńkowski (1986).

Happy and sad words

The situations that make us feel good or bad might be different for each of us, but what makes us similar is that we all have emotions and we experience emotions through our bodies. According to the trend of research in bioenergetics (Lowen, 1976), emotions could be considered physical events, in the sense that they produce a change in the flow of energy of our body. For example, excitement increases the flow of blood and produces an energetic drive that goes upwards. Depression diminishes the flow of blood and energy and produces a drive that goes downwards. Since emotions are an important part of our lives and of our bodily experiences, idiomatic expressions related to emotions are common in every language. In the English classroom, work on idioms and emotions could be organized.

In the following activity the teacher presents, using gestures and an appropriate tone of voice, some common idioms used to express happiness such as 'I'm over the moon', 'I'm in seventh heaven', 'I'm as merry as a cricket' and some idioms to express sadness as 'I'm down', 'I'm down in the mouth', 'I'm in low spirits'.

The class is invited to think of what the expressions related to happiness have in common (they illustrate the idea of metaphorically going up and reaching the sky, moving around and jumping) and what characterizes the expressions related to sadness (they illustrate the idea of going down, assuming shrinking positions with the body because of low energy or enthusiasm). Finally, the students are asked to compare the English idioms with sayings used in their mother tongue in similar circumstances and to find similarities and differences.

What about me?

The students are invited to think of situations when they feel sad and when they feel happy and to think of what they do in these situations. Successively they are asked to prepare drawings to illustrate their experiences and to write simple sentences, or simple comic strips and balloons. Before starting, the teacher can elicit some key words and sentences to prepare a vocabulary bank. Each child can then use or modify the suggested sentences according to his or her needs. Example of possible phrases:

'When I'm sad, I want to be alone', 'I want to cry', 'I want to talk to my mum', 'I want a hug', 'I want my favourite …', 'I want …'

'When I'm happy, I want to sing', 'I want to dance', 'I want to play', 'I want to chat with my friends', 'I want to hug my friends', 'I want …'

The students are also encouraged to use, for their comic strips, some of the idioms that have been presented in class. At the end they can share their work in small groups or with the whole class.

The purpose of this activity is to investigate the children's feelings, to make them aware of their reactions and consider that each of us, in similar situations, can react differently. Knowing what another student feels and does in a difficult situation is a way of getting to know each other better, to improve communication and mutual understanding.

Conclusion

The activities described in this chapter provide a general framework for working on the themes of diversity and tolerance, self-acceptance and self-confidence using children's literature. The materials can be adapted and modified according to the needs of different educational contexts. They can be used both by teacher trainers and teachers.

Picturebooks are incredible resources for language development and for personal and social growth. When listening to stories, children identify with the main characters; they feel sad or worried for the protagonists when they are in difficult situations and feel relieved when a solution is found. This identification process allows children to better understand their own emotions and to get to know other people's feelings as well.

Being able to recognize and manage emotions is an important step for developing emotional intelligence, as Goleman (1995) states. Emotional intelligence and self-esteem are both important for personal growth and for effective learning. The Council of Europe's Common European Framework of Reference (1998) underlines that a language learner, in order to be successful, needs to possess both the ability to learn and the ability to relate to otherness. Learners need to develop the existential competence that includes attitudes, values, personality traits and self-confidence, self-image and one's view of others. Since these factors deeply affect the process of learning, planning classroom work to enhance children's self-esteem and foster positive attitudes assumes a pivotal role.

Bibliography

Bradman, T., illus. Ross, T. (2009), *Michael*. London: Andersen Press.
Kostecki-Shaw, J. S. (2008), *My Travelin' Eye*. New York: Henry Holt and Company, LLC.
Pieńkowski, J. (1986), *Faces*. London: Puffin Books.
Traverso, P., illus. Massari, A. (2010), *The Owl's Song*. Genoa: Cideb.

References

Asher, J. (1982), *Learning Another Language Through Actions: The Complete Teacher's Guide Book*. Los Gatos: Sky Oaks Productions.
Bettelheim, B. (1989), *The Uses of Enchantment*. New York: Random House, Vintage Books.
Cardarello, R. (1995), *Libri e Bambini: La Prima Formazione del Lettore*. Firenze: La Nuova Italia.
Coopersmith, S. (1967), *The Antecedents of Self-Esteem*. San Francisco: Freeman & Co.
Council of Europe (1998), *Common European Framework of Reference for Languages: Learning, Teaching, Assessment*. Strasbourg: Modern Languages Division.
Ellis, G. and Brewster, J. (2002), *Tell it Again: The New Storytelling Handbook for Primary Teachers*. Harlow, UK: Longman.
Goleman, D. (1995), *Emotional Intelligence*. New York: Bantam Books.
Lowen, A. (1976), *Bioenergetics*. London: Conventur LTD.
Petter, G. (2007), *La Narrativa nella Scuola. Il Lavoro sul Testo e l'Incontro con l'Autore*. Trento: Erickson.
Piaget, J. (1962), *The Language and Thought of the Child*. New York: Norton.
Reasoner, R. (1992), *Building Self-Esteem in the Elementary Schools*. California: Consulting Psychologists Press Inc.
Revell, J. and Norman, S. (1997), *In Your Hands*. London: Saffire Press.
Rogers, C. (1969), *Freedom to Learn*. Columbus, OH: Merrill.
Wright, A. (1996a), *Storytelling with Children*. Oxford: Oxford University Press.
— (1996b), *1000 Pictures for Teachers to Copy*. Harlow: Longman.

18

The 'Art' of Teaching Creative Story Writing

Maria Luisa García Bermejo and Maria Teresa Fleta Guillén

Teaching children is a very inspirational and rewarding job and in order to make the learning stimulating and memorable to young learners, teachers need to explore new methodologies and be innovative at all times. One way to involve students effectively in the learning process is by promoting creativity across the curriculum; creativity understood as part of normality, and of everyday actions and ideas (Halliwell, 1993, p. 69). Trying out new ideas and making connections is as important as literacy and it should be at the heart of all teaching, from Kindergarten to college, from preschool and primary levels to university level. Creativity can be promoted through the production of stories, and learners can benefit from writing and from listening to their own stories in class. Storytelling is an old form of teaching and stories are excellent vehicles for natural language acquisition. For many authors, stories contain all the necessary ingredients for teaching and learning because they appeal to the whole child and to different learning styles (Garvie, 1990; Halliwell, 1992; Gardner, 1994; Moon, 2000 and Wright, 2006).

In the following sections we explore methodologies that focus on the effectiveness of using creative story writing as a central pedagogical resource for teaching English as a foreign/ additional language (EFL).

Stories for EFL teaching and learning

Since students are increasingly being introduced to EFL at school at a young age, there is a need to know more about the manner in which young learners approach the target language in order to consider how it is presented in the classroom. Children are language receptive and at an early age they learn foreign languages they are exposed to in natural child-directed speech but not if the information is presented to them through a television or audiotape (Kuhl, 2004, p. 841). Young learners learn new languages equipped with a set of instincts, skills and characteristics that enable them to extract and abstract information for meaning, pronunciation and grammar (Halliwell, 1992, p. 3). Therefore, as children learn languages implicitly, by listening to them and by speaking them, it seems logical to think that the linguistic environment where the exposure to natural linguistic data takes place becomes an essential factor for foreign language learning, because it determines the amount of linguistic data that children have access to.

At school, the teachers are the main and, in many cases, the only language facilitators and to provide children with the best exposure to authentic uses of the foreign language, teachers may need to make changes in their use of the foreign language (Moon, 2000, p. 14). Young learners should start working on the new grammar and use the target language from day one through different activities. Activities such as routines, transitions, songs, chants, rhymes, role play, drama and art offer the possibility to present language in the early years; and undoubtedly, stories are among the best teaching resources to attune the young learners' ears, to engage them in conversations and to help them to develop literacy skills. Both teachers and students can benefit from story making and from storytelling.

Traditionally stories have been used to entertain and to educate children of different languages, ages and abilities. During a story-time session, teachers and pupils share language, content and feelings, and when teachers read picturebooks to EFL learners, they are not only helping them to understand language and content, but also to develop positive attitudes towards the target language. Besides, by having access to picturebooks in class, young learners are introduced to the book language: to spacing, to punctuation and to the fact that books are read from left to right and from top to bottom.

The language in storybooks is contextualized and provides clues to meaning for understanding the texts. As McRae (1991) stresses, literature with a small 'l' opens up new avenues for language and literacy learning and teaching. Thus, the language in nursery rhymes, fairy tales, stories, comics, songs, TV series or computer games contains representational language that can be included in the materials which have a formative influence on young learners: 'any kind of material with imaginative or fictional content that goes beyond the purely *referential*, and brings imaginative interaction, reaction and response into play' (McRae, 1991, p. vii). Unlike in textbooks, the language in stories is not referential but representational and the characters think, interact, cry, shout or smile as in real life.

In this sense, stories should be considered an essential part of the language teaching and learning because they allow learners to experiment with the language and to make indirect and unconscious language learning meaningful. When students listen to stories read aloud in the classroom, they have access to vocabulary, intonation, grammatical structures and formulaic language within a context; at the same time, they develop an understanding of the plot. Cameron (2001, p. 40) points out that when foreign language learners are read stories in class, they get the meaning of the words from the book illustrations and through the context:

> Children listening to a story told in a foreign language from a book with pictures will understand and construct the gist, or outline meaning, of the story in their minds. Although the story may be told in the foreign language, the mental processing does not need to use the foreign language, and may be carried out in

the first language or in some language-independent way, using what psychologists call *mentalese*.

Stories appeal to the young learners' age, interests and curiosity, and by telling stories in class, teachers are offering students opportunities for holistic learning. Wright (2000, p. 3) considers that stories contain all the ingredients for language and content learning: 'Stories are the cornflakes of the classroom. Cornflakes contain a wide range of nutritional elements. A plate of cornflakes a day provides a good basic set of the elements we need. Stories are similar'.

Children are familiarized with the structure of stories, and with the formulaic language that goes with them in all languages, from very early on. Expressions such as: 'Once upon a time . . .', 'and they lived happily ever after' or '. . . and this is the end of the story' are not new to young L2 learners as they have heard this kind of formulaic language while listening to stories in their mother tongue. The teaching methodologies presented in this chapter help teachers and learners in their task of teaching and learning language and content through the means of writing, reading, telling and listening to stories in EFL.

Being creative in the EFL classroom through story making and storytelling

In the past, education has focused more on the ability to recall and retell stories accurately than on preparing students to become creative themselves, but the relationship between *teaching creatively* and *teaching for creativity* is an integral one (Jeffrey et al., 2004, p. 84). Teaching should be considered a form of 'art' because although creativity cannot be planned to make learning effective, teachers are creative in class when they make teaching and learning more interesting (Pugliese, 2010, p. 15). One way in which teachers and children can become creative in the classroom is by having the opportunity to test ideas out in their own ways through creative writing. Creative story writing can help to develop the children's first steps in literacy, and the teachers' own teaching skills. Young learners see teachers as their models, so teachers themselves must be prepared to experiment with creative experiences and have the chance to demonstrate the courage of being creative, of feeling what it is like to go through the creative process and the associated difficulties.

The underlying rationale to teaching literacy through creative story writing is to engage students at all levels (young and adult learners) in the learning process by making them use the target language actively in an environment that stimulates all areas of development (physical, emotional and cognitive) promoting, thus, holistic learning. As stated by Boden (2001, p. 102): 'Creativity is not the same thing as knowledge, but is firmly grounded in it. What educators must try to do is to nurture the knowledge without killing the creativity'.

By going through the creative writing process, students and teachers are able to explore creativity and to develop oral and written language.

The creative writing process

The aim of this section is to offer practitioners suggestions for planning a range of stimulating activities that promote creative writing, taking into consideration variations in the learners' age as well as differences associated with the learning contexts.[1] The project comprises four strands: inspiring learners through music, art and movement; creating opportunities to explore writing and illustrating; encouraging independent and group work; and exploring stories in EFL from the viewpoint of the writer, reader and listener. Table 18.1 illustrates how the activities can be implemented in the classroom focusing on the idea that writing is a combination of process and product that includes brainstorming, writing and editing (Sokolik 2003, p. 96).

Table 18.1 Sequences in the creative writing process

Phase 1	**Pre-writing,** visualization and brainstorming. Students visualize and give a name to a character.
Phase 2	**Gathering in groups,** getting to know each other Students exchange information; choose a character to write the story about.
Phase 3	**Writing and illustrating** the body of the story. Students edit the story.
Phase 4	**Publishing and presenting** the final product in class Students read/tell the story to the other students and answer questions.

As we will see below, the creative writing process consists of a series of interrelated sequences that integrate experiences as a scaffold to foster thinking, creativity, active learning, multiple intelligences, collaborative learning and also to develop oracy and literacy in EFL. Following Pugliese (2010, p. 21), the aim of writing creatively is to lead a group of students on a path of discovery with a certain degree of flexibility and skill for improvisation.

Phase 1: Pre-writing, music and art for inspiration

Traditionally, school learning has been based on textbooks and teacher's explanations in class, and has put emphasis on language skills and mathematics. However, since Howard Gardner proposed the theory of the Multiple Intelligences (MI) in 1983 many educators are using different methodologies that take into account the fact that individuals have different learning styles and possess several intelligences which should be developed. As Gardner (1995, p. 208) notes: 'We are not all the same, we do not all have the same kinds of minds, and education works most effectively for most individuals if (...) human differences are taken seriously'. To Gardner, we are thought to possess at least eight different avenues for learning (Linguistic, Mathematical, Spatial, Musical, Kinaesthetic, Interpersonal, Intrapersonal and Naturalistic), and each individual is thought to possess a combination of these intelligences with the capacity to develop all eight intelligences to a reasonably high level. We all have different intelligence profiles to the extent that not only we do learn differently, but we teach differently too. Thus, teachers can contribute to the development of their students' abilities by presenting content in different ways and by offering students a variety of activities.

There are many ways in which teachers can engage the learners' imagination and create a writing mood in the classroom, but music and art are among the best resources to be used as initial stimulus for inspiration. The musical intelligence is one that develops first and it runs parallel to the linguistic intelligence; there seems to be a natural connection between music, language, movement and thinking which suggests that incorporating musical activities into the daily instruction activates different centres of the brain at the same time: hearing, language and motor control skills. There exists a close correlation between music and literacy since both of them help to train the brain to the rhythmical patterns and to the qualities of sound. Thus, the first step of the creative writing process is to invite the learners to listen to a piece of music or, alternatively, to watch a piece of art while listening to the music to make up a story.[2] While listening independently to different types of music, the learners can draw pictures to reflect their moods and thoughts. They can be asked to visualize a character, draw it and also think of words to describe it because according to Palmer et al. (2003, p. 55) creative writing is about recreating and preserving experience as well as playing with words, ideas and patterns. This activity taps into the learners' creativity by using visualization as a learning strategy and by making connections; and as Wright (2006, p. 17) points out: 'Making new connections is what creativity is! Wandering and wondering without clear goals is more important than linear thinking if you want to make new connections and to discover new things'.

At this stage, the learners can be asked to express their emotions by moving freely to the music, as they think their character would move, using different types of movements (for levels: high, low and medium; for speed: fast and slow; for directions: backwards, forwards or sideways; and for movements: jumping, skipping or running). Moving freely to the music is particularly of interest for very young learners because they need to be engaged in activities that require large movements before they can progress to the finer motor control skills needed for writing. This activity helps to review the quality of movement skills, reinforces vocabulary in the target language and helps to develop facets of the kinaesthetic and musical intelligences.

Phase 2: Gathering in groups, collaborative work

Working collaboratively in small groups allows the students of all ages to practise different language skills and to use the language in meaningful contexts. Students working in groups develop their interpersonal intelligence putting into practice one of the most demanded competences nowadays, the social competence. Cooperative learning is considered to be an effective tool to enhance students' achievement, by improving and promoting positive relations and by increasing the liking among students for class, school, learning and self (Johnson et al., 1988; Kagan, 1988).

This phase promotes collaborative learning by making the most out of the classrooms as a real cooperative learning environment. At this stage, students can gather in groups of three or four and work on brainstorming associations, talk about their characters and decide on one or more characters to write the story about. The creative writing process offers students the opportunity to talk about what interests them and be immersed in the language which in turn helps their language to develop (Cameron et al., 2010, p. 24). While working in groups, students share ideas, exchange viewpoints and solve problems; they listen and talk to their companions, read and write, and what is more important they interact in the target language.

The purpose of this phase is to facilitate better peer learning opportunities by building up and strengthening the classroom dynamics and by putting to work the intrapersonal and linguistic intelligences.

Phase 3: Writing and illustrating

Drafting, flow charts and interaction

At this stage, the learners can draw pictures related to the story behind the music or behind the pictures used before for visualization. Flow charts or other type of visual organizers are particularly useful for pre-writing activities as they help the learners to sequence the information on the story and to use space in order to memorize it better. The students create a story map and integrate the information of the key incidents into a flow chart consisting of five or more spaces for the opening, build up, problem, resolution and ending (Corbett, 2003, p. 10). Some children find it easier to organize the information with the visual support that the graphic organizers provide rather than with linear information; they find it easier to illustrate what they know rather than to say it, because they see what they think first. The flow charts are a supportive aid for the students during pair or group interaction, as they work as a guideline while telling their stories to their peers.

At this stage, the students express their ideas through the drawings and through the written word. They create lists of words associated with their characters and settings to practise vocabulary: nouns, verbs and adjectives to describe the characters and settings; and connectors and basic words to make links between ideas. They go from simple language (words) to more complex language (sentences). As teachers dealing with young learners know, the children learn words easily; however, they forget them just as easily; so they need learning strategies that offer them the greatest chance of remembering new words. Therefore, making lists of words is particularly useful to promote emerging writing and it gives young learners the opportunity to revise spellings and meanings. In the same way, when learners have the chance to create and express their own messages with their own words in spontaneous communication, the words they have been using are close at hand and they are more easily retrieved from memory.

The main objective of this activity is to help learners to develop literacy skills in the target language and therefore, to work on the area of linguistic intelligence. Flow charts on the other hand can be used individually, in pairs or with the whole-class group to help students to activate previous knowledge and to organize ideas.

Storybook editing

During this phase the students work on the texts and the illustrations of their books. For that purpose, they may use the skeleton notes in the flow charts as the content for their own writing and transfer the information in the flow charts into a book format. They give books page numbers, front covers and back cover 'blurbs' about the content and authors. The book format is based on the fairy-tale structure and the five or more spaces of the flow chart correspond to the number of pages of the book. At this stage learners can be provided with resources for book making:

paper and card in assorted colours, sizes and shapes
pens, pencils, sharpeners, rulers, rubbers, felt-tip pens and crayons
scissors, stapler, hole punch and sellotape
paper binders and clips, paper fasteners, elastic bands, string, pipe cleaners
dictionaries

The purpose of this part of the project is to encourage learners to take responsibility for their writing and to work on the linguistic and spatial intelligences. The whole process becomes purposeful by editing the storybooks and by writing and illustrating them.

Phase 4: Publishing and presenting, sharing sessions

At this stage, the learners have the opportunity to read their stories aloud to different audiences and by doing so to work on storytelling skills: holding the book so the audience can see; getting the audience curious and interested using the front and the back covers; making eye contact with the audience while reading the story; encouraging involvement and active participation by using a loud and clear voice and pausing for dramatic effect; using voice-volume, intonation and tone to convey meaning and emotions. They can read and share their stories with other classes, and a display can be put up with all the examples of the students' work. As Gardner (1994, p. 203) puts it, listening to and telling stories may have a great significance on the young child's life: 'story hearing and telling is a very special, almost religious experience for the young child, one which commands his absolute attention and seems crucial in his mastery of language and his comprehension of the world (. . .)'.

By writing, illustrating and telling their own created stories, the students develop all four skills plus the cognitive and developmental skills, which in the case of children is particularly important because the cognitive development and the language development go hand in hand.

By helping the children to become storytellers, teachers give them opportunities that will help them both inside and outside the language classroom (Spiro, 2006, p. 7).

Implications for teacher development

These techniques are effective to teach EFL, the mother tongue or any additional language. Creative writing projects provide child and adult learners with activities that cover almost all areas of learning, especially those designed to control and to manipulate language. During the creative writing process, the teachers' talk time is minimized in favour of activities that motivate the learners and get them involved in creative activities. This type of teaching involves both sides of the brain: the visual-spatial right hemisphere and the linguistic left hemisphere, thus favouring the model of teaching intended to develop the linguistic, creative, personal and social areas of learning.

From the creative point of view, the learners develop ideas in their own way and they experiment with stories from the viewpoint of the story maker, the storyteller and the listener by making thinking visible through illustrating, writing and telling their stories. Writing creatively engages the students in highly interactive activities: in doing them and in talking about them, thus in using representational language. They play with ideas, words and grammatical patterns; and they live and share their stories from the vantage points of the visual, kinaesthetic, spatial, interpersonal, intrapersonal and linguistic intelligences. Creative story writing can be used with all kinds of learners: children, adults, beginners or advanced level students. It is an ideal means for interacting with teachers or with peers and for putting theory into practice.

Music, art and movement are very valid tools for inspiration and for stimulating the students' speech in terms of input and output opportunities. Thus, the stimuli that teachers consider adequate for each occasion and for each particular group of learners can become a teaching/learning resource and an important foundation for literacy. The students' brains work in complex patterns, so graphic organizers can help students to predict, sequence, organize and interpret the information for their stories. They help to make thinking visible and for some students visual information is more memorable.

In order to organize time and space for creative writing sessions, practitioners should take into consideration time allotting, arranging the room to facilitate the work in groups, assigning students in groups of three or four, making the groups as heterogeneous as possible, planning activities that promote interdependence, teaching the basic concepts and group strategies, assisting students with the task when needed and evaluating students' learning. The final product, the stories, shows that being immersed in EFL through creative writing activities gives the students ample opportunities to develop literacy skills making use of natural linguistic processes.

Notes

1   These methodologies have proven to have worked with child and adult learners. The young learners (ages 5–8) were from the British Council Bilingual School of Madrid and from Bosque School in Madrid where CLIL methodology had been implemented. The adult learners (ages 18–38) were from the School of Education at the Madrid Complutense University.
2   Examples of music and art used for visualization: Grieg (*Peer-Gynt*: 'In the Hall of the Mountain King' and 'March of the Dwarfs' Op.54/3), Vivaldi ('Summer', Presto)

and Brahms ('Lullaby', 'Waltz in A-flat major' Op. 39/15). The picture 'The Scream' by Munch with Hovhaness (Symphony No.2: 'Mysterious Mountain', Op.132, III. Andante Expressivo).

References

Boden, M. A. (2001), 'Creativity and knowledge', in A. Craft, B. Jeffrey and M. Leibling (eds), *Creativity in Education*. London: Continuum.

Cameron, L. (2001), *Teaching Languages to Young Learners*. Cambridge, UK: Cambridge University Press.

Cameron, L. and McKay, P. (2010), *Bringing Creative Teaching Into the Young Learner Classroom*. Oxford: Oxford University Press.

Corbett, P. (2003), *How to Teach Story Writing at Key Stage 1*. Oxon: David Fulton Publishers.

Gardner, H. (1983), *Frames of Mind: The Theory of Multiple Intelligences*. New York: BasicBooks.

— (1994), *The Arts and Human Development: A Psychological Study of the Artistic Process*. New York: BasicBooks.

— (1995), 'Reflections on Multiple Intelligences: Myths and messages', *Phi Delta Kappan*, 77(3), 200–9.

Garvie, E. (1990), *Story as a Vehicle: Teaching English to Young Children*. Clevedon: Multilingual Matters.

Halliwell, S. (1992), *Teaching English in the Primary Classroom*. London: Longman.

— (1993), 'Teacher creativity and teacher education', in D. Bridges and T. Kerry (eds), *Developing Teachers Professionally*, London: Routledge.

Jeffrey, B. and Craft, A. (2004), 'Teaching creatively and teaching for creativity: distinctions and relationships', *Educational Studies*, 30:1, 77–87. Available online at www.tandfonline.com/doi/pdf/10.1080/0305569032000159750

Johnson, D. W., Johnson, R. and Holubec, E. J. (1988), *Cooperation in the Classroom*. Edina, MN: Interaction Book Company.

Kagan, S. (1988), *Cooperative Learning Resources for Teachers*. Riverside, CA: University of California.

Kuhl, P. (2004), 'Early language acquisition: Cracking the speech code', *Nature Reviews Neuroscience*, 5, 831–43 (November).

McRae, J. (1991), *Literature with a Small 'l'*. London and Basingstoke: Macmillan.

Moon, J. (2000), *Children Learning English*. Oxford: Macmillan-Heinemann.

Palmer, S. and Corbett, P. (2003), *Literacy: What Works?* Cheltenham: Nelson Thornes.

Pugliese, Ch. (2010), *Being Creative: The Challenge of Change in the Classroom*. Peaslake: Delta Publishing.

Sokolik, M. (2003), 'Writing', in D. Nunan (ed.), *Practical English Language Teaching*. New York, NY: McGraw-Hill.

Spiro, J. (2006), *Storybuilding*. Oxford: Oxford University Press.

Wright, A. (2000), 'Stories and their importance in language teaching. Humanising language teaching', *Pilgrims*, Year 2; Issue 5, September. Accessible at www.hltmag.co.uk/sep00/martsep002.rtf.

— (2006), 'Being creative: Things I find useful', *Children & Teenagers: C&TS. The Publication of the Young Learners Special Interest Group*, IATEFL. 06(1), 17–19.

19

Stories as Symphonies

Andrew Wright

Words are only manifested if they are transmitted through non-verbal modes of communication. Words are thus never experienced as solo instruments but in duet or symphony. In the world of language teaching, I contend, through analogy, that 'word language' is studied as if it were a solo instrument and this is equivalent to studying the words of *Figaro* but not Mozart's music or the drama. I submit that this choice of focus in language teaching conflicts with our experience of language.

Non-verbal modes manifesting and complementing, or only complementing, words in stories

The voice and typography (including handwriting) may manifest the word and not contribute aspects of meaning (or only minimally). Most non-verbal modes, however, may manifest the word and contribute extra complimentary meanings or even offer meanings which conflict with the meaning of the word. 'Sorry!' spoken with irritation and impatience means that the speaker is not sorry!

Oral storytelling:

   Voice (manifesting and complementing words)
   Body (complementing words)
   Clothes (complementing words)
   Drama (complementing words)
   Settings and props (complementing words)
   Pictures (complementing words)
   Sound effects (complementing words)
   Music (complementing words)
   Camera techniques in film storytelling (manifesting and complementing words)
   Editing techniques in film storytelling (manifesting and complementing words)

Written storytelling:

Typography (manifesting and complementing)
Graphic design: size, shape, layout (complementing words)
Graphic features (complementing words)
Illustrations (complementing words)
Card, paper, cloth, computer screen (complementing words)

Note: other non-verbal modes of communication, not listed here, tell stories, for example architecture and sculpture.

Words as one instrument in the orchestra of communication

Three of the non-verbal modes listed above, voice, body and clothes (including body decoration), probably have a history longer than that of the word. Each of the above has its own wide range of potential meanings. These meanings are sometimes idiosyncratic but are often widely interpreted in the same way. Which of the lines below is peaceful, which is nervous and which is angry? In extensive informal tests (see Figure 19.1) I have found a huge consensus of agreement in this matching exercise in countries around the world: they were matched as (a) peaceful (b) nervous and (c) angry.

Story writers, storytellers, artists, designers, musicians and film directors have built up a rich repertoire of forms for communicating a wide range of meanings in their different non-verbal modes, which are far from the mere slaves of word language. The meanings offered by non-verbal communication have been developed over, in some cases, thousands of years and have been followed by students of the history of art over many centuries, for example, by my own professor, E. H. Gombrich, most famously, through his book, *The Story of Art*. This notion of the 'orchestration of communication' is far from being a new way of looking at things! In spite of this, I contend that 'word language' is largely treated as a solo instrument in the world of language teaching. Given the ease with which we can, with technology, choose any typeface and graphic

Figure 19.1 Three expressive lines.

arrangement on our computers; find a thousand pictures; YouTube a talking head and so on ... given all of this perhaps it is time to refocus our study of 'word language' as an orchestral, not a solo instrument.

Examples of non-verbal modes of communication

In this second part of my text I would like to recall examples from my own work (see, for example, Wright, 2008) of how words are experienced as part of orchestration rather than as solo instruments. My focus will chiefly be placed on the orchestration of communication in storytelling: oral telling and picturebooks.

Oral storytelling

Voice

'It's not what she said but how she said it that hurt me!' Isn't this experience very common? Try saying, 'Thank you', and clearly not meaning it. Or, 'I love you', and clearly not meaning it. In this case the non-verbal communication is more powerful than the words being offered. The voice can represent, heighten or contradict the meaning of the words spoken. 'I love you', in verbal content, is the most positive thing you could wish to hear, but if stress and a rising tone is placed on 'you', and if the body of the speaker is sunken and despondent with no vertical thrust, as well, then it is not such a happy message! A falling intonation suggests to me that the speaker 'has got it all sorted out', whereas a rising tone suggests the speaker is lively and open to new ideas. A harsh voice suggests harshness and a soft voice, gentleness. Regional or less common accents have been used in the theatre for centuries to offer associative meanings, for example, the grave diggers in *Macbeth* express their earthy common sense, natural wisdom and humour with their regional accents.

The storyteller may use his or her voice as a neutral teller one moment but the next might express the feelings of the person described. The words might be a neutral description but the teller might speak very slowly, lean forwards and look anxiously, when saying, 'He slowly opened the door.' In this case the teller is playing three instruments at the same time: words, voice, body; the words are neutral and the voice and body are expressive of tentative anxiety. The teller is two people at the same time: the neutral teller and the referred to protagonist.

Body

I think it is ridiculous to assert a precise contribution to meaning through body communication, as suggested by the 'picture dictionary' of actors' gestures represented in Figure 19.2. At any one moment, so much depends on context. What is certain is that body communication is extremely important in supporting the meaning of associated words, heightening meaning or offering different meanings. In my storytelling I think I usually begin my body movement a second before speaking the words the movement

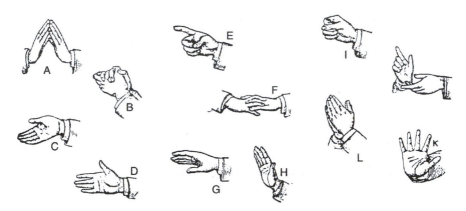

Figure 19.2 Modelled on a nineteenth-century 'picture dictionary' of gestures for actors, © Andrew Wright.

relates to. It might well be that this prompts the listener and viewer to hypothesize a meaning which is then confirmed or contradicted by the associated words and in this way the listener/viewer experiences interaction, and might even have the feeling that he or she has helped to make the story. In one story, before I say, 'A sailor slit open the throat of his sweetheart.' I already bend down, lift my chin twisting it slightly to expose my neck and slowly draw the forefinger of my right hand, representing a knife, across my throat. Listeners to my storytelling often tell me they see the scenes I describe so vividly. I believe it is largely because of my very slight body movements, which are not arbitrary or idiosyncratic to me, but help to suggest settings, objects, people and their feelings and relationships. Additionally, I use my voice not only to articulate the words but to emphasize the hissing sounds of the knife, 'A **sailor slit** open the **thr**oat of his **sw**eetheart.'

Clothes

Normally tellers simply wear the clothes they feel comfortable in when telling stories and hope that the magic of their telling will enable them to be narrator, protagonist and antagonist in turn. Some tellers might wear old-fashioned clothing, like a Victorian waistcoat. Other tellers put on scarves, hats or coats to quickly simulate their different characters. For my work with children I often wear one of my story jackets, covered with animals, princesses, boxes of treasure or moons. Children seem to like my jackets … indeed I have met grown-ups who say to me, 'Are you the man in the story jacket who came to our school twenty years ago?'

  The clothes we wear carry meanings. A tale tells of the much loved Turkish Hoja who was only allowed in to a wedding when he wore his best clothes so he poured the soup down his silken shirt and stuffed meat and potatoes into his jacket pockets declaring 'you invited these clothes to the wedding not me so I must feed my clothes … you didn't let me enter in my old clothes and I am the same person'.

Settings and props

It is true that a story can be so powerful as to make people forget where they are; fantasy can be more real than reality. At the same time a real object, for example, a real basket and real food and drink, in the telling of *Little Red Riding Hood*, can lead to that magical blend of the reality of the real and the imagined. Tellers can also use objects metaphorically. When I toured as a teller in Japan a local storyteller told me that he was trained as a teller using a white handkerchief and a fan for every tale he told. For example with the handkerchief he could create a mountain with the cloth draped over his fist and with the fan he could walk up the mountain. He kindly gave me a cloth and a fan, to try out this Rakugo technique (Figure 19.3).

Objects can 'mean' themselves with all their associations or can symbolize something else – the invitation to the listener viewer to supply the goal of the metaphor invites the listener viewer to take part in the story making and telling.

Pictures

Many, many years ago I was inspired by a man in a market place, in Damascus, showing pictures and telling stories. I have done the same thing using the pictures I painted for television to illustrate a story I am telling in the classroom. Figure 19.4 shows an example from my story 'The Floating World', in which a boy and his dog enter a world with no pull of gravity and where everything floats about. They look through a window, then as storyteller I say, 'Two babies were having a fight. One baby was throwing a fridge at another baby and the other baby was throwing his mother at the first baby.' The picture supplies far more information than the text and the children enjoy savouring all the crazy things that even babies can do if they lose all sense of gravity.

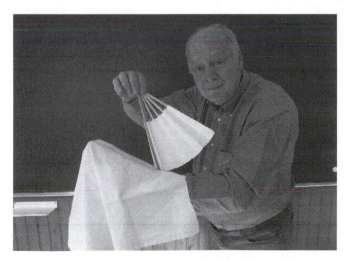

Figure 19.3 'The mountain was very high but he climbed and climbed and climbed. He climbed all day and all night.'

Stephen and Thumbolt peered through another window. There were two bad-tempered babies throwing things at each other. One was throwing a fridge and the other was throwing a lady sitting in an armchair, perhaps it was his mother. The air was full of objects flying about and bumping into each other. Everything was light and easy to throw and nothing was broken or bruised.

10

Figure 19.4 *The Floating World* (West German Television) 'Two babies were having a fight.' © Andrew Wright.

Pictures in books always offer more information than is referred to in the words of the story. In deciding whether the values, perceptions and behaviours represented in a storybook, are acceptable food to feed to your students, look very demandingly at the pictures, not just the words. Some illustrations represent a child but offer meanings related to children that you might find unacceptable. Cute faces and bodily postures of little children, I assert, may offer meanings as deadly for the mind as sweetened drinks are for the body, see my example of questionable illustrations in Figure 19.5. Pictures in children's books should be examined very closely for the values and perceptions they are offering: read the 'small print' in the pictures!

The style and content of story illustrations both add so much information.

Sound effects

Sound effects in my oral telling are usually supplied by the listeners. In one story I invite all the listeners to howl like wolves: that is a time when it is wonderful to have a very large audience! I once had an audience of 450 grown-ups, in a TESOL Toronto conference, watching a small group of children acting out a story I was telling. I asked the grown-ups to make the sound of wind in a forest, to wave their arms like branches of trees in a storm, to hoot like owls and to stamp their feet like falling branches. Having got the audience occupied, the children and I got on with the story. I believe that contributing in these ways provided the audience with experience additional to the words of the story and the sight of the children acting out the events.

Figure 19.5 A 'sugary' girl and a 'sour' boy © Andrew Wright.

Music and rhythm

A sense of and a need for rhythm must go very deep in our formation as human beings. Music and rhythm give us a sense of dramatic and emotional meanings of great complexity. Music and rhythm cannot directly support literal meanings but rather offer enriching complementary meanings.

Storytelling through film

The richness of non-verbal communication is at its greatest in filmmaking. The credits at the end of the film scroll down the list of hundreds of artists contributing their verbal and non-verbal communication skills, which are orchestrated by the director. In contrast to the lone storyteller every actor in a film can be chosen for his or her appropriateness of physique, manner, voice and then carefully dressed for the part. Settings and props and sound effects can have all the richness of reality but heightened with the selection and emphasis of art. Camera techniques and editing each represent specialist non-verbal modes offering great subtlety of meanings illustrating the text but also complementing or conflicting with it. Such is the power of the whole orchestra of communication in filmmaking that the words of the story may not be so important or memorable. We all know this. But if this is the case why is language not studied as a symphony in the language classroom?

Storytelling through books

In a children's book, words are manifested through typography, ink and paper. The words are, furthermore, complemented by graphic design and illustration. A lot of instruments playing their parts! Aren't we all affected by the feel of a book? The quality, weight, texture and colour of the paper, card or cloth? Part of our response is pure sensuality and part association: 'it must be good quality', 'it must be valuable', 'it might be very old', 'perhaps the story is old and full of enduring meanings'.

What can the language teacher do?

Language teachers do not normally receive any support in developing their understanding and skills in the teaching of 'orchestral communication' as discussed in this chapter. This is a mountainous stumbling block on which Harry Potter's wand could have little effect. So, what can language teachers do to help children develop their compositional, conducting and performance skills in communicative orchestration? In the third part of my chapter, I will make suggestions, each of which would require its own chapter to offer more detailed ideas.

Activities that combine verbal and non-verbal modes of communication

Involve non-verbal communication arts from the first lesson:

Say Hello

In the first lesson the children can try to say the word, 'Hello' in different ways, using a variety of voices, facial and body movements. They can discuss, in the mother tongue, what each of these, 'mini performances', might mean and in which contexts they might occur.

Add an adjective

The children can transform a noun from a generalized abstract notion into a living individual exemplar by qualifying it adjectively and by heightening it vocally. For example,

Cat ... Fat cat

Cat is a general notion. With the addition of a single adjective we are beginning to sense the presence of a particular cat. However, vocalize the two words and gently heighten emphasis on the sound both have in common and the two sounds that are different. Even move the body to express the staccato rhythm inherent in the phrase. We now have a living image rather than a dry and distant general notion. We have art: content and vibrant form.

Extend this creative exploration: Black, fat, lazy cat. We have lift off! Literature extends from here to Shakespeare's *Macbeth*.

Communication teachers unite!

Cooperate with the teachers of art, music, drama and IT: an interdisciplinary project. You might produce a story together:

drafted in the English lesson
illustrated in the art lesson
set to music in the music lesson
dramatized in the drama lesson
IT'd in the IT lesson and published on YouTube!

A case study: Oetzi

I would like to describe, in some detail, a project week which I have been conducting for 17 years for the same school in Austria. In the project week that took place in 2011 there were 30 students aged 11 to 12 who had been using English as their main language of instruction for just under 2 academic years. I was the project leader and there were two teachers accompanying the class (or three teachers for classes with higher numbers) who were responsible for the health and safety of the children. The teachers also gave editorial support to the students during the working sessions.

Summary of the project

I stipulated that the subject of the project would be Oetzi the Iceman's last days of life. Oetzi, was found in melting ice at 3,200 metres in the Otztal Alps, in 1991. He was an early copper-age hunter who had died of a flint arrowhead lodged in his chest shot from the back through his left shoulder blade 5,300 years ago. (In spite of the presence of the arrowhead in his chest, some scientists believe the actual cause of death was a blow to the head.)

The students studied the facts known about Oetzi, arising out of years of scientific investigations. They then each wrote a story about Oetzi's last hours or a story about the life of someone associated with Oetzi and how they might have been affected by his death. The children were told that all their stories and illustrations would be in a book, which would be published and distributed to families, the school and elsewhere. Here is the introduction:

> This is a collection of imaginative stories about the last hours of Oetzi who died high in the Alps over 5000 years ago and was found in 1991 in the ice, which had preserved him. The stories were written by the children of 2M Lisa, Europagymnasium, Auhof, Linz. The children were aged eleven and twelve when they did this work. The project week lasted for four days during five calendar days and took place at Lindenhof, Spital am Pyhrn in April 2011.
>
> What a remarkable achievement, and in English! (Wright, 2011: unpublished)

We guided the students through a series of steps in which they took on the roles of professional people, and did so splendidly.

You are a researcher: Facts and feelings about the time

The students considered the known facts derived from books and the internet about Oetzi and his time. They watched a film about Oetzi and made comprehensive notes on facts and impressions they might find useful in their own story making. They also went to the forest, ground corn with a quern, baked bread over an open fire, made axes and jewellery. They went for a long walk and made notes on how Oetzi might have felt and what he might have seen and experienced on his own walk up the mountainside. They tried archery and vertical surface climbing, all relevant to their first-hand research.

You are a writer: Drafting story ideas

The next step was to produce two different story seeds, that is very short summaries of stories and to try them out on other children. Following this the students designed flow charts of their stories staking out the main stages and adding key details. In this way they could all see if their story was clear, logical and potentially interesting to other people (children and teachers).

You are a writer: Beginning writing

Before getting into the story writing we worked on how to make a story really engaging through being as precise as possible:

> 'went up the mountain' ... walked ... walked slowly ... walked slowly sometimes falling into the deep snow ...

> 'flower' ... small flower ... small, deep blue flower ... small, deep blue flower pushing through the dirty snow of winter in a shadowed pocket of the hillside ...

This enabled us to make sure that their style was not a generalized description but a living creation of particular moments communicated with sensitive reference to the qualities of the moment. More examples: the darkness, the smell of wood smoke, the snap of twigs in the forest, the splash of blood on bright snow.

You are a writer: Writing the story

The students drafted their stories onto the grid structure chosen for the final book. (Due to time pressure the children wrote only one part of their story plan.) They then marked off the places where they wanted to have illustrations. Other students and the teachers read their stories and gave feedback based on: clarity, interest, logic and consistency. The focus was on clarity and interest rather than on grammatical accuracy.

You are a graphic designer: Designing the pages

I gave them an introduction to the notion of a grid and the possible ways of designing pages based on the grid.

You are a typographic designer: The title

The titles were individually chosen and individually designed. The aim was to produce a professional-looking book and not just a 'kid's exercise book'.

You are an illustrator

I gave a very brief introduction to ways of drawing people in action and into the art of illustration, for example making key actions large in the picture. The children created their pictures. In the cases where they thought I had done a picture for them they put my initials on the picture.

You are a graphic designer: Cover designs

Some students finished the project week by designing a cover for the class book. The designs were displayed and they voted for the one they wanted for the cover.

You are a song writer: Oetzi songs, poems and prayers

Some of the children found time to create, write, rehearse and perform songs, poems and prayers related to aspects of Oetzi's life.

Process or product?

Our aim was and is to help the students to enjoy themselves and to help them develop intellectually, creatively and socially. Process in this project week is thus much more important than the finished product. On the other hand, the book as a product provided an aim and set a standard, which affected the process. It also enabled the children to share their experience with all those who wished to read the book. There are some mistakes in the English the children used in their stories. Of course there are! The children were only 11 or 12 when they wrote these stories in their second (or third) language and after studying English for 2 years. We have left most of the mistakes in because we want the children to give their work to you. How hard the children worked! What good will! They drove themselves to do their best, hour after hour. The teachers gave, beyond the call of duty, their time, energy, talent and care.

The children wrote the story, designed the title, designed the page and illustrated the text; they 'played four communicative instruments' in creating their story. Figure 19.6 provides a glimpse in black and white of their coloured pages.

Conclusion

The theme of the chapter has been that the voice manifests the spoken word and adds its own extra meanings and that typographic design manifests the written word

he was old and had bad knees.
So I decided to follow him
and help him. I took my own
arrows and bow and my flint
knife. I grabbed one animal fur
to keep me warm and some
food. And then I walked
slowly and attentively into the
forest and up the mountain

Figure 19.6 A glimpse of a major publishing venture (created by Sandra Kleiner, aged 12).

and adds its own range of meanings. Accompanying the voice and the typographic design are many other non-verbal modes each adding a range of meanings, some complementary to an associated text and some in conflict. I contend that this orchestration of languages is part of our everyday experience and that the knowledge and skill in combining verbal and non-verbal modes is fundamental to successful communication. I also contend that this experience of communication is given little or no recognition in schools and young people are given little or no support in developing effective communication skills in this broader understanding of orchestral communication.

References

Gombrich, E. H. (1995), *The Story of Art* (16th edn). London: Phaidon Press.
Wright, A. (2008), *Storytelling with Children* (2nd edn). Oxford: Oxford University Press.

20

Conclusion

Christiane Lütge

The chapters in this volume set out to bring together contributions to the field of children's literature in the EFL classroom from diverse backgrounds. The term children's literature – itself not homogeneous in scope – is most commonly used to cover all literature for children and adolescents and includes so vast a variety of texts that it is almost impossible to establish a coherent theoretical approach or teaching methodology. Moving between fairy tales and nursery rhymes, graphic narratives and young adult literature, 'traditional' as well as contemporary themes, canonical texts and new formats introducing electronic fictions, EFL teachers find themselves faced with challenges and chances alike. The most important ingredient for any literature EFL classroom may be enthusiasm on the part of the reader, the most significant requirement on the part of the teacher may be to foster and keep this enthusiasm alive and let it grow and flourish. The significance of children's literature for different levels of the EFL classroom with a possible progression through various developmental stages needs to be more systematically exploited, therefore the contributions in this volume were compiled with a view to four different fields with manifold interconnections.

Extensive reading

The first part furnishes insights into extensive reading. The authors report on empirical research carried out in a number of contexts, from primary education to teacher education. The chapters focus on second language acquisition benefits as well as on the benefits to self-esteem, the acquisition of world knowledge and deeper understandings and ultimately to the development of an affective bond to books. The tremendous value of extensive reading for EFL contexts plays a major role here (Krashen, 2007). In fact, reading children's literature and young adult fiction in the literature EFL classroom can provide all the advantages of extensive reading and in-depth intensive reading, as well as offering opportunities for learning the important interpretive skills of reading between the lines and reading against the text (Bland, 2012, p. 214). Reading skills and reading habits are important and develop in close connection. Certain reading strategies are important for the EFL classroom, such as predicting, which entails an anticipation of what the text is likely to provide in terms of information or narrative. Apart from extensive reading, also known as voluntary or pleasure reading, intensive reading is important for the EFL classroom, too, in that it involves in-depth work on literature which in a selective manner focuses on for instance structural or thematic aspects of a text. Interpretive reading, moreover, assumes a certain analysis or community reading – a group interpretation of a complex text which is at first hand and by a single reader in isolation may be difficult to fully understand (Ahrens, 2012, p. 187).

Interestingly, it is extensive reading (free voluntary reading or pleasure reading) that is mentioned most often in connection with children's literature as it is seen as important for language acquisition, furthering reading skills and world knowledge. However, this should not evoke the impression that the connection between children's literature and extensive reading is to be found in an inferior quality of children's literature. In fact, the potential of children's literature for second language learning and reading skills via pleasure reading (Krashen, 2004) needs to be acknowledged more sincerely – without denying the beneficial aspects of intensive reading and the development of multiple literacies through children's literature.

Visual literacy

Among the insufficiently explored learning opportunities for the English language lesson, particularly the visual elements of literary texts need to be considered in more detail. Accordingly, the chapters in the second part of this volume focus on the potential afforded by multimodal texts in contemporary children's literature for language acquisition, cultural understanding and particularly visual and literary literacy. The 'visual turn' in language teaching through picturebooks or graphic novels demands much more of the learners than to read images alongside texts. The 'cocreation with the author or artist' and the creation of 'nonlinear formats' (Goldstone, 2001, pp. 362–3) have established a new quality in children's literature. Again, it has to be pointed out that the seemingly obvious connection of children's literature and pictures, for example in picturebooks, does not imply a trivial connection lacking the depths of 'real' quality literature. The potential of multimodal texts is manifold and there are connections both with extensive reading and intercultural learning, the major topic of Part III.

Inter- and transcultural learning

The third part of this volume discusses the potential of multicultural children's and young adult literature for the EFL classroom. The contributions refer to aspects of inter- and transcultural learning and diversity. Considering the increasing heterogeneity of student populations, the chapters in the third part address issues of developing teaching units based on various intercultural encounters, on 'doing identity', on various forms of otherness and the representation of minorities and the effects of migration in children's literature. Children's literature can play a major role in the development of intercultural awareness from the earliest years onwards. With its variety of topics referring to manifold occurrences of 'self' and 'other', children's literature has an enormous potential for one of the most prominent themes in second language education.

Empowerment and creativity

The fourth part offers key chapters on literary experiences and creative production: the benefits of children's literature as a model for linguistic patterning, language play and diversity of expression. Here, empowerment through creative reader response and ideas for creative writing are at the centre of interest. The connection between creativity, linguistic empowerment and enthusiasm for (children's) literature – as a basic ingredient for successful language learning – becomes obvious yet again. Indeed, a fascinating challenge may be seen in the fact that children's literature comes in various shapes, sizes and forms and that it lends itself to various discussions, interpretations and (re)readings.

Future developments

Thinking about possible future developments of children's literature in EFL teaching, it seems probable that new forms of literacies will emerge that call for changes in methodology. According to Kimberley Reynolds, it is highly likely that changing forms and formats will establish the area where the greatest change within children's literature will occur in the near future. Electronic fictions pose new challenges and may lead to new kinds of skills and approaches: 'Of greatest interest here is not whether the effects of new technologies have been beneficial or damaging to children's literature, but how they can be studied' (Reynolds, 2011, p. 206). A new chapter opening into children's literature research and – given a certain time lag – also into second language education may be triggered by electronic fictions for children. The connection with media literacy and the concept of multiliteracies may be of special importance for future developments in EFL contexts, especially with a view to teaching issues: 'The question for future research is whether new kinds of skills and approaches will be required to deal with the complexities of the transmedia environment, which is generating both new fictions for children and new ways of reading' (Reynolds, 2011, p. 207).

References

Ahrens, R. (2012), 'Introduction: Teaching literature', in M. Eisenmann and T. Summer (eds), *Basic Issues in EFL Teaching and Learning*. Heidelberg: Winter, pp. 181–9.

Bailey, A. (2011a), 'Using research libraries, archives and collections', in M. O. Grenby and K. Reynolds (eds), *Children's Literature Studies: A Research Handbook*. Houndmills, Basingstoke: Palgrave Macmillan, pp. 45–53.

— (2011b), 'Case study – working in the British library', in M. O. Grenby and K. Reynolds (eds), *Children's Literature Studies: A Research Handbook*. Houndmills, Basingstoke: Palgrave Macmillan, pp. 53–6.

Bland, J. (2012), 'Critical education potential with young adult literature in language education: The Harry Potter series in the literature class', in M. Eisenmann and T. Summer (eds), *Basic Issues in EFL Teaching and Learning*. Heidelberg: Winter, pp. 203–14.

Connolly, R. (2011), 'Using manuscripts to research children's literature', in M. O. Grenby and K. Reynolds (eds), *Children's Literature Studies: A Research Handbook*. Houndmills, Basingstoke: Palgrave Macmillan, pp. 56–60.

Dalrymple, N. (2011), 'Case study – working with the Seven Stories archive', in M. O. Grenby and K. Reynolds (eds), *Children's Literature Studies: A Research Handbook*. Houndmills, Basingstoke: Palgrave Macmillan, pp. 60–2.

Goldstone, B. (2001), 'Whaz up with our books? Changing picture book codes and teaching implications', *The Reading Teacher*, 55(4), 362–70.

Grenby, M. O. and Reynolds, K. (eds) (2011), *Children's Literature Studies: A Research Handbook*. Houndmills, Basingstoke: Palgrave Macmillan.

Krashen, S. (2004), *The Power of Reading* (2nd edn). Portsmouth, NH: Heinemann.

— (2007), 'Extensive reading in English as a foreign language by adolescents and young adults: A meta-analysis', *International Journal of Foreign Language Teaching*, 3(2), 23–9.

Pearson, L. (2011), 'Finding secondary material', in M. O. Grenby and K. Reynolds (eds), *Children's Literature Studies: A Research Handbook*. Houndmills, Basingstoke: Palgrave Macmillan, pp. 62–9.

Reynolds, K. (2011), 'Afterword', in M. O. Grenby and K. Reynolds (eds), *Children's Literature Studies: A Research Handbook*. Houndmills, Basingstoke: Palgrave Macmillan, pp. 206–8.

Additional Materials and Resources

In the following, we would like to point out a number of organizations, websites and ejournals that can guide teachers, teacher educators and researchers of children's literature through the dazzling array of materials. The following collection intends to bring together both theoretical and practical aspects of children's literature. As an explicit focus on second language acquisition is scarce, the examples from this collection address broader issues of teaching children's literature. They have been chosen, though, with an application within EFL contexts in mind. Furthering the impact of children's literature in educational contexts and highlighting its significance also in foreign language learning – both major goals of this volume – will hopefully be on the EFL agenda both critically and most prominently in the future.

An excellent compilation of children's literature archives, collections and resources can be found in Grenby/Reynolds (2011, chapter 2). Five sub-chapters on topics such as 'Using research libraries, archives and collections' (Bailey, 2011a), 'Case study – working in the British Library' (Bailey, 2011b), 'Using manuscripts to research children's literature' (Connolly, 2011), 'Case study – working with the Seven Stories archive' (Dalrymple, 2011), 'Finding secondary material' (Pearson, 2011) provide starting points for research and practical application alike.

Organizations

The Children's Literature Assembly (www.childrensliterature.org): an organization dedicated to bringing children's literature and advocates of children's literature together.

Children's Literature Association (www.childlitassn.org): a non-profit association of scholars, critics, professors, students, librarians, teachers and institutions dedicated to the academic study of literature.

International Research Society for Children's Literature (www.irscl.com): an international scholarly organization established to support and promote research in the field of children's literature.

Society of Children's Book Writers and Illustrators (www.scbwi.org): an organization for both new and experienced writers and illustrators working in the area of children's literature.

Websites

Carol Hurst's Children's Literature Site (www.carolhurst.com): Free literature-based classroom units, reviews of great books for kids, ways to use them in the classroom, free teaching guides and activities.

Children's Literature (www.childrenslit.com): An independent website that critically reviews more than 5,000 children's books annually.

Children's Literature Network (www.childrensliteraturenetwork.org): *Children's Literature Network* connects, informs, and educates those who have an interest in children's and teen books, authors and illustrators.

International Children's Digital Library (http://en.childrenslibrary.org/): Collection of children's books that represent outstanding historical and contemporary books from throughout the world.

http://picturebooksinelt.blogspot.de/ A picturebook blog by Sandie Mourão, a freelance English language teacher, teacher trainer and materials writer based in Portugal, who is passionate about picturebooks and wants to share that passion.

Osborne Collection of Early Children's Books (www.torontopubliclibrary.ca/osborne/): A collection of over 80,000 rare and notable children's books.

The Children's Literature Web Guide (http://people.ucalgary.ca/~dkbrown/) A website featuring discussion boards, book lists and resources for teachers, all related to books for both children and young adults.

Journals

Children's Literature Association Quarterly (http://muse.jhu.edu/journals/childrens_literature_association_quarterly/): Each issue features an editorial introduction, refereed articles about research and scholarship in children's literature, and book reviews.

Children's Literature in Education. An International Quarterly (www.springer.com/education+%26+language/linguistics/journal/10583): Children's Literature in Education has been a key source of articles on all aspects of children's literature for almost 40 years.

Children's Literature in English Language Education, CLELE (www.clelejournal.org): a new, bi-annual, comprehensively peer-reviewed on-line journal for scholars, teacher educators and practitioners involved in using and researching children's literature in the field of English learning as a second, additional or foreign language.

The Journal of Children's Literature Studies (www.piedpiperpublishing.com/journals.htm): This journal is published three times a year and includes research papers on all aspects of children's literature, childhood and books for children.

Index

Index

77351687R00137

Made in the USA
Middletown, DE
20 June 2018